Occupational Health
Disparities

APA/MSU SERIES ON MULTICULTURAL PSYCHOLOGY

Series Editor: Frederick T. L. Leong

Conducting Multinational Research: Applying Organizational Psychology in the Workplace
  Edited by Ann Marie Ryan, Frederick T. L. Leong, and
  Frederick L. Oswald

Occupational Health Disparities: Improving the Well-Being of Ethnic and Racial Minority Workers
  Edited by Frederick T. L. Leong, Donald E. Eggerth, Chu-Hsiang (Daisy)
  Chang, Michael A. Flynn, J. Kevin Ford, and Rubén O. Martinez

Occupational Health Disparities

Improving the Well-Being of Ethnic
and Racial Minority Workers

EDITED BY Frederick T. L. Leong, Donald E. Eggerth,
Chu-Hsiang (Daisy) Chang, Michael A. Flynn, J. Kevin Ford,
and Rubén O. Martinez

AMERICAN PSYCHOLOGICAL ASSOCIATION
WASHINGTON, DC

Published by
American Psychological Association
750 First Street, NE
Washington, DC 20002
www.apa.org

To order
APA Order Department
P.O. Box 92984
Washington, DC 20090-2984
Tel: (800) 374-2721; Direct: (202) 336-5510
Fax: (202) 336-5502; TDD/TTY: (202) 336-6123
Online: www.apa.org/pubs/books
E-mail: order@apa.org

In the U.K., Europe, Africa, and the Middle East, copies may be ordered from
American Psychological Association
3 Henrietta Street
Covent Garden, London
WC2E 8LU England

Typeset in Goudy by Circle Graphics, Inc., Columbia, MD

Printer: Sheridan Books, Chelsea, MI
Cover Designer: Beth Schlenoff Design, Bethesda, MD

The opinions and statements published are the responsibility of the authors, and such opinions and statements do not necessarily represent the policies of the American Psychological Association.

Library of Congress Cataloging-in-Publication Data

Names: Leong, Frederick T. L., editor.
Title: Occupational health disparities : improving the well-being of ethnic and racial minority workers / edited by Frederick T.L. Leong, Donald E. Eggerth, Chu-Hsiang Chang, Michael A. Flynn, J. Kevin Ford, Rubén O. Martinez.
Description: Washington, DC : American Psychological Association, [2017] | Series: Cultural, racial, and ethnic psychology book series | Includes bibliographical references and index.
Identifiers: LCCN 2016038811 | ISBN 9781433826924 | ISBN 1433826925
Subjects: LCSH: Industrial hygiene—Moral and ethical aspects. | Minorities—Employment. | Minorities—Health and hygiene.
Classification: LCC HD7261 .O335 2017 | DDC 363.11089—dc23 LC record available at https://lccn.loc.gov/2016038811

British Library Cataloguing-in-Publication Data
A CIP record is available from the British Library.

Printed in the United States of America
First Edition

http://dx.doi.org/10.1037/0000021-000

CONTENTS

CONTRIBUTORS

Thomas A. Arcury, PhD, Director, Center for Worker Health, Professor and Vice Chair for Research, Department of Family and Community Medicine, Wake Forest School of Medicine, Winston-Salem, NC

Krista Brockwood, PhD, Researcher and Project Manager of the SERVe Project, Oregon Health & Science University, Portland

Maria Julia Brunette, PhD, Associate Professor, Department of Work Environment, University of Massachusetts Lowell

Chu-Hsiang (Daisy) Chang, PhD, Associate Professor of Psychology, Department of Psychology, Michigan State University, East Lansing

Donald E. Eggerth, PhD, Research Psychologist, Training Research and Evaluation Branch, National Institute for Occupational Safety and Health, Cincinnati, OH

Michael A. Flynn, MA, Social Scientist, Training Research and Evaluation Branch, National Institute for Occupational Safety and Health, Cincinnati, OH

J. Kevin Ford, PhD, Professor of Psychology, Department of Psychology, Michigan State University, East Lansing

Ellen Ernst Kossek, PhD, Basil S. Turner Professor of Management and Research Director of the Susan Bulkeley Butler Center for Leadership

Excellence, Purdue University Krannert School of Management, West Lafayette, IN

Frederick T. L. Leong, PhD, Professor of Psychology, Department of Psychology, Michigan State University, East Lansing

Stanton Mak, MA, Department of Psychology, Michigan State University, East Lansing

Rubén O. Martinez, PhD, Director, Julian Samora Research Institute, Michigan State University, East Lansing

Rafael Moure-Eraso, PhD, CIH, Professor Emeritus, Work Environment Department, University of Massachusetts Lowell

Sara A. Quandt, PhD, Associate Director, Center for Worker Health and Professor, Department of Epidemiology and Prevention, Division of Public Health Sciences, Wake Forest School of Medicine, Winston-Salem, NC

Rashaun Roberts, PhD, Research Psychologist, Division of Applied Research and Technology, National Institute for Occupational Safety and Health, Cincinnati, OH

Lois E. Tetrick, PhD, Professor, Department of Psychology, George Mason University, Fairfax, VA

Rebecca Thompson, PhD, Assistant Professor, Division of Applied Behavioral Sciences, University of Baltimore, Baltimore, MD

Brad Wipfli, PhD, Research Assistant Professor, Oregon Institute of Occupational Health Sciences, Oregon Health & Science University, Portland

SERIES FOREWORD

I am happy to introduce the second volume in the APA/MSU Series on Multicultural Psychology. The goal of the series has been to emphasize multicultural theories and research in psychology and thereby expand on the traditional Eurocentric focus of mainstream psychology. In addition, a related aim is to provide the field with resources that will serve as guideposts for advancing multicultural perspectives in theory, research, and practice in psychology.

The book series was launched as part of the activities of the Consortium for Multicultural Psychology Research at Michigan State University (MSU). In 2007, I was hired to lead the Multicultural Initiative at MSU and established the Consortium for Multicultural Psychology Research to achieve the mission "to generate and apply psychological science to increase our understanding of multicultural issues in both domestic and international contexts." The consortium is an integral part of the Department of Psychology at MSU.

Learning from the enduring and highly successful Nebraska Symposium on Motivation, the consortium sought to establish the MSU Symposium on Multicultural Psychology to counter the current dominance of Eurocentric models and methods within the field. The MSU Symposium is part of an integrated approach of the consortium to infuse multicultural perspectives and mind-sets within the Department of Psychology and other social sciences at MSU as well as the field of psychology in general.

With conference funding from the National Institute for Occupational Safety and Health (NIOSH), the second MSU Symposium on Multicultural Psychology was convened in the fall of 2011 and focused on "Occupational Health Disparities among Racial and Ethnic Minorities: Formulating Research Needs and Directions." This book is derived from that second symposium and reflects the goals of NIOSH's National Occupational Research Agenda (NORA), which investigates the causes, impacts, and possible solutions to the disproportionate rates of disease, injury, and fatality that minority groups suffer from when compared with the population in general. These groups include women workers, aging workers, young workers, and workers from particular racial/ethnic backgrounds, although this book focuses on the latter. Specifically, NIOSH had launched a program focused on occupational health disparities (see https://www.cdc.gov/niosh/programs/ohd/), which was aimed at "improving surveillance of vulnerable populations and identifying methods, intervention approaches, and dissemination tools to better reach these populations." This program examined occupational health disparities through the lens of socioeconomic status, discrimination, and work organizations, a perspective also taken by the contributors to this volume.

Despite this NIOSH program, the literature on occupational health disparities among racial and ethnic minorities remained sparse. With the publication of the national report *Unequal Treatment*, the nation's health system began to pay attention to this pattern of health disparities among racial and ethnic minorities.[1] *Unequal Treatment* also galvanized the nation's scientific community's attention to this significant problem in our health system. This volume represents one aspect of that development by inviting leading experts to examine the nature, causes, and consequences of occupational health disparities among racial and ethnic minorities in terms of policy, research, and interventions.

—Frederick T. L. Leong
Series Editor

---

[1]Institute of Medicine. (2003). *Unequal treatment: Confronting racial and ethnic disparities in health care.* Washington, DC: National Academies Press.

PREFACE

FREDERICK T. L. LEONG, DONALD E. EGGERTH,
AND MICHAEL A. FLYNN

According to a recent report from the World Health Organization (WHO) Commission on the Social Determinants of Health, "a girl born in Sweden will live 43 years longer than a girl born in Sierra Leone."[1] The report goes on to observe that "in Glasgow, an unskilled, working-class person will have a lifespan 28 years shorter than a businessman in the top income bracket in Scotland" (see Footnote 1, p. 5). Commenting on these sobering statistics of health disparities around the world in an invited address, Vicente Navarro (2009) of Johns Hopkins University noted that

> the mortality differentials among countries are enormous. But such inequalities also appear within each country, including the so-called rich or developed countries. . . . We could add here similar data from the United States. In East Baltimore (where my university, the Johns Hopkins University, is located), a black unemployed youth has a lifespan 32 years shorter than a white corporate lawyer. Actually, as I have documented elsewhere, a young African American is 1.8 times more likely than a young White American to die from a cardiovascular condition.

[1]Navarro, V. (2009). What we mean by social determinants of health. *Global Health Promotion, 16,* 5–16.

Race mortality differentials are large in the US. . . . In the same study, I showed that a blue-collar worker is 2.8 times more likely than a businessman to die from a cardiovascular condition. (p. 5)

The challenges of health disparities for racial and ethnic minorities in this country have been publicized in the scientific community by reports such as *Unequal Treatment* and articles like Navarro's (2009) address.[2] However, much less attention and research have been focused on occupational health disparities (OHDs) among racial and ethnic minority groups. Despite an increasing number of immigrant and nonimmigrant racial and ethnic minorities in the United States, little is known about OHDs among these populations. Worker groups in the United States have differential exposure to workplace hazards, and in many cases, these hazards are disproportionately experienced by racial and ethnic minorities. As a result, any research and policy efforts to address health disparities among racial and ethnic minorities will also need to address the differential impacts of working conditions on their health. These OHDs are exacerbated by barriers resulting from language issues, socioeconomic factors, and cultural beliefs and attitudes. Therefore, a multicultural perspective on OHDs is needed to understand the unique barriers and stressors that they encounter in the workplace. This volume will provide a state-of-the-art review of the literature as well as a road map to guide future research to address the challenges in OHDs among racial and ethnic minorities.

---

[2]Institute of Medicine. (2003). *Unequal treatment: Confronting racial and ethnic disparities in health care.* Washington, DC: National Academies Press.

Occupational Health
Disparities

INTRODUCTION

FREDERICK T. L. LEONG, DONALD E. EGGERTH,
CHU-HSIANG (DAISY) CHANG, MICHAEL A. FLYNN,
J. KEVIN FORD, AND RUBÉN O. MARTINEZ

For several decades, the National Institute for Occupational Safety and Health (NIOSH) has recognized that some workers groups have suffered disproportionate rates of disease, injury, and fatality compared with the population in general. NIOSH prioritized research investigating the causes, impacts, and possible solutions to these disparities in its National Occupational Research Agenda (NORA). The populations most frequently studied were women workers, aging workers, young workers, and workers from particular racial/ethnic backgrounds.

These research efforts yielded a wealth of descriptive information about the individual groups studied. However, it became clear that general methodological approaches for successfully conducting intervention research with majority populations were not well suited to working with many racial/ethnic minority groups. Traditional methodological approaches were particularly ineffective with Latino immigrant workers as they did not account for

http://dx.doi.org/10.1037/0000021-001
Occupational Health Disparities: Improving the Well-Being of Ethnic and Racial Minority Workers, F. T. L. Leong,
D. E. Eggerth, C.-H. Chang, M. A. Flynn, J. K. Ford, and R. O. Martinez (Editors)

differences such as language, culture, and immigration status. As researchers came to identify better ways to reach these groups, it was recognized that culturally sensitive approaches were not just better practice for these groups but also generated better science and could fruitfully be adapted to other populations as well.

The mission of the NIOSH Occupational Health Equity (OHE) program (formerly the Occupational Health Disparities program) is to "promote research, outreach, and prevention activities that reduce health disparities for workers who are at higher risk for occupational injury and illness as a result of social and economic characteristics historically linked to discrimination or exclusion" (http://www.cdc.gov/niosh/docs/2016-142/; NIOSH, 2016). *Health disparities* are differences in disease incidence, mental illness, or morbidity and mortality that are closely linked with social, economic, and/or environmental disadvantage. It is important to note that the NIOSH program envisioned its efforts to eliminate occupational health disparities (OHDs) as aligned with and congruent with the overriding goals of the Healthy People 2020 initiative (U.S. Department of Health and Human Services, 2016): to achieve health equity, eliminate disparities, and improve the health of all groups (https://www.healthypeople.gov/2020/about/foundation-health-measures/Disparities).

This volume has been produced to address health disparities within a discrete life domain—the workplace—focusing on OHDs experienced by racial and ethnic minorities. Some chapters in this book are the fruit of the NIOSH initiative. All chapters present evidence-based principles of occupational health psychology (OHP) to address numerous sociocultural factors and improve the well-being of minority workers—including Latinos, African Americans, and Asian Americans—in a variety of industries (e.g., farming, food service, transportation, nursing, office work). We hope that this book will serve as both an impetus and a framework for guiding future research, interventions, and policy formulations that will help reduce OHDs among the millions of racial and ethnic minorities that make up our workforce.

AN OVERVIEW OF OCCUPATIONAL HEALTH PSYCHOLOGY

Although the field of OHP is relatively young, its core concern—the well-being of workers—has existed as long as humans have worked for others. OHP is a multidisciplinary field drawing together anthropology, economics, ergonomics, epidemiology, medicine, nursing, psychology, and public health. OHP has implications, both policy and practice, for law, management, public health, and job design. The scholarly roots of OHP can be traced back for more than a century, but it is only in the past few decades that OHP has emerged and coalesced into a distinct field of activity. Indeed, OHP did not exist as a specialty when most of the authors of this volume were in graduate school.

In many respects, OHP is analogous to family therapy models in which individual family members are always conceptualized within the context of the family system. Interventions are not aimed at individual family members but are intended to reshape the functioning of the entire family system, nudging it toward better health. Similarly, most OHP interventions are intended to change entire organizations or workgroups—to the benefit of individual workers. In part, this stance arises from the philosophic orientation of the larger occupational health community—that well-being is the responsibility of employers, not individual workers. It can also be argued that having one target for change (the work organization) rather than many (the individual workers) represents better economy of effort and also offers greater opportunities for developing interventions that are generalizable across multiple settings. Regardless of the merits of this orientation, it has become clear that such approaches are better suited to larger employers who have greater resources to dedicate to implementing and sustaining such processes. For example, models of safety culture conceptualize it as a top-down emanation reflecting company policies and management decisions that color the remainder of the workplace, including which behaviors are rewarded, and which are discouraged, in the work environment (Zohar, 2003). This model has been most successfully applied to larger companies having a clear, hierarchical structure and a highly skilled and/or unionized workforce. When companies have clear lines of power, their incentive to retain hard-to-replace workers and the need of management to respond to pressure from an organized workforce all combine to facilitate the success of interventions intended to bring about organization change using a top-down approach.

However, in small business situations, the line between owner/manager and worker is often blurred—particularly in family-operated businesses—and this conceptualization is harder to apply. In work settings employing less-skilled workers, who are easily replaced, there is often less incentive for management to make changes that would retain dissatisfied employees. Compounding this situation, these less skilled workers often have little social franchise and are not unionized. In such situations, there is neither economic nor political pressure for management to make changes to improve the well-being of workers without a corresponding increase in profits. The plight of these worker groups, many of whom are ethnic/racial minorities, falls within the realm of occupational health equity. Although focused on the workplace, occupational health equity is part of the larger intersection between public health and social justice that is referred to as the *social determinants of health*.

The social determinants of health have been defined as the "conditions in which people are born, grow, live, work, and age. . . . These circumstances are shaped by the distribution of money, power and resources at global, national and local levels, which are themselves influenced by policy choices" (World Health Organization [WHO], 2014). Although often an unintended consequence of social policies, how societies organize themselves affects who gets sick or injured, who receives treatment, who is healthy, and who is not. When these social arrangements contribute to differences in health (e.g., rates of infection and injury, exposure to chronic conditions or risk factors, poorer treatment outcomes) among specific groups, they are often referred to as *health disparities* or *health inequity*.

When viewed within the framework of social determinants of health, it is clear that work must be conceptualized globally—as an integral and inter-active part of one's entire life. The NIOSH Total Worker Health (TWH; NIOSH, 2016) initiative recognizes that both work-related factors and health factors beyond the workplace jointly contribute to the many safety and health problems that impact workers and their families. Traditionally, programs addressing workplace safety were offered in isolation from pro-grams addressing supposedly nonwork "lifestyle" issues (e.g., smoking cessa-tion, weight loss) that are also frequently offered by employers. The TWH approach argues that this separation is artificial and that workers are better served by combining all such efforts into a coordinated and comprehensive well-being program.

As the next section discussing the history of OHP makes clear, this focus on worker well-being was not an initial aim of the scholarly activities that eventually gave rise to the field. Indeed, increasing productivity was the pri-mary aim of these early efforts. Although this discussion can easily be framed in traditional terms of an adversarial relationship between labor and manage-ment, each side pursuing conflicting goals, the TWH approach argues that it is more fruitful to conceptualize worker well-being activities as a win–win situation for both workers and employers.

HISTORY OF OCCUPATIONAL HEALTH PSYCHOLOGY

Industrial–organizational psychology in the United States began in the early part of the 20th century with the rise of scientific management, its emphasis on time and motion studies to increase worker efficiency and productivity, and the demands of World War I. Scientific management sepa-rated "thinkers" from "doers" in the workplace, leading to the transfer of knowledge of production from workers to "scientific managers." As a spe-cialty, industrial psychology combined knowledge from experimental and behavioral psychology and put it at the "service of commerce and industry" (Münsterberg, 1913). The emphasis of industrial psychology was on increasing industrial output by developing rational approaches to the problem of managing workers.

In particular, the focus was on mental testing and motivation. The aim was to use psychological methods to identify personalities that were, by their mental qualities, fit for particular types of work. The specialty would later be applied by the U.S. Army to classify and assign military personnel. The pioneering studies of the Hawthorne plant of Western Electric Company in the late 1920s and early 1930s examined the influences of environmental factors (lighting and other workplace factors) and drew attention to the demand characteristics of research studies and to the influence of the work group in the productivity of its members (Mayo, 1933, 1949; Roethlisberger & Dickson, 1939; Whitehead, 1938). Known as the *Hawthorne effect*, the findings of the study shed light on the importance of the social, psychological, and cultural features of work, as well as the relationship between workplace conditions and worker motivation.

The human relations dimensions of worker productivity gained further momentum through the work of Abraham Maslow, who argued that repressive environments inhibited individuals from self-actualization (Barling & Griffiths, 2011). In other words, psychologically healthy individuals were more likely to be motivated to work (Maslow, 1965) and less likely to be alienated from their productive selves through repressive work environments, as Karl Marx (1867/1976) argued late in the 19th century.

Another major influence in the development of OHP was the work of Arthur Kornhauser, who started his applied career focusing on the development of trade tests for the U.S. Army during World War I (Zickar, 2003). He viewed the use of tests as a useful approach to help people find fitting employment and for management to select good employees. By 1930, however, he began to critique industrial psychology for being obligated to management, arguing that selection procedures and training programs were evaluated with regard to efficiency and without regard for worker satisfaction. He then began to study "worker feelings," including job satisfaction, boredom, and the fullness of life within modern industry (Kornhauser, 1930).

Because of the close relationship between industrial psychology and management, a focus on the issues of concern to labor was minimal (Gordon & Burt, 1981). Indeed, labor unions regarded industrial psychology with distrust and suspicion. Consequently, concerns for the health and safety of workers took two separate paths: one in which labor unions were directly concerned with the hazards of the workplace, and the other—that of industrial psychology—giving indirect attention to these issues in the pursuit of increased worker productivity. As industrial psychology continued to integrate studies from different fields and subfields, including medicine and clinical psychology, it gave increased attention to the dimensions of the workplace and their role in generating stress and depression among workers. By the beginning of the second half of the 20th century, an emerging interdisciplinary subfield had begun to take form within a broadening overlap among other emergent subfields, including industrial psychology, management, public health, preventive medicine, industrial engineering, industrial medicine, and nursing (Macik-Frey, Quick, & Nelson, 2007).

By the 1950s, the field of public health had begun to include occupational and environmental health, within the context of an organization, as topics across a broadening range of disorders and health risks (Macik-Frey et al., 2007). Many studies within this period focused on stress and productivity, and as the human relations school continued to influence the emerging subfield of occupational health psychology, more and more attention was given to the influences of work environments on the physical and psychological aspects of employees. By the 1970s, many studies were underway on the psychosocial aspects of work, and with the passage of the Occupational Safety and Health Act of 1970 (OSH Act), several institutional mechanisms were implemented to "assure safe and healthful working conditions for working men and women," including the Occupational Safety and Health Administration (OSHA), NIOSH, and the independent Occupational Safety and Health Review Commission.

Leading up to the passage of the OSH Act was the collaboration set in motion in 1969 between the Employment Standards Administration of the U.S. Department of Labor and the Institute for Social Research—the Social Environment and Mental Health and the Organizational Behavior programs at The University of Michigan. This collaboration was based on a series of Quality of Employment Surveys conducted between 1969 and 1977 and variously supported over time by the U.S. Department of Labor, NIOSH, and other federal agencies. The surveys were conducted to meet the need for reliable data on the varying conditions of employment and the behaviors, attitudes, and problems associated with employment among employed adults. There was also an interest in the general changes occurring in society that related to work and in developing the technological capacity for monitoring such changes (Quinn & Staines, 1979).

In 1971, the secretary of health, education, and welfare commissioned a task force to examine health, education, and welfare issues in relation to employment (Sauter & Hurrell, 1999). The seminal report, *Work in America*, highlighted (a) the general dissatisfaction with jobs among workers; (b) the psychosocial aspects of worker health; (c) the physical and mental health costs of jobs; (d) the recommendation that work be redesigned to allow workers to participate in decision-making processes affecting their lives; (e) worker self-renewal programs that allow for additional education and training and for worker mobility; and (f) the role of federal policy in relation to the creation of jobs, manpower, and welfare to improve the quality of working life in America (O'Toole & Members of the Special Task Force to the Secretary of Health, Education, and Welfare, 1972).

With these studies came a surge of further research on occupational stress and its effects on worker productivity and health. During the 1980s, studies sought to identify work-related psychological injuries, distress, and disorders among the top 10 occupational health risks by NIOSH (Quick et al., 1997). At the same time, management studies continued to focus on the organizational dimensions of occupational health and safety, including the coining and use of the concepts *safety climate* and *safety performance* (Macik-Frey et al., 2007). By 1990 the term *occupational health psychology* had been coined by Raymond, Wood, and Patrick (1990), and NIOSH put forth its national strategy to prevent work-related psychological disorders (Sauter, Murphy, & Hurrell, 1990), acknowledging that there was not an adequate national surveillance system to assess the scope of the psychological health disorders. Following this there was an emphasis on the development of surveillance systems that could lead to early identification of health problems within populations, identification of health risk factors, and development of intervention and treatment approaches to prevent disorders and improve health (Macik-Frey et al., 2007).

Over the past decade and a half, NIOSH has collaborated with the American Psychological Association (APA) in launching a series of initiatives to promote the new field of OHP. These include graduate training programs in OHP; a series of international conferences on work, stress, and health; establishment of the Society for Occupational Health Psychology (SOHP); and the founding of the *Journal of Occupational Health Psychology*. Over the years, the journal has published articles across a broad range of the topics, including burnout, work–family issues, violence, safety, job insecurity, substance abuse, leadership, aging, workaholism, positive organizational behavior, and more. As the range of studies broadens, new topics signal scholarly shifts in the specialty, with positive health and positive psychology gaining recent attention (Macik-Frey et al., 2007). More recently, the topic of OHDs has gained increased attention, and in 2011 NIOSH held a national conference on Eliminating Health and Safety Disparities at Work. At the same time, changes at the macro level have also affected the conditions and organizational context of work. These include technology and globalization, both of which have had major impacts on work in the 21st century, both within the workplace and within the broader economic environment.

Globalization has brought recognition to the notion of a global workforce and the need to protect the health, safety, and welfare of its members. At the same time, economic restructuring has resulted in flatter companies, leaner production processes, and new management policies. These changes provide numerous new dimensions of work life to study. However, it is important to keep in mind that globalization is not the result of objective evolutionary processes (Paul & O'Brien, 2006). Rather, it is the result of deliberate policies and practices based on the ideology of free-market fundamentalism better known as *neoliberalism*. Although OHP recognizes legislation as an important factor in worker health and safety, it does not have a salient focus on policies and legislation. As a consequence, it tends to accept the changing context of firms and corporations as given and tends to study its effects rather than considering the possibility of changing the policies that are influencing the nature and context of work today—that is, recognizing the trajectory of a society based on free-market fundamentalist policies, which tend to run against the mission of occupational health organizations. It may be that the study of occupational health must be broadened to include sociological and political theory to expand its influence on the improvement of worker health and safety conditions. Indeed, perhaps occupational health can be viewed as the nexus by which the distribution of power in society and its influence on the work lives of employed adults can be examined and ultimately altered.

RECENT DEVELOPMENTS IN OHDS AMONG RACIAL AND ETHNIC MINORITIES

The nature and extent of OHDs among racial and ethnic minorities can be better explained by describing several recent developments that have provided the context for the current volume.

Healthy People 2000

From a federal government perspective, the current focus on health disparities research can be traced back to the national Healthy People 2000 initiative. In his update, Koh (2010) pointed out that the initiative was launched by the U.S. Department of Health and Human Services in 1979. It was based on a systematic approach to health improvement at the national level and identified baseline data and 10-year targets by monitoring outcomes and evaluating the effects across the country. In addition, it also included multiple iterations during the last 4 decades.

In their overview of Healthy People 2000, Mason and McGinnis (1990) noted that the aims of the initiative were

> to increase the span of healthy life and reduce the disparities in health status experienced by different groups of Americans through the prevention of disease and disability. . . . Health promotion, health protec-

tion, and preventive services are employed as three broad approaches to improving the health status of the population. . . . In addition, objectives are established for improved surveillance and data systems, and a cross listing is provided for the objectives according to the age groups that are targeted. (p. 441)

Mason and McGinnis (1990) noted a mixed picture with regard to the outcomes being evaluated within the initiative. For example, although death rates declined for three of the leading causes of death among Americans (i.e., heart disease, stroke, and motor vehicle crashes), many of the gains in the 1980s were not shared by certain population groups. The national monitoring discovered that certain high-risk groups were bearing a disproportionate share of disease, disability, and premature death compared with the general population. It was this pattern of findings that gave rise to the attention to health disparities among different groups in the country. Specifically, Mason and McGinnis (1990) observed that

> health disparities between the poor and those with higher incomes are almost universal for all dimensions of health. Those disparities may be summarized by the finding that people with low incomes may have death rates twice that of people with adequate incomes. Poverty reduces a person's prospects for long life by increasing the chances of infant death, chronic disease, and traumatic death. For the coming decade, perhaps no challenge is more compelling than that of equal opportunity for good health. (p. 443)

From their review of the status of the Healthy People 2000 initiative, Mason and McGinnis (1990) concluded that special attention was needed to reduce and eventually eliminate these health disparities in death, disease, and disability rates experienced by these groups compared with the general population. Thus, the nation's attention was directed to the health disparities uncovered by the Healthy People initiative.

The Institute of Medicine's *Unequal Treatment* Report

A concomitant of the U.S. history with regard to racial and ethnic minorities is the inequities experienced by these groups in the nation's health system. Whereas research on such racial and ethnic differences in access to and quality of health care has a long history, critical attention to the problem was catalyzed by the national report *Unequal Treatment* (Institute of Medicine, 2003). In some sense this report was the culmination of the undeniable pattern of health disparities among racial and ethnic minorities uncovered by the national monitoring undertaken in the Healthy People initiative. *Unequal Treatment* stimulated greater attention to the topic and galvanized the country's scientific community's attention to this problem. One example of this development is the transition of the National Center on Minority Health and Health Disparities to the National Institute on Minority Health and Health Disparities in 2010. The promotion of the center to that of an institute represents the recognition by National Institutes of Health of the increasing importance of minority health disparities and provides a more central structure for addressing this national challenge.

The abstract from *Unequal Treatment* (Institute of Medicine, 2003) provides an excellent summary of the health disparities identified in the study:

> Racial and ethnic minorities tend to receive a lower quality of healthcare than non-minorities, even when access-related factors, such as patients' insurance status and income, are controlled. The sources of these disparities are complex, are rooted in historic and contemporary inequities, and involve many participants at several levels, including health systems, their administrative and bureaucratic processes, utilization managers, healthcare professionals, and patients. Consistent with the charge, the study committee focused part of its analysis on the clinical encounter itself and found evidence that stereotyping, biases, and uncertainty on the part of health care providers can all contribute to unequal treatment. The conditions in which many clinical encounters take place—characterized by high time pressure, cognitive complexity, and pressures for cost containment—may enhance the likelihood that these processes will result in care poorly matched to minority patients' needs. Minorities may experience a range of other barriers to accessing care, even when insured at the same level as Whites, including barriers of language, geography, and cultural familiarity. Further, financial and institutional arrangements of health systems, as well as the legal, regulatory, and policy environment in which they operate, may have disparate and negative effects on minorities' ability to attain quality care. (p. 1)

Since the publication of *Unequal Treatment*, the scientific literature has grown exponentially. For example, a search of PsycINFO for the decade before the release of the Institute of Medicine report for research on "health disparities" yielded 5,244 entries (1999–2009). Using the same search term in PsycINFO for just the last 4 years yielded over 8,573 entries (2010–2014). This translates to an average of 524 articles per year before *Unequal Treatment* and an average of 2,143 articles per year afterward, a 400% increase.

In 2014, Smedley and Myers (2014) provided an updated review of the research progress with regard to health disparities in a special issue of the *Journal of Social Issues*. As represented by the articles in that special issue, health disparities continue to remain a major problem for racial and ethnic minorities. Indeed, in their guest editors' introduction to the issue, Smedley and Myers (2014) pointed to the mechanisms of racism and discrimination as key factors in the health status of people of color. They had organized the special issue as an attempt to connect research on racism and how it "operates at the interpersonal, internalized, institutional, and structural levels" (Smedley & Myers, 2014, p. 382) to maintain these health disparities and concluded that policy strategies are needed to mitigate the racism—health relationship underlying this national problem.

OHD According to NIOSH

NIOSH's program on OHDs (NIOSH, 2012) recognized that both general and occupational health disparities have a disproportionate impact on racial and ethnic minorities and those with lower socioeconomic status:

> As the workforce becomes more diverse, it has also become clear that there are disparities in the burden of disease, disability, and death experienced by certain population groups, including low-income workers and racial/ethnic minorities. The public health research community has conducted many excellent studies which document the growing disparities in rates of health outcomes such as cardiovascular disease, cancer, and mental health, as well as in the access to and quality of care. Although not as well researched, current statistics indicate that disparities also exist in the rates of occupational illnesses and injuries. Occupational hazards are known to be distributed differentially; workers with specific biologic, social, and/or economic characteristics are more likely to have increased risks of work-related diseases and injuries. Therefore, one of the priority areas established by the National Occupational Research Agenda (NORA) in 1996 was improving research to define the nature and magnitude of risks experienced by these special populations and to develop appropriate intervention and communication strategies. (NIOSH, 2012)

METHODOLOGICAL CONCERNS IN OHD RESEARCH

Research in OHD, much like cross-cultural and cross-national research in any other topic areas, faces particular challenges. The first challenge is *measurement equivalence*, which refers to the extent to which instruments or scales maintain their meaning and calibration across samples with different cultural or national backgrounds (Sanchez, Spector, & Cooper, 2006). Measurement equivalence is of particular importance when the instrument is based on self-reports. For example, researchers may compare burnout symptoms assessed by a set of self-reported questionnaire items across different racial or ethnic groups. These scales are often developed and validated in the mainstream (e.g., racial or ethnic majorities) samples, with minimum attention paid to establishing the measurement equivalence when they are applied to samples with different cultural backgrounds (Stewart & Nápoles-Springer, 2003). As such, diverse group members' (e.g., racial or ethnic minorities) scores on these scales may reflect not only their true scores on the construct that the scale intends to assess (e.g., burnout) but also their potential biases, rendering the comparison between groups difficult to interpret.

Moreover, when conducting research on OHDs, researchers often have to adapt the established scales or interview protocols from its original language (e.g., English) to the native language because the target population (e.g., immigrants) may not be sufficiently fluent in English. In this case, researchers typically use the translation-back-translation procedure (Brislin, 1980), such that the items are first translated into the target language (e.g., Mandarin) by the first translator and then are translated back to their original language (e.g., English) by a second, independent translator. The back-translated items are compared with the original items so that discrepancies can be identified and resolved. Although the translation-back-translation procedure can result in a version of the scale in an alternative language that is similar in meaning compared with its original version, some researchers have questioned the extent to which this procedure can produce precise matches in connotative meaning between versions of the same scale (e.g., Chang & Spector, 2011). In particular, Chang and Spector (2011) discussed the possibility that while an item may appear to have the same meaning across two languages, its relative standing on the construct it intends to measure may be different across two languages. For example, English-speaking participants may interpret an item as reflecting a mild symptom of burnout, whereas Mandarin-speaking participants may interpret the same item as indicative of a more severe symptom of burnout. In this case, participants' responses to the same item, although seemingly equivalent, may actually reflect their different standings on the construct of burnout.

In addition to a rigorous translation-back-translation procedure, measurement equivalence may be statistically established (Nye & Drasgow, 2011). Two approaches are often used to test the measurement equivalence. The first approach uses the differential item functioning analysis within the item-response theory framework to assess whether individuals with the same standing on a variable but from different groups assessed by the scale have the equal observed scores. This approach allows researchers to determine whether items behave differently across different samples (Chang & Spector, 2011; Nye & Drasgow, 2011). A second approach is the confirmatory factor analysis to compare the mean and covariance structure. This approach allows researchers to compare the factor structure of a set of items and may establish equivalence based on a set of more stringent (e.g., equivalent means and covariance) versus relaxed (e.g., similar factor structure with nonequivalent loadings) criteria (Vandenberg & Lance, 2000). The confirmatory factor analysis also allows researchers to examine the equivalence of multiple scales at the same time (Chang & Spector, 2011). Both approaches can be useful in evaluating measurement equivalence for OHDs research that involves comparing multiple groups with different backgrounds.

Finally, even objective records (e.g., occupational fatality or injury rates) or assessment (e.g., objective socioeconomic status) may have measurement equivalence concerns (Stewart & Nápoles-Springer, 2003). For example, Braveman, Cubbin, Marchi, Egerter, and Chavez (2001) found that different objective indicators of socioeconomic status, such as education level and income, were interpreted differently across racial and ethnic groups. They cautioned researchers interested in health disparities to select the appropriate measure of socioeconomic status that is based on clear conceptual justification.

A second methodological challenge in research on OHDs is sample equivalence. *Sample equivalence* refers to the extent to which the samples involved in a health disparity comparison study are different in only the factor that is presumably resulting in the disparity (e.g., gender, race, ethnicity; Sanchez et al., 2006). Sample equivalence is important because it helps rule out potential confounding variables that may explain the observed differences in occupational health and safety indicators between the groups. For example, researchers may collect data from U.S.-born versus foreign-born farm workers to compare their exposure risk to chemicals used in pesticides. Although these two groups may appear to be equivalent in their occupation, there may be other differences between them (e.g., educational background, English fluency) that may contribute to the differential exposure risk for the two groups. These confounding variables add to the difficulty in interpreting the results.

Because it is not always possible to have case-controlled or matched samples to ensure sample equivalence, one way that researchers can address the sample equivalence challenge is by including additional measures of potential confounding variables in their study. These variables can then be empirically tested and controlled in the analysis to help establish the statistical equivalence between the samples (Chang & Spector, 2011). This approach relies on researchers to accurately anticipate the potential confounding variables and to carefully plan for their assessment. Alternatively, Chang and Spector (2011) argued that replication of the findings across multiple samples and study sites may be another way to help rule out some confounding variables.

Finally, a third methodological concern for research on OHDs is the assessment of the specific factors that may explain the disparity between groups. Although the first step for research on OHDs is to establish the existence of disparities between groups, extending beyond the initial step to identify the mechanisms underlying these disparities can represent some methodological challenges. This is in part because the root cause of OHDs may be complex and reflect multilevel processes that have dynamic and reciprocal effects on each other and on disparities. Thus, researchers need to design and use measures that can capture these processes to better understand the factors contributing to OHDs (Chang & Spector, 2011).

OVERVIEW OF THIS BOOK

Through its OHE program, NIOSH has sought to examine how some worker groups suffer disproportionate rates of disease, injury, and fatality compared with the population in general. This volume, based on a conference grant from NIOSH, is an extension of those efforts. Specifically, we organized the Michigan State University (MSU) Symposium on Multicultural Psychology, which generated this volume, to provide a review of the current state of the field and to formulate research needs and identify directions for future research and interventions to address OHDs. This volume follows the organization structure of the conference and therefore has been organized into three tracks of policy, research, and interventions. This tripartite organization is important because these three dimensions are interrelated and inform each other. Leading experts in these three areas were invited to present at the MSU Symposium and then prepare a more in-depth exposition of the ideas and issues presented at the conference.

All too frequently in the public health literature, occupational safety and health is treated as a bottom-up phenomenon. Injuries, fatalities, and efforts at their reduction are often conceptualized as factors, usually in terms of dollars and cents, impacting the overall economy. In Chapter 1, Martinez makes a strong argument that decisions made at the highest levels contribute significantly to the health inequities experienced by workers. Martinez draws clear connections between global economic policy and the significant OHD experienced by Latino workers, particularly immigrants, in the United States. Clearly, it is time to recognize that just as mandating implementation of health and safety measures in the workplace can impact economic bottom lines, policies aimed at the broader economy can lead to unintended hardship and tragedy in the workplace.

Moure-Eraso and Brunette argue in Chapter 2 that employment conditions are an important factor influencing the health of Latino workers. They hold that employment conditions are one of the nine social determinants of health identified by the WHO Commission on Social Determinants of Health. Employment conditions, however, are influenced by broader structural and community factors such as labor markets, social discrimination, work organizations, government regulatory agencies, educational systems, population characteristics, and linkages between the provision of health services and employment. These factors impact the conditions of employment and the levels of risk of exposure to hazards, and consequently they impact the health of Latino workers. Moure-Eraso and Brunette provide a demographic overview of OHDs experienced by Latinos, including fatal occupational rates for native- and foreign-born Latino workers. They apply the WHO Social Determinants Framework of Employment Conditions and Health to Latino workers, which includes structural, individual social status, and intermediate factors (employment conditions), and they identify critical structural and intermediate intervention points.

In Chapter 3, Tetrick discusses how OHDs are largely driven by social status associated with the occupations and, therefore, reflect the general health disparities in the society. Racial and ethnic minorities are more likely to be employed in occupations with lower pay and prestige and higher risks of exposure to chemical, physical, and biological hazards. This tendency is similar across males and females. Although workers of these low-status occupations tend to suffer higher rates of occupational illnesses and injuries, Tetrick discusses additional mechanisms through which social status as reflected by occupation may have implications for employees' health and well-being. In particular, employees in these low-status occupations may perceive that they have low social status and restricted access to health care and experience more unfairness and stress associated with their low income. These psychological factors may mediate the effects of occupation status on workers' health.

Chapter 4 by Arcury and Quandt details the process and progress of a multiyear, multiphasic intervention intended to reduce the exposure of Latino immigrant agricultural workers and their families to insecticides. The discussion of the participatory action approach used by this project could serve as a primer for both scholarship and fieldwork for researchers new to this area. Arcury and Quandt remind us that true application of this approach requires engaging community partners as true equals and a willingness to commit professionally to the long-term well-being of a community that risks economic and political backlash through participation in research. However, if one is willing to shoulder these burdens, the rewards are great. Professionally, one is offered the rare opportunity to see research efforts translate directly into improving the well-being of a community, and as success breeds success, one is naturally led to the next research topic ad infinitum.

According to Chapter 5 by Roberts, stress is an internationally recognized health and safety risk factor and has become increasingly visible in the field of occupational disease as research supports the link between occupational stress and problems in health and safety. It contributes to a number of outcomes that threaten organizational success, and stress-related health and safety problems result in considerable losses to industry. An extensive literature indicates that a variety of stressors that are associated with the way jobs are designed, along with other working conditions, contribute to problems in health and safety. It is particularly crucial for stress interventions to be developed for African Americans, who—along with other minority groups—have disparities that reflect inequalities in many aspects of life and are differentially exposed to race-related stressors. African Americans may be more likely than other groups to contend with racial/ethnic discrimination in the workplace.

Chapter 6 by Leong, Chang, and Mak provides a brief history and a demographic overview of Asian Americans with an emphasis on socioeconomic status and OHDs. It presents a process-oriented model for organizing the literature on OHDs and Asian Americans that includes risk/hazards (environmental and individual), human exposure and internal dose factors (bio-physiological, psychological, and behavioral), and health effect outcomes (disparities in symptoms and costs associated with occupational injuries and illnesses). The chapter concludes with sets of research and policy recommendations for addressing the OHDs experienced by Asian Americans.

In Chapter 7, Quandt and Arcury provide key insights into the development of safety training programs for low-wage immigrant workers in manual occupations. First they highlight the need for effective training programs as one way to address OHDs. They summarize the characteristics of effective training programs in general using examples from studies conducted with immigrant workers. They discuss the need for tailoring materials for the target audience and review the characteristics of immigrant workers that shape their training needs. They present a framework for using OSH research to develop training program and provide a detailed example from their own research using the model to create a training program on pesticide safety. They end the chapter with a discussion of procedures for developing effective training activities and materials that can be used in training programs for immigrant workers and provide some final thoughts on research to practice.

Chapter 8 by Kossek and her colleagues focuses on interventions that change the organization of work to reduce work–family conflict and therefore influence employee and family health. Organizational job and demographic population groups often covary in ways that shape work–family and job demands, which creates workplace structures and cultures that systematically influence employee well-being on and off the job. The chapter discusses the content and customization of the Work, Family, and Health Network (WFHN) intervention, which is a large-scale randomized field control work–family and health study. Kossek and her colleagues review the intervention in depth and highlight key findings. They also delineate implications for future research and policy.

Finally, the Afterword by Chang, Ford, and Martinez provides a comprehensive review of OHDs that synthesizes key points presented throughout the book. It identifies common themes and recommends new directions for research, best practices for implementing interventions, and the implications of policy as they relate to addressing OHDs among racial and ethnic minorities.

The purpose of this volume is to provide a review of the major challenges of OHDs experienced by racial and ethnic minorities in this country. These challenges are discussed from the perspectives of research, practice, and policy, with the goal of empowering those three communities in their efforts to reduce the current set of OHD within our increasingly diverse country.

REFERENCES

Barling, J., & Griffiths, A. (2011). A history of occupational health psychology. In J. C. Quick & L. E. Tetrick (Eds.), *Handbook of occupational health psychology* (2nd ed., pp. 21–34). Washington, DC: American Psychological Association.

Braveman, P., Cubbin, C., Marchi, K., Egerter, S., & Chavez, G. (2001). Measuring socioeconomic status/position in studies of racial/ethnic disparities: Maternal and infant health. *Public Health Reports, 116,* 449–463. http://dx.doi.org/10.1016/S0033-3549(04)50073-0

Brislin, R. (1980). Translation and content analysis of oral and written materials. In H. Triandis & J. Berry (Eds.), *Handbook of cross-cultural psychology: Volume 2. Methodology* (pp. 389–444). Boston, MA: Allyn and Bacon.

Chang, C.-H., & Spector, P. E. (2011). Cross-cultural occupational health psychology. In J. Quick & L. Tetrick (Eds.), *Handbook of occupational psychology* (2nd ed., pp. 119–137). Washington, DC: American Psychological Association.

Gordon, M. E., & Burt, R. E. (1981). A history of industrial psychology's relationship with American unions: Lessons from the past and directions for the future. *International Review of Applied Psychology, 30,* 137–156. http://dx.doi.org/10.1111/j.1464-0597.1981.tb00134.x

Institute of Medicine. (2003). *Unequal treatment: Confronting racial and ethnic disparities in health care.* Washington, DC: National Academies Press.

Koh, H. K. (2010). A 2020 vision for healthy people. *The New England Journal of Medicine, 362,* 1653–1656. http://dx.doi.org/10.1056/NEJMp1001601

Kornhauser, A. W. (1930). The study of work feelings. *Personnel Journal, 8,* 348–353.

Macik-Frey, M., Quick, J. C., & Nelson, D. L. (2007). Advances in occupational health: From a stressful beginning to a positive future. *Journal of Management, 33,* 809–840. http://dx.doi.org/10.1177/0149206307307634

Marx, K. (1976). *Capital: A critique of political economy* (Vol. 1). New York, NY: Penguin Books. (Original work published 1867)

Maslow, A. H. (1965). *Eupsychian management: A journal.* Homewood, IL: Irwin-Dorsey.

Mason, J. O., & McGinnis, J. M. (1990). Healthy People 2000: An overview of the national health promotion and disease prevention objectives. *Public Health Report, 105,* 441–448.

Mayo, E. (1933). *The human problems of industrial civilization.* New York, NY: Macmillan.

Mayo, E. (1949). *Hawthorne and the Western Electric Company, the social problems of an industrial civilisation.* New York, NY: Routledge.

Münsterberg, H. (1913). *Psychology and industrial efficiency.* New York, NY: Houghton Mifflin. http://dx.doi.org/10.1037/10855-000

National Institute for Occupational Safety and Health. (2012). *Occupational health disparities: Program description.* Retrieved from: http://www.cdc.gov/niosh/programs/ohd/

National Institute for Occupational Safety and Health. (2016). *Total worker health.* Retrieved from http://www.cdc.gov/NIOSH/twh/

Nye, C. D., & Drasgow, F. (2011). Effect size indices for analyses of measurement equivalence: Understanding the practical importance of differences between groups. *Journal of Applied Psychology, 96,* 966–980. http://dx.doi.org/10.1037/a0022955

Occupational Safety and Health Act of 1970, Pub. L. No. 91-596, 84 Stat. 1590 (1970). Retrieved from https://www.osha.gov/pls/oshaweb/owadisp.show_document?p_table=oshact&p_id=2743

O'Toole, J., & Members of the Special Task Force to the Secretary of Health, Education, and Welfare. (1972). *Work in America.* Washington, DC: U.S. Department of Health, Education, and Welfare. (ERIC Document Reproduction Service No. ED070738).

Paul, J., & O'Brien, R. (Eds.). (2006). *Globalization and economy, Vol. 4: Globalizing labour.* London, England: Sage.

Quick, J. C., Camara, W. J., Johnson, J. V., Sauter, S. L., Hurrell, J. J., Jr., Piotrkowski, C. S., & Spielberger, C. D. (1997). Creating healthier workplaces: The American Psychological Association/National Institute of Occupational Safety and Health cooperative agreement. Introduction and historical overview. *Journal of Occupational Health Psychology, 2,* 3–6. http://dx.doi.org/10.1037/1076-8998.2.1.3

Quinn, R. P., & Staines, G. L. (1979). *The 1977 Quality of Employment Survey: Descriptive statistics, with comparison data from the 1969–70 and the 1972–73 surveys.* Ann Arbor: Survey Research Center, Institute for Social Research, University of Michigan.

Raymond, J. S., Wood, D. W., & Patrick, W. K. (1990). Psychology doctoral training in work and health. *American Psychologist, 45,* 1159–1161. http://dx.doi.org/10.1037/0003-066X.45.10.1159

Roethlisberger, F. J., & Dickson, W. J. (1939). *Management and the worker.* Cambridge, MA: Harvard University Press.

Sanchez, J. I., Spector, P. E., & Cooper, C. L. (2006). Frequently ignored methodological issues in cross-cultural stress research. In P. T. P. Wong & L. C. J. Wong

(Eds.), *Handbook of multicultural perspectives on stress and coping* (pp. 187–201). Dallas, TX: Spring. http://dx.doi.org/10.1007/0-387-26238-5_9

Sauter, S. L., & Hurrell, J. J., Jr. (1999). Occupational health psychology: Origins, content, and direction. *Professional Psychology: Research and Practice, 30*, 117–122. http://dx.doi.org/10.1037/0735-7028.30.2.117

Sauter, S. L., Murphy, L. R., & Hurrell, J. J., Jr. (1990). Prevention of work-related psychological disorders. A national strategy proposed by the National Institute for Occupational Safety and Health (NIOSH). *American Psychologist, 45*, 1146–1158. http://dx.doi.org/10.1037/0003-066X.45.10.1146

Smedley, B. D., & Myers, H. F. (2014). Conceptual and methodological challenges for health disparities research and their policy implications. *Journal of Social Issues, 70*, 381–391.

Stewart, A. L., & Nápoles-Springer, A. M. (2003). Advancing health disparities research: Can we afford to ignore measurement issues? *Medical Care, 41*, 1207–1220. http://dx.doi.org/10.1097/01.MLR.0000093420.27745.48

U.S. Department of Health and Human Services. (2000). *Healthy People 2010: Understanding and improving health* (2nd ed.). Washington, DC: Government Printing Office.

U.S. Department of Health and Human Services. (2016). *Healthy People 2020: Disparities*. Retrieved from https://www.healthypeople.gov/2020/about/foundation-health-measures/Disparities

Vandenberg, R. J., & Lance, C. E. (2000). A review and synthesis of measurement invariance literature: Suggestions, practices, and recommendations for organizational research. *Organizational Research Methods, 3*, 4–70.

Whitehead, T. N. (1938). *The industrial worker* (Vols. 1 and 2). Cambridge, MA: Harvard University Press.

World Health Organization. (2014). *Social determinants of health*. Retrieved from http://www.who.int/social_determinants/sdh_definition/en/

Zickar, M. J. (2003). Remembering Arthur Kornhauser: Industrial psychology's advocate for worker well-being. *Journal of Applied Psychology, 88*, 363–369. http://dx.doi.org/10.1037/0021-9010.88.2.363

Zohar, D. (2003). Safety climate: Conceptual and measurement issues. In J. C. Quick & L. E. Tetrick (Eds.), *Handbook of occupational health psychology* (pp. 123–142). Washington, DC: American Psychological Association.

I

POLICY

1

LATINO OCCUPATIONAL HEALTH AND THE CHANGING REGULATORY CONTEXT OF WORK

RUBÉN O. MARTINEZ

This chapter provides an overview of the changing regulatory context of work for Latinos and the occupational health risks they experience in the workplace. In particular, American neoliberalism's emphasis on deregulation weakens safety and health protections for workers. In this context it is important to examine the occupational safety and health of Latinos, the largest ethnic minority group in the country. Despite the downward trend in fatal occupational injury rates among all racial/ethnic groups over the past half century, Latinos continue to have the highest rates. Fatal work injuries are highest among foreign-born Latino workers, who have experienced increases in work-related deaths since the 1990s. However, the political climate in the country may be changing. The presidential candidate debates in 2016 have raised public concerns about worker rights and questions about the system that favors corporations. It may be that political values and beliefs are

I am thankful to Michael Flynn for his critical comments and contributions on earlier versions of the manuscript. His suggestions greatly improved the final product.

http://dx.doi.org/10.1037/0000021-002
Occupational Health Disparities: Improving the Well-Being of Ethnic and Racial Minority Workers, F. T. L. Leong, D. E. Eggerth, C.-H. Chang, M. A. Flynn, J. K. Ford, and R. O. Martinez (Editors)

shifting from neoliberalism toward a greater emphasis on the Common Good. Even as neoliberal legislators continue to promote policies that augment the neoliberal policy environment, changes in political values are likely to transform the policy context over time. Should that occur, we can expect that working conditions for Latinos and other workers will improve through more collectivist-oriented policy changes.

THE CHANGING REGULATORY CONTEXT
OF WORK AND LATINOS

Occupational health is a function of occupational safety practices, which are shaped by, among other things, politics and the policies that stem from them (Abrams, 2001; Berman, 1977, 1978; Mogensen, 2006a; Pouliakas & Theodossiou, 2013; Wood, 1995). In turn, class and racial struggles provide the context in which occupational safety policies are developed and implemented (Rosner & Markowitz, 1987; Wood, 1995). Today, occupational safety occurs within the regulatory context shaped by neoliberalism, the most powerful political movement of the past 4 decades (Martinez & Rocco, 2016; Mogensen, 2003, 2006a). As used here, *neoliberalism* refers to the political economic movement of the past half century that promotes free market fundamentalism and economic freedom for individuals and firms (Martinez, 2016). It is in this context that the conditions of work and occupational safety and health of workers play out and result in occupational health disparities among the major racial and ethnic groups (Leong, Eggerth, Flynn, Roberts, & Mak, 2012).

Latinos became the second largest ethnic group in the country at the turn of the 21st century, following White Americans in population size and replacing African Americans as the largest racial minority group. In this precarious position Latinos have become the nation's "canaries in the coal mines" for understanding the impact of neoliberalism on minority workers. This chapter focuses on the regulatory context of work and identifies occupational health patterns among Latinos by highlighting occupational injuries, mortalities, and diseases. The view is that it is important to examine occupational safety among Latinos in the nation's industries, and given the few studies on the occupational health and safety of Latino workers, it is important to bring them into the mainstream of research on worker safety and health. It is argued that the ideology of limited government and deregulation, core emphases of neoliberalism, weakens safety and health protections for workers and that Latinos, by virtue of being concentrated in occupations with relatively higher rates of workplace injuries and fatalities, are at greater risk than workers from other subpopulations.

Neoliberalism in this country emphasizes, among other things, a political philosophy of radical individualism, limited government, and flexible labor (Martinez, 2016). The emphasis on radical individualism centers on individual responsibility for economic well-being and achievement, with all people expected to take care of themselves and their families. Under limited government, the primary policy emphases are deregulation; privatization; and consistent with radical individualism, the elimination of social programs through the reduction of taxes, especially taxes on corporations. Flexible labor emphasizes maximum flexibility for firms and corporations to determine the terms and conditions of employment to minimize the impact of economic downturns. Flexible labor also seeks to minimize benefits to workers and is antithetical to organized labor and other forms of fixed costs to firms. Its primary approach emphasizes part-time and temporary employment, with a recent turn by firms toward opting out of workers' compensation programs, which are state-based employer insurance programs that provide compensation to workers injured at work. Of the major emphases of neoliberalism, it is deregulation that has the principal effect on the workplace and its safety features. Deregulation has included legislative, legal, and administrative approaches intended to allow employers to determine safety practices in the workplace with minimum government intervention (Bain, 1997; Cooper, 2009).

The Changing Economy and Workplace

The world of work today is considerably different from that of the recent past and continues to change because of the influence of several factors. For example, neoliberalism and technology each have had major impacts on the workplace, with the former changing the policy context and the latter changing the nature of work by influencing communications and equipment. Neoliberalism has had a tremendous effect on the economy in general, with market liberalization leading both to the runaway plant phenomenon of the 1980s, when manufacturing firms in this country moved to developing countries to reduce the costs of labor, and to increased regional economic integration efforts during the 1990s (e.g., the North American Free Trade Agreement, or NAFTA). The decline of manufacturing and the growth of the service sector (often called economic restructuring) across the country displaced millions of workers through job losses and redistributed them across occupations, industries, and geographic regions (Lee & Mather, 2008). Altogether, these shifts have set in motion a "race to the bottom" in which the living standards of millions of U.S. workers have declined over the past several decades (Tonelson, 2000).

A hostile environment toward organized labor, the decline of labor union influence, the rise of part-time/temporary employment, and the declining value of the minimum wage have exacerbated the situation by negatively impacting access to health care and other employment benefits for workers even as the Affordable Care Act has been implemented. The rise of part-time employment is a result of the shift of employment from manufacturing toward trade and service industries, which are linked to secondary labor markets characterized by low wages, low skill sets, and high employee turnover rates (Shaefer, 2009). It is also the result of firms adopting secondary labor market processes to reduce costs, including avoiding having to pay employee benefits (Tilly, 1991). Finally, since the 1980s, the share of prime-age men classified as *nonemployed* has steadily risen at the same time that labor force participation among women has increased and begun to converge with that of men (Bednarzik, Hewson, & Urquhart, 1982; Lee & Mather, 2008).

The displacement of workers from their jobs has probably engendered the greatest economic misery. During the 1980s, the number of displaced workers through job loss remained at approximately 10 million across the decade (Podgursky, 1992). More recently, during the period of the Great Recession of 2007–2008 more than 8 million jobs were lost. Between 2009 and 2011, there were 12.9 million displaced workers across the country (Bureau of Labor Statistics [BLS], 2012b). Most widely impacted were low-skilled workers in construction, retail, and manufacturing industries (Killingsworth, Grosskopf, & Hernandez, 2012; Podgursky, 1992).

Minorities have traditionally been hardest hit by economic downturns and have borne a heavier burden stemming from widespread job displacement and the Great Recession (Aguirre & Martinez, 2014; Gardner, 1995; Kletzer, 1991; Kochhar, Fry, & Taylor, 2011; McKernan, Ratcliffe, Steuerle, & Zhang, 2013; Smeeding, 2012). Between 1981 and 1992, Latinos had the highest job displacement rates (between 2.9% and 4.8%) of major racial/ethnic groups (Whites from 2.4% to 3.8%, Blacks from 2% to 3.8%; Gardner, 1995). The result has been widespread increases in poverty, as millions of families were put at financial risk and in precarious financial situations (Mishel, Bivens, Gould, & Shierholz, 2012; Navarro, 1998). In 2014, Latinos had a poverty rate (23.6%) that was nearly 2.5 times that of Whites (10.1%; DeNavas-Walt & Proctor, 2015), with the gap slightly reduced from previous years.

With the rise of neoliberalism in the late 1970s, particularly in the form of deregulation, workplace safety became less of a critical public concern than it had been in previous years (Mogensen, 2006b). With the passage of the Occupational Safety and Health Act in 1970 came the assurance of a safe and healthful workplace for working men and women (Mogensen, 2003). Little did workers know that a major political movement was underway that would lead to persistent political attacks on social and environmental regulations, including workplace safety regulations.

At the same time that neoliberal policies were undermining the regulatory context, technology changed the workplace by providing new tools that altered the way workers carry out their duties. Perhaps because of the racial division of labor, Latino workers, who are concentrated in certain occupations within key sectors of the economy, were affected in ways different from those in other occupations (Richardson, Ruser, & Suarez, 2003). For example, within the division of labor, communications technology has had a greater impact on white-collar than on blue-collar occupations, where manual labor remains central. This is particularly the case in agricultural, landscape, construction, and other occupational sectors in which Latinos are found in significant numbers.

Additionally, neoliberalism has influenced the dynamics and cycles of the economy, which has experienced 11 recessions since 1945 (Killingsworth, Grosskopf, & Hernandez, 2012); contributed to the lack of stable employment; depressed wages; contributed to the rise of part-time employment; and increased the number of family members (men, women, children, and elders) having to work to maintain a middle-class lifestyle with regular access to health care. The displacement of workers over the past four decades has led not only to increased rates of downward and geographical mobility but also to major shifts in the skill sets required of workers. As firms adjust to changes in the economy, particularly with the rise of electronic communications, nanotechnology, and green industries, the skill sets of the labor force require alignment with those demanded by emerging and changing occupations. The misalignment between skill sets and jobs have required massive investment in the "retooling" of workers.

Overall, workers in general are more vulnerable today under neoliberal policies than they were under Keynesian policies of the middle 20th century when there were progressive efforts to address dangers in the workplace (Abrams, 2001). Not only has job insecurity increased, there has been an intensification of the racial division of labor as racial and ethnic groups compete for jobs. Not surprisingly, the result has been that occupational and industry instabilities have led to persisting occupational segregation for Latinos (Alonso-Villar, Gradin, & del Rio, 2012; Watts, 1995). Indeed, one can expect that during periods of economic instability and increased competition for jobs, racial tensions will increase, and the dominant group will use whatever mechanisms are at its disposal to secure and maintain employment for its members. Ironically, between 1983 and 2002, occupational segregation declined for Blacks while it increased for Latinos (Queneau, 2009), with occupational segregation persisting into the present for each subpopulation (Hamilton, Austin, & Darity, 2011). At the same time, pay inequality and occupational segregation intensified for immigrant Latinos (Catanzarite, 2000). Further, Hudson (2007) suggested that citizenship is at least as important as race and gender in channeling workers into less desirable, more dangerous jobs, and Flynn, Eggerth, and Jacobson (2015) provided a view on how this occurs for those workers with undocumented status. It is during this period (1983–2002) that Latinos experienced rapid population growth and eclipsed Blacks as the largest racial minority group in the country.

Deregulation and Workplace Safety

The pursuit of "economic freedom" by neoliberals has led to the decline of the enforcement of health and safety standards in the workplace and a climate in which employers are encouraged to comply voluntarily with occupational health and safety standards (Scholz, 1984). Deregulation takes two forms: (a) weakening or eliminating existing safety regulations and (b) reducing resources to regulatory and enforcement agencies so that they are unable to carry out their mission. Although the contemporary deregulation movement began in the 1970s, when a coalition of interests sought the deregulation of the transportation industry, it wasn't until the 1980s that the Occupational Safety and Health Administration (OSHA) became one of the primary targets of deregulation efforts (Maakestad & Helm, 1989). Between 1980 and 1987, for instance, the number of inspectors was reduced by 25%, and citations and penalties dropped dramatically during the same period. Since that period there have been numerous reports by the U.S. Government Accountability Office (GAO) highlighting weaknesses at OSHA and providing recommendations on how to improve its performance (GAO, 1990, 2002, 2012, 2013a, 2013b). These include concerns about lax penalties and the length of time taken by OSHA in its rulemaking process. As such, it is doubtful that the agency can effectively carry out its public mission in a context where there is legislative hostility toward regulation in general and toward occupational health and safety standards enforcement in particular.

In 2007, the Subcommittee on Employment and Workplace Safety of the Committee on Health, Education, Labor, and Pensions of the U.S. Senate held a hearing titled *Is OSHA Working for Working People?* (2007). There it was acknowledged that since the passage of the Occupational Safety and Health Act in 1970, there has been significant progress in reducing work-related injuries, fatalities, and exposure to toxins, but that progress has slowed in recent years and may be reversing. The slowing of progress and possible reversal are the result of underfunding, reduced staff, limited enforcement capabilities, lax penalties, and agency limitations on promulgating new standards. Moreover, with changes that have occurred in the workplace, new hazards, along with persisting ones, continue to place workers in the path of harm. Not only are there inconsistencies across states, but also across industries. In this context, it is likely that Latino workers, who are dispropor-tionally represented in more dangerous industries, are at risk of greater safety and health risks at their workplaces than members of other population groups (Byler, 2013; Strong & Zimmerman, 2005). It is the occupational health pat-terns among Latinos that are the focus in the next section.

Latino Workers and Occupational Health

According to the BLS (2014), Latinos comprised 16% of the nation's labor force in 2013 and are projected to increase to 19.8% by 2024 (Toossi, 2015). Non-Hispanic Whites comprised 64.6% of the labor force in 2014 and are projected to decrease to 59.6% by 2024 (Toossi, 2015). Latinos in the labor force have the lowest median age (36.9), followed by Blacks (39.3), Asians (41.2), and non-Hispanic Whites (43.6; BLS, 2012a). The pattern is expected to remain through 2020. Latinos have the highest participation rate (66%) in the labor force among the largest population groups (Whites, 63.5%; Blacks 59.2%), with Native Hawaiian and Other Pacific Islanders having the highest rate (70%; BLS, 2014). Among adult men (20 years of age and older), Latinos have the highest participation rate (81.1%), whereas among women, Blacks have the highest participation rate (61.8%, with Latinas having a rate of 58.5% and White women having a rate of 58.2%). The median weekly earnings for full-time wage and salary Latino workers in 2013 were $578, compared with $802 for Whites, $629 for Blacks, and $942 for Asians. The overall patterns were similar for men and women (BLS, 2014).

Table 1.1 presents the annual percentage averages of employed and the percentage of total employed persons 16 years of age and older by major occu-pational categories by race/ethnicity for 2013. In terms of their distribution across major occupational categories, among the groups, Latinos were least represented (20.2%) in management, professional, and related occupations, compared with Whites (38.8%), Blacks (28.7%), and Asians (49.6%). On the other hand, they were most represented in the categories of service (26.7%); natural resources, construction, and maintenance operations (15.4%); and production, transportation, and material moving occupations (16.5%). At a more specific level, they were most overrepresented among miscellaneous agricultural workers (50%), grounds maintenance workers (45%), and maids and housekeeping cleaners (44%, not shown in table; BLS, 2014), where they comprise large percentages of employees. With respect to total persons employed, the figures in Table 1.1 show that with the exception of Whites, and relative to other racial groups, Latinos are most overrepresented in natu-ral resources, construction, and maintenance operations (26.5%); service occupations (23.1%); and production, transportation, and material moving occupations (21.9%).

TABLE 1.1

Percentage Employed and Percentage of Total Employed Persons 16 Years of Age and Older in the Workforce by Major Occupational Categories by Race/Ethnicity, 2013 Annual Averages

| | Race/Ethnicity | | | | | | | |
| | Latinos | | Whites | | Blacks | | Asian | |
Occupational category	% Employed	% of Total	% Employed	% of Total	% Employed	% of Total	% Employed	% of Total
Management, professional, and related occupations	20.2	8.3	38.8	81.9	28.7	11.2	49.6	7.4
Service occupations	26.7	23.1	16.8	74.8	25.6	15.8	17.1	5.4
Sales and office occupations	23.1	14.4	23.3	80.5	24.3	9.7	19.9	5.2
Natural resources, construction, and maintenance operations	15.4	26.5	9.9	87.2	5.7	7.0	3.6	2.2
Production, transportation, and material-moving occupations	16.5	21.9	11.4	77.4	15.7	14.9	9.7	4.6

Note. Latinos may be of any race and are included among Whites. They are most concentrated among Whites, Blacks, and Asians. They are most concentrated among Whites, which has the effect of reducing their differences with the dominant group. The "% of total" is the measure of the members of a population category as part of the overall employed segment of the labor force. From *Labor Force Characteristics by Race and Ethnicity, 2013* (BLS Report 1050, p. 23) by the Bureau of Labor Statistics, 2014, Washington, DC: U.S. Department of Labor. In the public domain.

Table 1.2 shows the percentage employed for persons 16 years of age and older by industry and race/ethnicity for 2013 annual averages. The nation's labor force is distributed across 13 major industries, with the largest percentage working in education and health services (22.6%), followed by wholesale and retail trade (13.7%), professional and business services (11.7%), manufacturing (10.3%), and leisure and hospitality (9.4%). This distribution shows how little the nation's economy is based on manufacturing and how much of it is based on other industries. Private household services (0.5%), mining and other extraction activities (0.7%), agriculture and related industries (1.5%), information (2.1%), and wholesale trade (2.5%) have the lowest percentages of the labor force.

Relative to other racial groups, Latinos are most represented in agriculture and related industries (2.2%), construction (10.5%), wholesale and retail trade (13.6%), and leisure and hospitality (13.1%). By contrast, Latinos

TABLE 1.2
Percentage Employed Persons 16 Years of Age and Older
by Industry and Race/Ethnicity, 2013 Annual Averages

Industry	Race/Ethnicity				
	Total	Latinos	Whites	Blacks	Asian
Agriculture and related industries	1.5	2.2	1.7	0.4	0.4
Mining, quarrying, and oil and gas extraction	0.7	1.0	0.7	0.4	0.2
Construction	6.4	10.5	7.2	2.9	2.4
Manufacturing	10.3	10.4	10.5	8.8	12.5
Durable goods	6.4	5.6	6.7	4.9	8.3
Nondurable goods	3.8	4.7	3.8	3.9	4.2
Wholesale and retail trade	13.7	13.6	13.8	13.1	12.8
Wholesale trade	2.5	2.6	2.7	1.8	2.2
Retail trade	11.1	11.1	11.1	11.2	10.6
Transportation and utilities	5.2	5.3	4.8	7.8	4.0
Information	2.1	1.4	2.1	2.0	2.2
Financial activities	6.8	5.1	7.0	5.9	7.5
Professional and business services	11.7	11.7	11.7	9.8	14.9
Education and health services	22.6	16.4	21.9	28.3	22.4
Leisure and hospitality	9.4	13.1	9.1	9.4	11.2
Other services	5.0	5.8	5.0	4.4	6.1
Other services, except private households	4.4	4.7	4.4	4.0	5.8
Private households	0.5	1.2	0.5	0.4	0.3
Public administration	4.7	3.5	4.4	6.8	3.5

Note. Latinos may be of any race and are included among Whites, Blacks, and Asians. They are most concentrated among Whites, which has the effect of reducing their differences with the dominant group. From *Labor Force Characteristics by Race and Ethnicity, 2013* (BLS Report 1050, p. 34) by the Bureau of Labor Statistics, 2014, Washington, DC: U.S. Department of Labor. In the public domain.

are least represented in comparison with other racial groups in education and health services (16.4%), financial activities (5.1%), and information (1.4%). As the second-largest population group in the nation, it is particularly interesting that they have such limited presence in public administration (3.5%) compared with Blacks (6.8%), who have nearly twice the rate in that sector.

Occupational Health Disparities

Occupational health disparities denote disproportionate rates of workforce injuries, fatalities, illnesses, and health outcomes by socioeconomic status and race/ethnicity due to work activities and workplace environments. For Latinos, disparities are linked to structural inequalities based on class, gender, and institutional racism (Strong & Zimmerman, 2005). Disparities occur in contexts of uneven regulatory environments that also are linked to and reflect institutional racism, structured inequalities, and power differentials (Krieger et al., 2006).

Latinos, especially immigrants, are more likely to be concentrated at the lower end of the occupational structure, where vulnerabilities are more common and enforcement of safety standards less likely (Orrenius & Zavodny, 2009). Additional factors on the job, such as language barriers (Lashuay & Harrison, 2006; National Research Council, 2003; Rhodes, 2006); lack of knowledge about workplace safety procedures and regulatory protections (Arcury, Estrada, & Quandt, 2010; Lashuay & Harrison, 2006; Pransky et al., 2002); and fear of retaliation for raising workplace concerns, including mistreatment, or attempting to unionize (Smith-Nonini, 2003) also contribute to the occupational health disparities for Latinos, especially immigrants. Finally, undocumented status contributes to vulnerabilities and intense exploitation (Flynn, 2010; Flynn, Eggerth, & Jacobson, 2015; Walter, Bourgois, Loinaz, & Schillinger, 2002). This particular segment of the workforce (e.g., undocumented immigrant workers) has to seek information about occupational safety on its own as it does not have the same levels of access commonly available to other workers. That is, not only is safety information less likely to be available in Spanish, but undocumented workers are less familiar with their rights as workers than native-born workers, and they are less likely to request such information from their employers given their vulnerability because of their immigration status.

Official data and reports from agencies such as the BLS represent the most comprehensive data on workplace injuries and diseases. However, they are not perfect tools and often do not include variables specific to immigrant workers, such as immigration status of the victim or duration of time living in the United States, or they rely on employer records that frequently underreport injuries (Leigh, Marcin, & Miller, 2004) and are often missing basic demographic data such as race/ethnicity (Souza, Steege, & Baron, 2010). Therefore, these data should be taken as a low-bound estimate because of concerns about the underreporting of workplace injuries and diseases, particularly among minorities and immigrants.

Even with the underreporting, the data still indicate significant occupational health disparities and are useful in constructing a profile of the occupational health status of Latinos within the nation's industries (Azaroff, Levenstein, & Wegman, 2002; Cierpich et al., 2008; Russer, 2008). Between 1973 and 2007, the overall rate of workplace injuries and illnesses decreased from 11.0 to 4.2 per 100,000 full-time equivalent workers (OSHA, 2008). Similarly, the rate of fatal work injuries decreased from 5.3 in 1992, when there were 6,217 workplace fatalities, to 3.7 in 2007, when there were 5,657 workplace fatalities (OSHA, 2008). In 2007, the industries with the highest fatality rates (per 100,000 workers) were agriculture, forestry, fishing, and hunting (27); mining (25); transportation and warehousing (16); and construction (10). Decreases in the fatality rates for each industry sector occurred from 2007 to 2014, with the exception of construction, which remained basically the same: agriculture, forestry, fishing, and hunting (568; 24.9), mining (181; 14.1), transportation and warehousing (735; 13.5), and construction (874; 9.5; BLS, 2015a)—industries in which Latinos are likely to be employed.

Nonfatal occupational injury and illness rates among Latinos are higher than those of non-Hispanics (Richardson, Ruser, & Suarez, 2003). Between 1998 and 2000, Latino men had the highest overall relative risk of 1.51 for nonfatal occupational injuries and illnesses (Richardson, Ruser, & Suarez, 2003). This compares with a relative risk of 1.07 for non-Hispanic White men and of 1.40 for non-Hispanic Black men. Although Latinas were not at greater risk (1.0) when compared with all working women (1.0) of that period, they were at greater risk when compared with non-Hispanic White women (0.76). Latinas, however, were at slightly lower risk than non-Hispanic Black women (1.06).

Table 1.3 presents the percentage of nonfatal occupational injuries and illnesses in private industry involving days away from work by nature of injury or illness and race/ethnicity for 2004. This table is presented because it highlights a major problem with data collection focused on comparing racial and ethnic groups on select categories of injuries and illnesses. The column in Table 1.3, labeled "R/E not reported" contains the highest reported outcomes, with nearly one third of reported cases involving injured or sick employees. The result is that the interpretability of the statistics in Table 1.3 is problematic and limited because there is no way to identify an accurate general pattern of injuries/illness involving "sick days" among employees by race/ethnicity. However, with the exception of Whites, the population size

TABLE 1.3

Percentage of Nonfatal Occupational Injuries and Illnesses
in Private Industry Involving Days Away From Work by Nature
of Injury or Illness and Race/Ethnicity, 2004

	Race/Ethnicity				
Injuries and illnesses	Latinos	Whites	Blacks	Asians	R/E not reported
Traumatic injuries and disorders	13.2	46.6	8.3	1.3	29.6
Systemic diseases and disorders	10.7	55.0	6.8	1.2	25.6
Infectious and parasitic diseases	2.4	60.7	7.1	—	29.2
Symptoms, signs, and ill-defined conditions	9.4	40.9	9.9	1.8	37.2
Other diseases, conditions, and disorders	10.0	33.2	11.6	1.3	42.5
Multiple diseases, conditions, and disorders	12.6	43.2	4.5	6.3	27.9
Nonclassifiable	23.4	35.7	4.1	4.5	31.0
Total	13.0	47.0	8.2	1.3	29.5

Note. Adapted from *Survey of Occupational Injuries and Illnesses In Cooperation With Participating State Agencies* (Table 73) by the Bureau of Labor Statistics, 2004, Washington, DC: U.S. Department of Labor. In the public domain.

of the Latino population relative to other racial groups suggests that Latinos are likely to be overrepresented in the "R/E not reported" category. Further, Latinos are overrepresented in "nonclassifiable injuries and illnesses," and this calls for further investigation.

A different measure of occupational health is the number of days away from work due to injury or illness. In 2014, the median number of days away from work for Latinos in private industry was 8, the same as that for Whites and Blacks (BLS, 2015e). The statistics were higher for all groups working in state government (Latinos, 9; Whites, 10; and Blacks, 14), whereas those for local government employees were the same or about the same (Latinos, 8; Whites, 8; and Blacks, 9) as their respective overall rate. Unfortunately, the most recent report on employer-reported workplace injuries by the BLS does not provide figures by race/ethnicity (BLS, 2015c). Fortunately, however, some rates are available through the 2014 National Census of Fatal Occupational Injuries that allow for the identification of patterns (BLS, 2015b).

In 2014, there were 4,679 fatal workplace injuries, of which 789 or 17% were among Latinos; 3,174 or 67.8% were among Whites; and 457 or 10% were among Blacks (BLS, 2015a). Of the fatalities among Latinos, 63.8% were among foreign-born workers. Overall, the figures for Latinos reflected an increase of 11.6% from the number of workplace fatalities in 2010, when the number (707) was lowest for the current century. Unfortunately, rates (per

100,000) were not provided (BLS, 2015a), and these increases may reflect the increasing size of the Latino labor force. The occupational categories in which the number of fatalities increased in recent years (2010 through 2014) among Latinos are: (a) service occupations; (b) natural resources, construction, and maintenance operations; and (c) production, transportation, and material moving occupations. This was the case for both native-born and foreign-born workers (BLS, 2015d).

Identifying potential occupational health disparities for chronic occupational illness is very difficult. The lag time between occupational exposures to toxins and the onset of the illness makes chronic occupational illnesses generally hard to document. Given this lag time, medical professionals and workers often do not associate the disease with potential exposures from the workplace. This is made even more difficult for Latinos for several reasons. For example, Latinos are more likely to change employers either because they are overrepresented in the temporary workforce or because they are overrepresented in industries, such as construction and agriculture, which require workers to routinely change employers and/or job sites. This makes tracking exposure to toxins even more difficult than for workers in more stable employment situations.

Even when occupational illness is identified, the increased mobility between job sites can make it difficult to identify where the exposure took place and whom to hold responsible for it. For example, it is generally reported that farmworkers have pesticide exposure and its sequelae often result from chronic exposure to small doses (Arcury & Quandt, 2011). However, the chronic nature of the exposure and the mobility of the workers make it difficult to attribute exposures to specific fields or employers. Latinos also have less access to routine medical care and checkups, which further complicates identifying occupational exposures and illnesses. Given the limitations of the current surveillance systems, the occupational health community is pushing for inclusion of occupational data fields in electronic medical records as a way of improving data collection on occupational illness (Filios et al., 2008). Although it is often assumed that higher rates of injuries for Latino workers likely signal higher rates of occupational illness, this often cannot be determined because of a lack of accurate data. This does not mean, of course, that a relationship is not present for Latino workers.

Table 1.4 shows fatal occupational injury rates by race/ethnicity for the years 1992 through 2008 and 2011 (official rates that are provided irregularly). There has been a consistent downward trend in fatal occupational injury rates among all groups (Latinos, non-Hispanic Whites, and non-Hispanic Blacks). In 2014, the overall rate for the groups as a whole was 3.3 per 100,000 workers. For Latinos, the rate went from 5.6 in 1992 to 3.9 in 2011, for non-Hispanic Whites it went from 4.9 to 3.5, and for non-Hispanic Blacks it went from 5.0 to 3.2. Comparatively speaking, Latinos have the highest rates among the groups, whereas non-Hispanic Blacks tend to have

TABLE 1.4
Fatal Occupational Injury Rates by Race/Ethnicity, 1992–2008, 2011

Year	Race/Ethnicity (%)		
	Latinos	NH-Whites	NH-Blacks
2011	3.9	3.5	3.2
2008	4.2	3.8	3.7
2007	4.6	3.8	3.9
2006	5.0	4.0	3.7
2005	4.9	4.0	3.9
2004	5.0	4.1	3.7
2003	4.5	4.0	3.7
2002	5.0	3.9	3.5
2001	6.0	4.2	3.8
2000	5.6	4.2	3.9
1999	5.2	4.4	4.1
1998	5.2	4.5	4.0
1997	5.1	4.6	4.8
1996	5.3	4.6	4.5
1995	5.4	4.7	5.1
1994	5.6	5.1	5.4
1993	6.5	4.9	5.3
1992	5.6	4.9	5.0

Note. The rate represents the number of fatal occupational injuries per 100,000 full-time equivalent workers. NH = non-Hispanic. Adapted from *Census of Fatal Occupational Injuries—Archived Data* by the Bureau of Labor Statistics. Washington, DC: U.S. Department of Labor. In the public domain.

the lowest rates relative to non-Hispanic Whites. The lower rate for non-Hispanic Blacks relative to non-Hispanic Whites first occurred in 1996 and has been relatively consistent since 1998. Only Latinos have had rates of 6.0 or greater, first in 1993 (6.5), then again in 2001 (6.0). The gap between Latinos and the other groups was greatest in 2001, when it reached 1.8 with non-Hispanic Whites and 2.2 with non-Hispanic Blacks. This points to the need to examine the factors related to the rise and decline of occupational injury rates and if they are the same across groups.

Table 1.5 shows fatal work injuries by race/ethnicity for the years 1992 through 2014. Overall, the number of fatal work injuries among Latinos increased from 533 in 1992 to a high of 990 in 2006, and since then has declined unevenly to 789 in 2014. Still, the number of fatal work injuries for Latinos increased between 1992 and 2014 by 48.1%. By contrast, the number of fatal work injuries among both Whites and Blacks declined. Among Whites, the number increased from 4,711 in 1992 to 5,019 in 1999, then decreased unevenly to 3,174 in 2014, reflecting an overall decline of 32.6%. Similarly, the number of fatal work injuries among Blacks increased from 618 in 1992 to a high of 695 in 1994, then decreased unevenly to 457 in 2014, reflecting an overall decrease of 26.1%. Also important to note is

TABLE 1.5
Fatal Work Injuries by Race/Ethnicity, 1992–2014

| | Fatal work injuries by race/ethnicity, 1992–2014 | | | | | | |
| | Latinos | | Whites | | Blacks | | |
Year	N	%	N	%	N	%	Total
2014	789	16.9	3,174	67.8	457	9.8	4,679
2013	817	16.7	3,125	64.0	439	9.0	4,585
2012	748	16.2	3,177	68.6	486	10.5	4,628
2011	729	15.8	3,257	70.7	433	9.4	4,609
2010	707	15.1	3,363	71.7	412	8.8	4,690
2009	713	15.7	3,204	70.4	421	9.2	4,551
2008	804	15.4	3,663	70.2	533	10.2	5,214
2007	937	16.6	3,867	68.4	609	10.8	5,657
2006	990	17.0	4,019	68.8	565	9.7	5,840
2005	923	16.1	3,977	69.4	584	10.2	5,734
2004	902	15.6	4,066	70.5	546	9.5	5,764
2003	794	14.2	3,988	71.5	543	9.7	5,575
2002	841	15.2	3,926	70.9	491	8.9	5,534
2001	895	15.2	4,175	70.8	565	9.6	5,900
2000	815	13.8	4,244	71.7	575	9.7	5,920
1999	730	12.0	5,019	82.9	627	10.4	6,054
1998	707	11.7	4,478	74.0	583	9.6	6,055
1997	658	10.5	4,576	73.4	661	10.6	6,238
1996	638	10.3	4,586	73.9	615	9.9	6,202
1995	619	9.8	4,599	73.3	684	10.9	6,275
1994	624	9.4	4,954	74.7	695	10.5	6,632
1993	634	10.0	4,665	73.7	649	10.3	6,331
1992	533	8.6	4,711	75.8	618	9.9	6,217

Note. Figures for the year 2001 exclude fatal work injuries resulting from the September 11 terrorist attacks. Total figures include Asians, Native Americans, and Others. Adapted from *Census of Fatal Occupational Injuries, 1992–2014,* by the Bureau of Labor Statistics, 2015, Washington, DC: U.S. Department of Labor. In the public domain.

the relative increase among Latinos of total fatal work injuries, which nearly doubled from 8.6% in 1992 to 16.9% in 2014. By contrast, the percentage of fatal work injuries among Whites decreased from 75.8% in 1992 to 67.8% in 2014, whereas that for Blacks remained relatively stable over time, having decreased slightly from 9.9% in 1992 to 9.8% in 2011. These figures reflect both the changing demographics of the labor force and the disproportionate number of fatal work injuries among Latinos. Although the increase reflects the relative growth of Latinos in the labor force, one is hard pressed to explain the disproportionate numbers. Further, it would be most helpful if official statistics were provided in terms of rates by 100,000 workers, as they would provide a clearer understanding of the disparities across groups.

Table 1.6 shows the number of fatal work injuries among Latinos by nativity status (i.e., whether individuals were born in the United States or

TABLE 1.6
Number of Fatal Work Injuries Among Latino Workers
by Nativity Status, 1992–2014

	Nativity status		
Year	Native born	Foreign born	Total
2014	286	503	789
2013	275	542	817
2012	264	484	748
2011	237	512	749
2010	266	441	707
2009	284	429	713
2008	301	503	804
2007	303	634	937
2006	323	667	990
2005	285	638	923
2004	306	596	902
2003	274	520	794
2002	263	578	841
2001	323	572	895
2000	321	494	815
1999	262	468	730
1998	302	405	707
1997	279	379	658
1996	267	371	638
1995	277	342	619
1994	288	336	624
1993	314	320	634
1992	258	275	533

Note. Figures for the year 2001 exclude fatal work injuries resulting from the September 11 terrorist attacks. *Nativity status* refers to whether a person is native born, that is, born in this country, or foreign born. Adapted from *Census of Fatal Occupational Injuries, 1992–2014,* by the Bureau of Labor Statistics, 2015, Washington, DC: U.S. Department of Labor. In the public domain.

in other countries) for the years 1992 through 2014. Overall, the number of fatal work injuries among Latinos increased from 533 in 1992 to 789 in 2014, reflecting an increase of 48%. Throughout, however, the rates among foreign-born Latino workers are higher than those for native-born Latino workers. The highest number of fatalities among foreign-born workers was 667 in 2006; that year was also among the highest number of fatalities (323) for native-born workers. The greatest gap between the two groups of workers occurred in 2005, when it reached 353. In other words, there were 353 more fatal work injuries among foreign-born workers than among native-born workers. The smallest gap of 17 occurred in 1992. Orrenius and Zavodny (2009) suggested that the *immigrant effect*, or the willingness of immigrants to work in riskier jobs, may explain the higher rates. They also suggested that low English-language proficiency and low educational attainment contribute to the overrepresentation in risky jobs.

The number of fatal workplace injuries among Latinos increased steadily during the 1990s and the early part of this century, reaching a high point in 2006 with 990 fatalities. It has declined since then but remains considerably higher than the figure of 533 in 1992. At the same time, the number and proportion of fatalities of foreign-born workers among Latinos increased significantly from the figure of 275 (51.2%) in 1992. This increase points to several potential problems and areas for possible intervention. Indeed, with the increasing fatality rates and workplace injuries among Latinos, OSHA has identified Latinos as a special emphasis population for targeted outreach activities, including providing Spanish-language resources such as a Spanish-language website, OSHA en Español; Spanish-language publications, including QuickCards and fact sheets on a range of topics; and a toll-free number, (800) 321-OSHA, with 24-7 access to a Spanish-speaking operator for compliance assistance information and other assistance. Still, given the decline in capacity to enforce workplace safety regulations and standards in a neoliberal environment, it is not likely that employers will address the safety needs of foreign-born Latinos. Effective interventions are needed that will increase not only the prevalence of safety practices among Latino workers but also bilingual programs in medical clinics and emergency rooms where they receive treatment (O'Connor, Loomis, Runyan, Abboud dal Santo, & Schulman, 2005).

DISCUSSION

The racial division of labor and occupational segregation have persisted and perhaps worsened for Latinos under neoliberal policies and practices. Occupationally, although employed in all economic sectors, Latinos tend to be overrepresented in leisure and hospitality services; agriculture and related industries; construction and maintenance operations; wholesale and retail trade (packers and packagers); and production, transportation, and material moving occupations. In general, they tend to be at the lower end of the occupational structure, where occupational hazards are more common and enforcement of safety standards is less prevalent.

Accurate data collection on workplace injuries and diseases is problematic (Kraus, 1985) and may have worsened under neoliberalism because there is less emphasis on making official data available by standard racial/ethnic categories in an effort to promote a colorblind order, but it may do nothing more than obscure racial disparities and reinforce hierarchical relations among the groups (Dovidio, Gaertner, & Saguy, 2015). Although workplace injuries and illnesses as a whole decreased over the past half century mainly to the policies adopted in the 1970s, the nation's workers face increasing workplace safety and health hazards because of the dismantling of the net of protections established during the 20th century.

Latinos are overrepresented in industries with the highest fatality rates and have the highest overall risk of nonfatal occupational injuries and illnesses among racial/ethnic groups. Despite the downward trend in fatal occupational injury rates among all groups, Latinos continue to have the highest rates. Latinos no longer experience more days away from work because of injury or illness, but this could reflect both their ethic of "hard work" and vulnerability in their employment that forces them to work even when ill or injured. Finally, fatal work injuries are highest among foreign-born Latino workers, who also have experienced increases in work-related deaths since the 1990s. Coupled with downward pressures on wages, persisting attacks by conservative legislators on health insurance coverage, and the steady dismantling of workplace safety protections and enforcement for workers, we can expect that working conditions for Latinos and other workers will continue to deteriorate, at least in some occupational sectors, in the coming years.

Well-intentioned efforts to provide safety and health support to Latino workers through targeted language programs are helpful but cannot address the scope of the problem in a neoliberal policy environment that is structural in nature and requires interventions across a range of related safety and health areas, but especially in the policy arena. At this point in time, neoliberal politics continue to hold sway, and labor organizations continue to struggle to have influence. However, as the presidential campaign of 2016 has demonstrated, some candidates have raised concerns about worker rights, and these issues are becoming part of the public discourse. In addition, nearly one in three young voters today favor socialism over capitalism, indicating that the political pendulum is moving away from neoliberal values and beliefs (YouGov, 2016). Still, it will take several years to reverse the damage that neoliberal policies have done to society in general and to workplace safety in particular, unless there is a major political shift in the near future that changes the direction of legislation toward promoting the Common Good.

CONCLUSION

The regulatory context of the work environment has changed dramatically over the past 40 years. The impact of neoliberalism on workplace safety has occurred through deregulation efforts grounded in an ideology of free market fundamentalism that have crippled the capability of regulatory agencies to effectively protect workers by promoting and maintaining safety standards in the workplace. Moreover, structural changes in the economy due to the liberalization of markets have resulted in a shift from full-time manufacturing jobs to service and part-time and temporary jobs that provide few, if any, benefits to workers, who by force of necessity, have to take whatever employment they can to subsist.

As these changes in the economy were occurring, the Latino population experienced dramatic growth. Latino workers became increasingly integrated into the economy's racial division of labor, becoming overrepresented in occupations at the lower end of the occupational structure where workplace hazards are more common and enforcement of safety regulations are less likely, especially in an environment characterized by dependence on employers to regulate themselves as part of a reliance on the supposed efficacy of market forces and a movement away from state regulation and intervention.

In this context Latino workers are at greater risk for workplace injuries and fatalities, as has been shown by official data, shortcomings of the data notwithstanding. It is not clear how much greater the risk is, however. Although there has been a consistent downward trend in fatal occupational injuries in general, the numbers continue to increase for Latinos in certain occupations, and Latinos continue to have the highest rates among the major population groups. Moreover, foreign-born Latinos have the highest occupational fatal injury rates, reflecting not only their concentration in hazardous jobs but also the consequences of language barriers and the lack of occupational infrastructure to meet their safety needs on the job. Finally, their overrepresentation in occupations with high rates of injuries ensures that Latinos are likely to continue to be vulnerable to occupational health problems in the future. This is particularly the case should the influences of neoliberalism and its reliance on market forces be more fully realized in the future.

In closing, it is important to note that there are some areas that are in need of additional research. For example, why did fatal injury rates increase at the turn of the century, then begin to decline? What interventions are most effective in reducing Latino workplace injuries and diseases, and why are workplace injuries and fatalities persistently higher among Latinos relative to other populations? Why are Latinos overrepresented among "nonclassifiable injuries and illnesses?" Systematic research into these areas will shed light on the approaches needed to more effectively address workplace safety issues that put the occupational health of Latinos at risk.

REFERENCES

Abrams, H. K. (2001). A short history of occupational health. *Journal of Public Health Policy, 22*, 34–80. http://dx.doi.org/10.2307/3343553

Aguirre, A., Jr., & Martinez, R. O. (2014). The foreclosure crisis, the American Dream, and minority households in the United States: A descriptive profile. *Social Justice, 40*(3), 6–15.

Alonso-Villar, O., Gradin, C., & del Rio, C. (2012). *Occupational segregation of Hispanics in U.S. Metropolitan areas* (Working Paper No. 2012–242). Retrieved from http://www.ecineq.org/milano/WP/ECINEQ2012-242.pdf

Arcury, T. A., Estrada, J. M., & Quandt, S. A. (2010). Overcoming language and literacy barriers in safety and health training of agricultural workers. *Journal of Agromedicine, 15*, 236–248. http://dx.doi.org/10.1080/1059924X.2010.486958

Arcury, T. A., & Quandt, S. A. (2011). Living and working safely: Challenges for migrant and seasonal farmworkers. *North Carolina Medical Journal, 72*, 466–470.

Azaroff, L. S., Levenstein, C., & Wegman, D. H. (2002). Occupational injury and illness surveillance: Conceptual filters explain underreporting. *American Journal of Public Health, 92*, 1421–1429. http://dx.doi.org/10.2105/AJPH.92.9.1421

Bain, P. (1997). Human resource malpractice: The deregulation of health and safety at work in the USA and Britain. *Industrial Relations Journal, 28*, 176–191. http://dx.doi.org/10.1111/1468-2338.00053

Bednarzik, R. W., Hewson, M. A., & Urquhart, M. A. (1982). The employment situation in 1981. *Monthly Labor Review, 105*(3), 3–14.

Berman, D. M. (1977). Why work kills: A brief history of occupational safety and health in the United States. *International Journal of Health Services, 7*, 63–87. http://dx.doi.org/10.2190/8M31-316B-GUEJ-FRCW

Berman, D. M. (1978). *Death on the job: Occupational health and safety struggles in the United States.* New York, NY: Monthly Review Press.

Bureau of Labor Statistics. (2012a). *Economic and employment projections* (Economic News Release). Retrieved from http://www.bls.gov/news.release/ecopro.toc.htm

Bureau of Labor Statistics. (2012b). *Worker displacement: 2009–2011* (Economic News Release, USDL-12-1719). Retrieved from http://www.bls.gov/news.release/disp.nr0.htm

Bureau of Labor Statistics. (2014). *Labor force characteristics by race and ethnicity, 2013* (BLS Report 1050). Retrieved from http://www.bls.gov/opub/reports/race-and-ethnicity/archive/race_ethnicity_2013.pdf

Bureau of Labor Statistics. (2015a). *Census of fatal occupational injuries charts, 1992–2014* [Preliminary data]. Retrieved from http://www.bls.gov/iif/oshwc/cfoi/cfch0013.pdf

Bureau of Labor Statistics. (2015b). *Census of fatal occupational injuries summary, 2014* (News release, USDL-15-1789). Retrieved from http://www.bls.gov/news.release/cfoi.nr0.htm

Bureau of Labor Statistics. (2015c). *Employer-reported workplace injuries and illnesses—2014* (News Release, USDL-15-2086). Retrieved from http://www.bls.gov/news.release/pdf/osh.pdf

Bureau of Labor Statistics. (2015d). *Fatal occupational injuries incurred by Hispanic or Latino workers, 2010–2014.* Retrieved from http://www.bls.gov/iif/oshwc/cfoi/hispanic.pdf

Bureau of Labor Statistics. (2015e). *Nonfatal occupational injuries and illnesses requiring days away from work, 2014* (News Release, USDL-12-2205). Retrieved from http://www.bls.gov/news.release/pdf/osh2.pdf

Byler, C. G. (2013). Hispanic/Latino fatal occupational injury rates. *Monthly Labor Review, 136*(2), 14–23.

Catanzarite, L. (2000). Brown-collar jobs: Occupational segregation and earnings of recent-immigrant Latinos. *Sociological Perspectives, 43*, 45–75. http://dx.doi.org/10.2307/1389782

Cierpich, H., Styles, L., Harrison, R., Davis, L., Chester, D., Lefkowitz, D., . . . Baron, S. (2008). Work-related injury deaths among Hispanics—United States, 1992–2006. *Morbidity and Mortality Weekly Report, 57*, 597–600.

Cooper, P. J. (2009). *The war against regulation: From Jimmy Carter to George W. Bush.* Lawrence: University of Kansas Press.

DeNavas-Walt, C., & Proctor, B. D. (2015). *Income and poverty in the United States: 2014* (U.S. Census Bureau Current Population Reports, P60-252). Washington, DC: U.S. Government Printing Office. Retrieved from https://www.census.gov/content/dam/Census/library/publications/2015/demo/p60-252.pdf

Dovidio, J. F., Gaertner, S. L., & Saguy, T. (2015). Color-blindness and commonality: Included but invisible. *American Behavioral Scientist, 59*, 1518–1538. http://dx.doi.org/10.1177/0002764215580591

Filios, M., Attfield, M., Graydon, J., Marsh, S., Nowlin, S., Sestito, J., . . . Storey, E. (2008). *The case for collecting occupational health data elements in electronic health records.* Retrieved from https://c.ymcdn.com/sites/www.cste.org/resource/resmgr/OccupationalHealth/TheCaseforCollectingOccHealt.pdf

Flynn, M. A. (2010). *Undocumented status and the occupational lifeworlds of Latino immigrants in a time of political backlash: The workers' perspective.* Unpublished master's thesis, University of Cincinnati, Cincinnati, Ohio. Retrieved from http://etd.ohiolink.edu/view.cgi?acc_num=ucin1280776817

Flynn, M. A., Eggerth, D. E., & Jacobson, C. J., Jr. (2015). Undocumented status as a social determinant of occupational safety and health: The workers' perspective. *American Journal of Industrial Medicine, 58*, 1127–1137. http://dx.doi.org/10.1002/ajim.22531

Gardner, J. (1995). Worker displacement: A decade of change. *Monthly Labor Review, 118*(4), 45–57.

Hamilton, D., Austin, A., & Darity, W., Jr. (2011). *Whiter jobs, higher wages: Occupational segregation and the lower wages of black men* (EPI Briefing Paper No. 288). Retrieved from Economic Policy Institute website: http://www.epi.org/files/page/-/BriefingPaper288.pdf

Hudson, K. (2007). The new labor market segmentation: Labor market dualism in the new economy. *Social Science Research, 36*, 286–312. http://dx.doi.org/10.1016/j.ssresearch.2005.11.005

Is OSHA working for working people? Hearing before the Subcommittee on Employment and Workplace Safety of the Committee on Health, Education, Labor, and Pensions, U.S. Senate, 110th Cong. (2007). Washington, DC: Government Printing Office. (S. Hrg. 110-40). Retrieved from http://www.gpo.gov/fdsys/pkg/CHRG-110shrg35165/pdf/CHRG-110shrg35165.pdf

Killingsworth, J., Grosskopf, K., & Hernandez, L. (2012). 'Retooling' recession displaced workers for green collar jobs. In *48th ASC Annual International Conference Proceedings.* Retrieved from http://ascpro0.ascweb.org/archives/cd/2012/paper/CERT113002012.pdf

Kletzer, L. G. (1991). Job displacement, 1979–86: How blacks fared relative to whites. *Monthly Labor Review, 114*(7), 17–25.

Kochhar, R., Fry, R., & Taylor, P. (2011). *Twenty-to-one: Wealth gaps rise to record highs between whites, blacks and Hispanics.* Washington, DC: Pew Research Center. Retrieved from http://www.pewsocialtrends.org/files/2011/07/SDT-Wealth-Report_7-26-11_FINAL.pdf

Kraus, J. F. (1985). Fatal and nonfatal injuries in occupational settings: A review. *Annual Review of Public Health, 6,* 403–418. http://dx.doi.org/10.1146/annurev.pu.06.050185.002155

Krieger, N., Waterman, P. D., Hartman, C., Bates, L. M., Stoddard, A. M., Quinn, M. M., . . . Barbeau, E. M. (2006). Social hazards on the job: Workplace abuse, sexual harassment, and racial discrimination—a study of black, Latino, and white low-income women and men workers in the United States. *International Journal of Health Services, 36,* 51–85. http://dx.doi.org/10.2190/3EMB-YKRH-EDJ2-0H19

Lashuay, N., & Harrison, R. (2006). *Barriers to occupational health services for low-wage workers in California. A Report to the Commission on Health and Safety and Workers' Compensation.* Oakland: California Department of Industrial Relations.

Lee, M. A., & Mather, M. (2008). U.S. labor force trends. *Population Bulletin, 63*(2), 1–20.

Leigh, J. P., Marcin, J. P., & Miller, T. R. (2004). An estimate of the U.S. Government's undercount of nonfatal occupational injuries. *Journal of Occupational and Environmental Medicine, 46,* 10–18. http://dx.doi.org/10.1097/01.jom.0000105909.66435.53

Leong, F. T. L., Eggerth, D., Flynn, M., Roberts, R., & Mak, S. (2012). Occupational health disparities among racial and ethnic minorities. In P. L. Perrewé, J. R. B. Halbesleben, & C. C. Rosen (Eds.), *The role of the economic crisis on occupational stress and well being, research in occupational stress and well being* (Vol. 10, pp. 267–310). Bingley, England: Emerald Group. http://dx.doi.org/10.1108/S1479-3555(2012)0000010011

Maakestad, W. J., & Helm, C. (1989). Promoting workplace safety and health in the post-regulatory era: A primer on the non-OHSA legal incentives that influence employer decisions to control occupational hazards. *Northern Kentucky Law Review, 17,* 9–52.

Martinez, R. (2016). The impact of neoliberalism on Latinos. *Latino Studies, 14*, 11–32. http://dx.doi.org/10.1057/lst.2015.48

Martinez, R., & Rocco, R. (2016). Introduction: Neoliberalism and Latinos. *Latino Studies, 14*, 2–10. http://dx.doi.org/10.1057/lst.2015.56

McKernan, S.-M., Ratcliffe, C., Steuerle, E., & Zhang, S. (2013). *Less than equal: Racial disparities in wealth accumulation.* Washington, DC: Urban Institute. Retrieved from http://www.urban.org/UploadedPDF/412802-Less-Than-Equal-Racial-Disparities-in-Wealth-Accumulation.pdf

Mishel, L., Bivens, J., Gould, E., & Shierholz, H. (2012). *The state of working America* (12th ed.). Ithaca, NY: Cornell University Press.

Mogensen, V. (2003). Occupational safety and health in a neoliberal world. *Working USA, 7*(2), 3–6. http://dx.doi.org/10.1111/j.1743-4580.2003.00003.x

Mogensen, V. (2006a). Introduction. In V. Mogensen (Ed.), *Worker safety under siege: Labor, capital, and the politics of workplace safety in a deregulated world* (pp. xiii–xxix). Armonk, NY: M. E. Sharpe.

Mogensen, V. (2006b). State or society: The rise and repeal of OSHA's ergonomics standard. In V. Morgensen (Ed.), *Worker safety under siege: Labor, capital, and the politics of workplace safety in a deregulated world* (pp. 108–139). Armonk, NY: M. E. Sharpe.

National Research Council. (2003). *Safety is seguridad: A workshop summary.* Washington, DC: National Academies Press.

Navarro, V. (1998). Neoliberalism, "globalization," unemployment, inequalities, and the welfare state. *International Journal of Health Services, 28*, 607–682. http://dx.doi.org/10.2190/Y3X7-RG7E-6626-FVPT

O'Connor, T., Loomis, D., Runyan, C., Abboud dal Santo, J., & Schulman, M. (2005). Adequacy of health and safety training among young Latino construction workers. *Journal of Occupational and Environmental Medicine, 47*, 272–277. http://dx.doi.org/10.1097/01.jom.0000150204.12937.f5

Occupational Safety and Health Administration. (2008). *OSHA fact book.* Washington, DC: OSHA Office of Communications.

Orrenius, P. M., & Zavodny, M. (2009). Do immigrants work in riskier jobs? *Demography, 46*, 535–551. http://dx.doi.org/10.1353/dem.0.0064

Podgursky, M. (1992). The industrial structure of job displacement, 1979–1989. *Monthly Labor Review, 115*(9), 17–25.

Pouliakas, K., & Theodossiou, I. (2013). The economics of health and safety at work: An interdisciplinary review of the theory and policy. *Journal of Economic Surveys, 27*, 167–208. http://dx.doi.org/10.1111/j.1467-6419.2011.00699.x

Pransky, G., Moshenberg, D., Benjamin, K., Portillo, S., Thackrey, J. L., & Hill-Fotouhi, C. (2002). Occupational risks and injuries in non-agricultural immigrant Latino workers. *American Journal of Industrial Medicine, 42*, 117–123. http://dx.doi.org/10.1002/ajim.10092

Queneau, H. (2009). Trends in occupational segregation by race and ethnicity in the USA: Evidence from detailed data. *Applied Economics Letters, 16*, 1347–1350. http://dx.doi.org/10.1080/13504850701367346

Rhodes, L. H. (2006). How safe are U.S. workplaces for Spanish speaking workers? In V. Mogensen (Ed.), *Worker safety under siege: Labor, capital, and the politics of workplace safety in a deregulated world* (pp. 72–96). Armonk, NY: M. E. Sharpe.

Richardson, S., Ruser, R., & Suarez, P. (2003). Appendix D: Hispanic workers in the United States: An analysis of employment distributions, fatal occupational injuries, and non-fatal occupational injuries and illnesses. In *Safety is Seguridad: A workshop summary* (pp. 43–82). Washington, DC: National Academies Press.

Rosner, D., & Markowitz, G. (1987). Introduction: Workers' health and safety—some historical notes. In D. Rosner & G. Markowitz (Eds.), *Dying for work: Worker's safety and health in twentieth-century America* (pp. ix–xx). Indianapolis: Indiana University Press.

Russer, J. W. (2008). Examining evidence on whether BLS undercounts workplace injuries and illnesses. *Monthly Labor Review, 131*, 20–31.

Scholz, J. T. (1984). Voluntary compliance and regulatory enforcement. *Law & Policy, 6*, 385–404. http://dx.doi.org/10.1111/j.1467-9930.1984.tb00334.x

Shaefer, H. L. (2009). Part-time workers: Some key differences between primary and secondary earners. *Monthly Labor Review, 132*(10), 3–15.

Smeeding, T. (2012). *Income, wealth, and debt and the Great Recession.* Stanford, CA: Stanford Center on Poverty and Inequality. Retrieved from https://www.stanford.edu/group/recessiontrends/cgi-bin/web/sites/all/themes/barron/pdf/IncomeWealthDebt_fact_sheet.pdf

Smith-Nonini, S. (2003). Back to "The Jungle": Processing migrants in North Carolina meatpacking plants. *Anthropology of Work Review, 24*, 14–20. http://dx.doi.org/10.1525/awr.2003.24.3-4.14

Souza, K., Steege, A. L., & Baron, S. L. (2010). Surveillance of occupational health disparities: Challenges and opportunities. *American Journal of Industrial Medicine, 53*, 84–94. http://dx.doi.org/10.1002/ajim.20777

Strong, L. L., & Zimmerman, F. J. (2005). Occupational injury and absence from work among African American, Hispanic, and non-Hispanic White workers in the national longitudinal survey of youth. *American Journal of Public Health, 95*, 1226–1232. http://dx.doi.org/10.2105/AJPH.2004.044396

Tilly, C. (1991). Reasons for continuing growth of part-time employment. *Monthly Labor Review, 114*(3), 10–18.

Tonelson, A. (2000). *The race to the bottom: Why a worldwide worker surplus and uncontrolled free trade are sinking American living standards.* Boulder, CO: Westview Press.

Toossi, M. (2015, December). Labor force projections to 2024: The labor force is growing but slowly. *Monthly Labor Review.* Retrieved from http://www.bls.gov/opub/mlr/2015/article/labor-force-projections-to-2024.htm

U.S. Government Accountability Office. (1990). *Occupational safety and health: Options for improving safety and health in the workplace* (Publication No. GAO/HRD-90-66BR). Retrieved from http://www.gao.gov/assets/80/77868.pdf

U.S. Government Accountability Office. (2002). *Workplace safety and health: OSHA can strengthen enforcement through improved program management* (Publication No. GAO-03-45). Retrieved from http://www.gao.gov/assets/240/236413.html

U.S. Government Accountability Office. (2012). *Workplace safety and health: Better OSHA guidance needed on safety incentive programs* (Publication No. GAO-12-329). Retrieved from http://www.gao.gov/assets/590/589961.pdf

U.S. Government Accountability Office. (2013a). *Workplace safety and health: Further steps by OSHA would enhance monitoring of enforcement and effectiveness* (Publication No. GAO-13-61). Retrieved from http://www.gao.gov/assets/660/651494.pdf

U.S. Government Accountability Office. (2013b). *Workplace safety and health: OSHA can better respond to state-run programs facing challenges* (Publication No. GAO-13-320). Retrieved from http://www.gao.gov/assets/660/653799.pdf

Walter, N., Bourgois, P., Loinaz, H. M., & Schillinger, D. (2002). Social context of work injury among undocumented day laborers in San Francisco. *Journal of General Internal Medicine, 17*, 221–229. http://dx.doi.org/10.1046/j.1525-1497.2002.10501.x

Watts, M. J. (1995). Trends in occupational segregation by race and gender in the U.S.A., 1983–92: A multidimensional approach. *The Review of Radical Political Economics, 27*(4), 1–36. http://dx.doi.org/10.1177/048661349502700401

Wood, P. J. (1995). The politics of industrial injury rates in the United States. *The Review of Radical Political Economics, 27*, 71–96. http://dx.doi.org/10.1177/048661349502700104

YouGov. (2016). *Table 1. Favorability of socialism*. Retrieved from https://d25d2506sfb94s.cloudfront.net/cumulus_uploads/document/467z1ta5ys/tabs_OP_Socialism_20160127.pdf

2

EMPLOYMENT CONDITIONS AS A SOCIAL DETERMINANT OF HEALTH IN LATINO POPULATIONS: POLICY INTERVENTIONS USING THE WHO SOCIAL DETERMINANTS MODEL

RAFAEL MOURE-ERASO AND MARIA JULIA BRUNETTE

The World Health Organization (WHO) Commission on Social Determinants of Health has defined *employment conditions* as one of the nine social determinants of health status of the general population (WHO, 2005).[1] In this chapter we analyze this factor in the Latino labor force and delineate intervention recommendations to improve Latino workers' occupational health. An increasing body of social science literature proposes

The work described herein was performed at the Department of Work Environment, College of Health Sciences, University of Massachusetts Lowell, One University Avenue, Lowell, Massachusetts. Grant sponsors are the National Institutes of Health, Centers for Disease Control and Prevention, and National Institute for Occupational Safety and Health (Grant No. T01OH008424-03).

[1]*Social determinants of health* are defined as major influences in health of populations from across the social and economic spectrum that affect the circumstances in which people live and work. The nine social determinants of health chosen by the World Health Organization (2005) are: (a) poverty and its manifestations; (b) inequity; (c) globalization; (d) food insecurity; (e) social exclusion and discrimination; (f) inappropriate housing; (g) safeguarding of early childhood development; (h) employment conditions, and (i) insufficient quality of health systems.

http://dx.doi.org/10.1037/0000021-003
Occupational Health Disparities: Improving the Well-Being of Ethnic and Racial Minority Workers, F. T. L. Leong, D. E. Eggerth, C.-H. Chang, M. A. Flynn, J. K. Ford, and R. O. Martinez (Editors)

that structural social inequality factors, including community factors, are strong and consistent determinants of disparities in health (Williams, 2003). Employment conditions include an external contextual domain composed of structural/community factors and an internal domain consisting of the exposure–disease spectrum (Moure-Eraso, 2006), both of which we examine as determinants of the gradient of health status in the Latino workers population. The most recent demographic profile of the Latino labor force in the United States and statistical evidence of the disparities in Latino occupational-induced mortality and morbidity are also presented. Interventions are discussed using the conceptual framework of the relationships between structural, community, and individual determinants of health inequalities developed by WHO (2005), and recommendations for future studies are provided.

DEMOGRAPHICS OF LATINO OCCUPATIONAL HEALTH DISPARITIES

Demographic data on the U.S. Latino population is presented in this section with details on the topics of temporal demographic changes, poverty and economic characteristics, leading causes of death, and occupational injury and diseases.

Demographic Changes

Immigration trends in the last decades of the 20th century have produced the most dramatic changes in the ethnic composition of the U.S. population since the first decades of that century (Brown, 2003). According to the latest data presented by the reputable Pew Hispanic Center (2013), there are approximately 41.7 million foreign-born Latino persons in the United States, of whom approximately 11.7 million are undocumented. It is estimated that the foreign born share of the nation's population will exceed historic highs between 2020 and 2025, reaching 15%. The historic peak shares were 14.8% in 1890 and 14.7% in 1910. The United States receives approximately 1 million immigrants each year, including both legally admitted and undocumented entrants who later receive amnesty and legal residence. Most of these recent immigrants are of working age (18–64 years old), and 95% live in metropolitan areas (Brown, 2003; Kandula, Kersey, & Lurie, 2004; National Research Council, 1996; Pew Research Center, 2008; Pransky et al., 2002). Foreign-born workers also are employed in the most hazardous industries, including agriculture, construction, and manufacturing, comprising 29%, 23%, and 19% of the U.S. workforce in these sectors, respectively (U.S. Census Bureau, 2011).

Today, Latinos are the fastest growing ethnic group and the largest minority group in the United States. Despite significant undercounting issues by the Census Bureau, they account for approximately 17% (51.9 million) of the U.S. population, and it is expected that 60% of the nation's population growth from 2005 to 2050 will be due to Latinos (National Research Council, 2003; Pew Research Center, 2008, 2013). When compared with other Hispanic country populations in North, Central, or South America, Latinos in the United States (or *Hispanic Americans*) rank among the top. In 2005, Hispanic Americans ranked fifth (37 million) among Latin American country populations, Brazil and Mexico being the largest with 182 and 106 million, respectively. By 2050, Hispanic Americans are projected to increase to 103 million, moving up to the third position in the ranking following Brazil and Mexico with estimated populations of 250 and 147 million, respectively (Economic Commission for Latin America and the Caribbean, 2002; U.S. Census Bureau, 2011). In addition, almost 36% of the U.S. Latino population is foreign born with Mexico, El Salvador, and Cuba being the countries of origin of the large majority (Pew Research Center, 2013).

Unfortunately, the majority of Latinos have been trapped within current work systems that do not offer decent and safe conditions of work. External factors, including structural and community factors, intensify the impact of unsustainable work systems on the well-being of millions of Latinos living and working in the United States.

Poverty and Economic Characteristics

There is vast evidence regarding the relationship between factors such as substandard living conditions, lifestyle factors, and lack of preventive services and increased risk of work injury and disability. Latinos may be at greater risk for occupational injuries and illnesses because of limited economic and political resources and poor living or working conditions (Pransky et al., 2002). In recent past decades, the poverty rate for Latinos has been consistently 2.5 times the rate for Whites. Latinos and African Americans, the groups that consistently have had the highest poverty rates of all ethnic/racial groups, shared the same highest rate in 2000, or 22% (LaVeist, 2005). Latino males are 1.5 times more likely to be unemployed and to be among the working poor than White males (De Jong & Madamba, 2001).

Likewise, according to the 2008 Pew Hispanic Center/Robert Wood Johnson Foundation Latino Health Survey, the percentage of Latinos who had no health insurance coverage was 60% for Latinos who were not citizens and not legal permanent residents and 28% for Latinos who were U.S. citizens or legal permanent residents—compared with the 17% reported for the general U.S. population. Considering that employment is the most important social conditioner for having access to health services in the United States, these medical care data reflect Latinos' inadequate employment conditions with regard to basic benefits such as health care—with the unauthorized immigrants being the ones in the most vulnerable situation.

An analysis of recent socioeconomic and health and safety data reveals that immigration status might be a significant risk factor in occupational health. Workers whose country of origin is not the United States have shown higher rates of work-related injuries and illnesses. Data show, for example, that among Latinos, the living and working conditions faced by those who are foreign born are significantly poorer. The percentage of Mexicans living in poverty in the United States is 1.5 times higher than the percentage of Mexican Americans (Katz & Stern, 2006). Immigrant underemployment is greater than that of the native born. Foreign-born Latinos are more likely to be engaged in high-risk occupations, with limited access to appropriate health care for work injuries. Census data from 1995 through 2000 showed that 59% (or 2,440) of the 4,167 fatal work injuries among Latino workers involved workers who were born outside of the United States. Moreover, the fatality rate for foreign-born Latinos (1996–2000) was 6.1 per 100,000 compared with a rate of 4.5 per 100,000 for native-born Latino workers. The rate for all workers over this same period was 4.6 per 100,000. Data from the Bureau of Labor Statistics (BLS) revealed that fatalities involving foreign-born Latinos in 2005 reached 625 fatal work injuries (compared with 292 for U.S.-born Latinos), up from 596 in 2004 (BLS, 2006).

Leading Causes of Death

Table 2.1 presents the leading causes of death for Latino and White males in 2002. The leading causes of death for Latino males in the first three age groups (working ages 15–34 years old) include accidents (unintentional injuries, including work-related injuries), assaults (homicide), and intentional self-harm (suicide). The death rates from assaults for Latinos are higher than the rates for Whites across all the age groups. The human immunodeficiency virus (HIV) is among the top three causes of death for Latinos in the 35-to-44 age group. The HIV death rate for Latinos is significantly higher than that for Whites. Death rates from accidents for Latinos are similar for all age groups, with an average of 48 deaths per 100,000. For workers age 45 and older, cancer and heart disease are the two major killers, with rates increasing over 400% from the previous age group. Working conditions are also recognized contributors to cancer mortality and heart disease, and that relationship might help explain the drastic increase of these two rates (Karasek & Theorell, 1990).

TABLE 2.1
Death Rates for the Leading Causes of Death for Latino and White Males in Selected Working Age Groups, 2002

Cause of death	15–19 years		20–24 years		25–34 years		35–44 years		45–54 years		55–64 years	
	Latino	White	Latino	White	Latino	White	Latino	White	Latino	White	Latino	White
Diseases of heart	1.6	2.2	3.4	3.3	6.1	8.8	**20.6**	**39.7**	**80.5**	**128.6**	**256.0**	**324.0**
Malignant neoplasm	4.9	4.2	5.5	5.9	6.3	9.1	18.4	30.5	**78.4**	**121.8**	**254.3**	**386.0**
Accidents (unintentional injuries, including work)	**45.8**	**51.0**	**60.0**	**66.4**	**43.0**	**49.3**	**48.5**	**54.7**	**48.7**	**52.3**	**43.5**	**43.5**
Cerebrovascular diseases	—	0.3	—	0.7	1.5	1.2	5.1	4.2	18.6	12.9	**45.0**	**35.6**
Diabetes	—	—	—	0.5	0.9	1.6	4.1	5.3	16.7	14.3	**58.9**	**39.6**
Chronic liver disease	—	—	—	—	1.6	1.2	13.5	9.7	44.2	27.1	**60.0**	**33.2**
Assault (homicide)	**25.5**	**8.2**	**32.9**	**12.9**	**19.8**	**8.9**	12.1	6.8	9.1	—	—	—
Chronic lower respiratory diseases	—	0.4	—	—	—	—	—	—	—	8.8	17.5	46.0
Human Immunodeficiency Virus (HIV)	—	—	—	—	5.1	3.3	**20.1**	**11.6**	23.1	9.8	15.0	—
Intentional self-harm (suicide)	**9.1**	**13.4**	**11.9**	**22.0**	**10.7**	**21.6**	11.2	26.2	11.3	27.0	—	24.3

Note. Bold numbers indicate substantial differences between Latinos and Whites. Adapted from "Deaths: Leading Causes for 2002," by R. N. Anderson and B. L. Smith, 2005, *National Vital Statistics Reports, 53*(17), pp. 23, 53–54. Centers for Disease Control and Prevention, U.S. Department of Health and Human Services, 2005. In the public domain.

EMPLOYMENT CONDITIONS AS DETERMINANT OF LATINO HEALTH   55

Occupational Injuries and Diseases

Latinos are frequently relegated to the most hazardous jobs. There is no doubt that the conditions of work and pay that they confront are unsatisfactory and represent serious hazards to their health and safety, especially in the construction, agricultural, and service industries. Language difficulties or workplace discrimination may result in inadequate safety training. If hurt on the job, immigrants may be less likely to obtain appropriate health care and may have increased risk for prolonged disability. The situation is exacerbated by inadequate health care benefits, lack of knowledge and awareness of available health services, and cultural barriers such as language preference and cross-cultural differences to accessing needed care (Pransky et al., 2002).

Latinos have higher rates of work-related fatal injuries than non-Latinos, as shown in Table 2.2. Unfortunately, fatal injuries for Latinos have been consistently increasing. More recent BLS data reveal that a total of 917 Hispanic or Latino workers suffered fatal injuries in 2005, up from 815 deaths in 2000. Foreign-born Latinos are exposed to the most hazardous jobs and consequently will be highly represented in the fatalities that belong to "hazardous" events (falls and contact with objects or equipment), as well as the known hazardous industry sectors such as agriculture and construction (see Table 2.3). For foreign-born Latinos, almost one out of three fatal occupational injuries occurs in construction (vs. 9% for U.S.-born Latinos). Likewise, almost 20% of these injuries take place in agriculture (vs. 9% for U.S.-born Latinos). All these numbers reveal the critical need to design effective interventions in these two industry sectors and revise current health and safety regulations targeted to this vulnerable population.

TABLE 2.2
Numbers and Rates per 100,000 of Fatal Occupational Injuries for Latino
Workers and Non-Latino Workers in the United States, 1995–2000

Year	Latino workers		Non-Latino workers	
	Number	Rate	Number	Rate
2000	815	5.6	5,068	4.2
1999	730	5.2	5,292	4.4
1998	707	5.2	5,314	4.5
1997	658	5.1	5,561	4.8
1996	638	5.3	5,535	4.8
1995	619	5.4	5,628	4.9

Note. From *Safety Is Seguridad* (p. 54), the National Research Council, 2003, Washington, DC: National Academies Press. In the public domain.

TABLE 2.3
Percent Distribution of Fatal Occupational Injuries for All Latino Workers,
Foreign-Born Latino Workers, and U.S.-Born Latino Workers
by Event and Industry Sector (1995–2000)

Frequency and percent for events and industry	All Latinos	Foreign-born Latinos	U.S.-born Latinos
Number	4,167	2,440	1,727
Percent	100	100	100
Event			
Transportation incidents	34	30	39
Assaults and violent acts	19	19	19
Contact with objects or equipment	17	19	15
Falls	16	18	12
Exposure to harmful substances	11	11	10
Fires, explosions	3	3	4
Industry			
Agriculture, forestry, fishing	15	19	9
Mining	3	2	4
Construction	28	31	23
Manufacturing	10	11	9
Transportation, public utilities	12	11	13
Wholesale trade	4	4	4
Retail trade	10	10	11
Finance, insurance, real estate	1	1	2
Services	12	10	14
Government	5	1	10

Note. From Safety Is Seguridad (p. 62), the National Research Council, 2003, Washington, DC: National Academies Press. In the public domain.

In addition, Latino males have a higher relative risk of nonfatal injury compared with all workers in each major industry sector (see Table 2.4). As reported by Richardson, Ruser, and Suarez (2003), this suggests that Latino workers tend to work in riskier jobs in each industry division.

STRUCTURAL, COMMUNITY, AND INDIVIDUAL FACTORS IN OCCUPATIONAL HEALTH OF LATINO WORKERS

The examination of employment conditions as causes of incidence of occupational disease and disease gradients among Latino workers is an exercise of social epidemiology. In this case, social epidemiology studies the manner in which the specific living environment of the Latino worker could affect the personal and collective health of his or her community. It must incorporate health status and the specific Latino living environment. We also have to examine how social policies impact cultural groups differently. But in addition

TABLE 2.4

Relative Risk of Nonfatal Occupational Injury and Illness for Male Workers by Race and Industry Division (1998–2000)

	All	White Non-Latino	Black Non-Latino	Latino
Total	1.12	1.06	1.39	1.50
Agriculture service, forestry, and fishing	1.69	1.47	1.77	2.11
Construction	1.70	1.68	1.76	1.80
Durable goods	1.30	1.26	1.46	1.76
Nondurable goods	1.11	1.03	1.26	1.48
Transportation and public utilities	1.67	1.56	2.11	2.16
Wholesale trade	1.70	1.63	2.84	2.32
Retail trade	0.94	0.94	1.14	0.98
Finance, insurance, and real estate	0.32	0.25	0.53	0.84
Service industries	0.65	0.55	1.01	1.15

Note. From *Safety Is Seguridad* (p. 68), the National Research Council, 2003, Washington, DC: National Academies Press. In the public domain.

to "mapping" relationships, we also need to elucidate issues of accountability and agency (Krieger, 2001). This means that it is necessary to identify the sectors in society (agency) that are responsible for the development of social policies that Latinos benefit from and consider the impacts (accountability) on health of such policies. For example, workers compelled to work with highly toxic substances (i.e., asbestos) for the benefit of corporations do this at a high risk to their health. This risk might be expressed as unaccounted for costs to the workers in the form of losses of health and income due to toxic exposures. *What causes* the population patterns of health and disease and *who is responsible* are central questions when examining the occupational health of Latinos (Krieger, 2001).

An important question related to the health of Latino workers is how employment conditions contribute to the distribution of psychosocial insults (causing stress, mental and heart disease). Other critical dimensions are how these conditions interact with pathogenic physical, chemical, or biological agents and how psychosocial insults are shaped by social political and economic policies (Cassel, 1976). The impact of these dynamics is different among various communities and causes inequalities in health. The identification of the causes of these inequalities will determine the nature of the interventions necessary to alleviate the differences in health status. Some of the external (meaning structural, such as regulations on working conditions) social determinants that influence occupational health are underemployment, income inequalities, lack of access to health systems (vs. access to health insurance), loss of social support because of movement of populations, lack of influence in society because of deficiencies in social participation, and social isolation (resulting from language and cultural barriers; Lahiri et al., 2006). We are proposing that these circumstances are a result of social discrimination that contributes to health inequalities that are recurrent in the occupational status of Latino workers.

Structural Factors

Examples of social (structural) factors with relevance to health are as follows:

- nature of labor markets, the presence of large informal sectors;
- existence of vulnerable population groups, for example, immigrant, illiterate, unskilled workers;
- existence of institutions of worker representation;
- quality of government regulatory structures;
- quality of educational systems; and
- linkages between employment and provision of health services.

All of these social factors shape employment effects on health and safety inequity (Hege, Vallejos, Apostolopoulos, & Lemke, 2015). These external factors may act directly by modulating exposure to hazards. For example, the nature of the labor market will determine the degree and strength of the labor organizations (unions). Strong unions will negotiate with employers for safer working conditions or access to health care, thereby alleviating the impact of unhealthy working conditions. Also, the social factor *quality of governmental regulatory structures* could, in turn, determine the quality and strength of occupational health and safety laws, improving the possibilities of prevention of accidents and occupational diseases. External factors may also act indirectly. For example, external economic factors might be conducive to generating higher incomes in the worker population; this in turn will determine access to better food, better shelter, better health services, and other health-related items (Lahiri et al., 2006).

Major influences on the health of any population come from across the social and economic spectrum that affects the circumstances in which people live and work. Social determinants of health are social conditions under which humans work and live (Tarlov, 1996). Employment conditions of Latino workers are one of the social determinants of health that explain cases of disease and incidence of disease, as well as the shifting gradients of disease. This has been recognized by international organizations at the level of all workers (WHO,

2005). Employment conditions, however, cannot be "boxed" exclusively within person–hazard interactions in worksites. External social determinants, such as current applicable immigration laws and health and safety regulations, need to be taken into consideration as relevant to working conditions. The boxed approach has tended to marginalize employment conditions as social determinants of health within a narrow workplace environment (Moure-Eraso, Flum, Lahiri, Tilly, & Massawe, 2006; Nuwayhid, 2004). The examination of worksite condition variables (chemical exposure, ergonomic hazards, and work organization) is only the first step in the investigation of health impacts. If we are searching for more comprehensive analysis of health determinants, it is necessary to also view worksite conditions in conjunction with external contextual variables (see the partial list of social factors previously mentioned). In the examination of these contextual external variables, it seems to us, a key contribution to the occupational health of Latino workers could be their marginal social status, which causes a substantial disparity in health compared with the general U.S. population (see Tables 2.1, 2.2, and 2.3).

Community Factors

An understanding of the occupational health status of Latinos is gained by identifying not only the specific worksite conditions but also the social context in which work takes place. This context includes the social relationships and shared interests that define the various Latino communities in the United States. Understanding comes from both the internal domain of occupational health (worksite exposure–disease spectrum) and the external contextual domain (social context, regulatory and legal climate, population characteristics; Nuwayhid, 2004). For example, the impact of shared knowledge of decent and safe employment conditions can have significant effects on workers' defensive behaviors when facing workplace hazards. This networking occurs among Latino day laborers who share communal and living experiences that help them become aware of better potential job choices.

The social context is substantially determined by the relative political power of the interacting social institutions. The reality of power in occupational settings is that necessary changes for risk protection are not under the control of the individual worker, but of the employer. Therefore, to achieve improvements in working conditions, the worker must devise and implement a collective approach (e.g., unionization). Because worksites are social institutions, changes almost always involve social groups—managers, supervisors and regulators, or workers and their organizations. Collective representation provides a readily available avenue for individuals to obtain change (Levenstein, Wooding, & Rosenberg, 2000).

In dealing with exposure to hazards, collective interventions create a supportive structural context for implementing many solutions. Two chief collective interventions that have proven effective are (a) government agencies charged with monitoring, regulating, and/or conducting education around workplace hazards; and (b) unions or producer associations undertaking similar actions (Dembe, 1996; Silverstein, Frumkin, & Mirer, 2000). The two can be particularly effective in combination. This requires that the community of workers develop a social strategy on hazard controls, have the political will to act to improve the risky conditions, and have the basic technical knowledge concerning their legal rights and occupational health issues (Moure-Eraso, 1999). A community (collective) approach beyond the power of single individuals seems to be an effective strategy to improve working conditions (Silverstein et al., 2000). An example is the unionization of workers, as has occurred to some extent in construction. Another important expression of collective interventions is the actions of employer associations' initiatives on workplace safety and health. By engaging employer association affiliates on the development of consensus on the implementation of safety interventions, positive changes could be achieved.

Work organization may also be a contributor to psychosocial stress and eventually chronic disease (Karasek & Theorell, 1990). Again, to effect any change in work organizations requires a community intervention by a collective. It could be unionized workers' actions, interventions of progressive employers' organizations, or intervention of a government agency (usually requested by the organized workers).

Individual Factors

In the United States, employment is the most important social condition for access to health services (Levenstein et al., 2000; Taylor & Murray, 2000). This could be in the form of some health insurance, workers' compensation, or ability to pay for services out-of-pocket. Employment is the primary means available of securing access to goods and services. For Latino workers, the first priority becomes employment. The priority of secure employment overrides any concern for the potential negative health impact that working conditions can inflict. In the United States, Latino workers most affected are a subgroup of mostly foreign-born Latinos. As mentioned previously, individual workers (particularly those that have an undocumented immigration status) lack the power to improve employment conditions on their own. Individual-level factors that are amenable to change, such as years of education, health behaviors, attitudes, et cetera, are heavily conditioned to opportunities that society and the community make available to individuals.

However, isolated individuals, on their own, cannot force society to offer them desirable socioeconomic opportunities and cannot bring about systematic changes. Organized collective action in the political arena, which includes the formation of social coalitions, has proven to be an effective vehicle to generate desirable socioeconomic opportunities and improve working and employment conditions (Silverstein et al., 2000).

The U.S. Latino worker tends to hold a high proportion of substandard jobs characterized by low wages; low activity control; high psychological demands; low peer and supervisory support; and unsafe, dangerous conditions (Lahiri et al., 2006). These job characteristics are defined by the current work organization system in a given workplace, and there is very little possibility for improvements through individual action. Interventions at the individual level do not seem to be effective in generating systematic change.

INTERVENTIONS AT THE STRUCTURAL, COMMUNITY, AND INDIVIDUAL LEVELS TO IMPROVE LATINO WORKERS' HEALTH

WHO's (2005) Commission of Social Determinants of Health developed a conceptual framework (model) of the relationships between structural (community) and intermediate determinants of health inequalities. We modified that scheme to make it specifically relevant to employment conditions and Latino health (see Figure 2.1). Structural determinants are those that generate social stratification in society. They include such traditional factors as income, education, and labor market (Lahiri et al., 2006).

The modified WHO model presented in Figure 2.1 shows two major groups of determinants that affect health and health equity—structural (external) and intermediate (internal). WHO constructed its framework with structural determinants (left side of Figure 2.1) as a spectrum of factors, eventually determining that collective health cannot be directly measured at the individual level (political–institutional environment, labor market, educational opportunities). These determinants flow from the social structure of a community (first column far left) toward intermediate determinants on the right (chemical exposures, work organization) and are modified by an individual's social status (ethnicity, gender). Intermediate determinants shape differences of exposure in the workplace. They flow from the social structures and, in turn, are the determinants of differences in health and well-being. A group's health and well-being, as well as health inequities, are defined then by the confluence of the structural variables with the intermediate variables modified by individual social status. The objective of the framework is twofold. First, it "maps" the relationships between the determinants, and

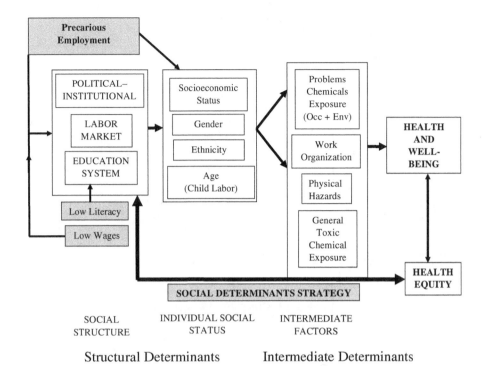

Figure 2.1. World Health Organization (WHO) social determinants framework of employment conditions and health applied to Latino workers. From *Towards a Conceptual Framework for Analysis and Action on the Social Determinants of Health* (Discussion Paper for the Commission on Social Determinants of Health) (p. 17), by the World Health Organization, 2005, Washington, DC: World Health Organization. Copyright 2005 by the World Health Organization. Adapted with permission.

second, it permits one to visualize the entry points of proposed interventions recommended to address Latino health inequalities (see Figures 2.2 and 2.3).

The interventions recommended are designed to decrease the differential exposures and vulnerabilities that are hypothesized to decrease the differential health consequences of the factors identified. It is expected that the sum of all the interventions to decrease negative health impacts (summarized in Figures 2.2 and 2.3) would in turn achieve decreases (upward) in social stratification by improving the social status of Latino workers.

Structural Determinants Interventions

Figure 2.2 identifies interventions at the social structural level. The oval boxes represent structural interventions, such as strengthening of adequate regulations and improvement of social facilities (education, health

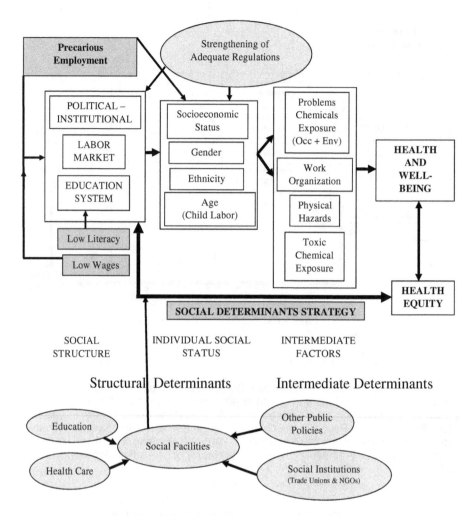

Figure 2.2. Structural interventions entry points in the World Health Organization (WHO) framework of employment conditions and health of Latino workers (interventions in oval shapes). From *Towards a Conceptual Framework for Analysis and Action on the Social Determinants of Health* (Discussion Paper for the Commission on Social Determinants of Health) (p. 17), by the World Health Organization, 2005, Washington, DC: World Health Organization. Copyright 2005 by the World Health Organization. Adapted with permission.

access). All these interventions will ultimately affect socioeconomic status. For example, the promulgation of new humane immigration policies (new laws and regulations) will require the engagement of political and community institutions and eventually will contribute positively to changes in the social structure. Further, the example of unionization is a typical local development in which individuals organized collectively to effect changes. There

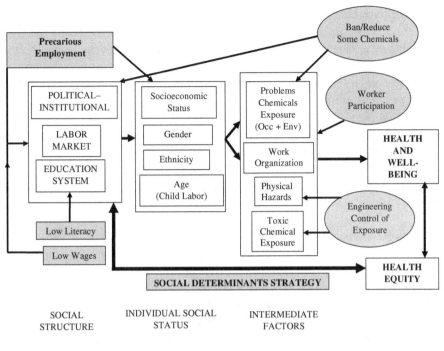

SOCIAL STRUCTURE   INDIVIDUAL SOCIAL STATUS   INTERMEDIATE FACTORS

Structural Determinants   Intermediate Determinants

Figure 2.3. Intermediate interventions entry points in the World Health Organization (WHO) framework of employment conditions and health of Latino workers (interventions in round shapes). From *Towards a Conceptual Framework for Analysis and Action on the Social Determinants of Health* (Discussion Paper for the Commission on Social Determinants of Health) (p. 17), by the World Health Organization, 2005, Washington, DC: World Health Organization. Copyright 2005 by the World Health Organization. Adapted with permission.

are other social action interventions to be contemplated, such as the control of underemployment, the narrowing of income inequalities (makes health insurance affordable), the counterbalancing of loss of social support caused by movement of populations, and the addressing of social isolation (language and cultural barriers). All these interventions deal with the lack of influence of Latinos as a group in the United States.

Improvements in working conditions (wages and benefits) are the outcome of a particular approach to national economic and social policy. Some improvements are related to human rights: social justice, equality, elimination of discrimination, freedom of association, collective bargaining, and so on. To be effective, actions and policies to improve employment conditions must be an integral part of a country's economic and social policy. These policies need to be carefully planned to have coherent and coordinated results.

Intermediate Determinants Interventions

Figure 2.3 identifies the interventions recommended at the level of intermediate factors to decrease differential exposures and their consequences. The intervention label *ban/reduce some chemicals* refers to scientifically recognized problem substances in the workplace, such as carcinogens, that should be banned or systematically reduced to eliminate or substantially reduce disease. There are two points of entry for this intervention: at the workplace level (intermediate factor) and at the political–institutional level of workplace regulation (social structure factor). Workplace organization and engineering control of exposures are two other interventions that have as point of entry the workplace and address intermediate factors.

Agents Responsible for Latino Health Inequalities

Figures 2.1, 2.2, and 2.3 may be described as webs of causation or conceptual frameworks of variables and interventions. Webs of causation tend to give descriptive snapshots of interrelationships of structural, community, and individual variables. However, those relationships accept social structures and interrelations as "natural environment," whereas in reality they are social constructs defined by relationships of power and class in the society. These webs do not show this power relationship or provide an explicit accounting of social agency (Moure-Eraso et al., 2006). We should address not only philosophical concerns but also those issues of accountability and agency determined by the power relationships between institutions and social classes (Krieger, 2001).

To claim exclusive emphasis in "fundamental social causes" does not necessarily offer principles for systematically thinking through *whether* specific public health and policy interventions are needed to curtail social inequalities in health and, if so, *which* ones (Krieger, 2001). We have to guard against interventions that are reduced to general exhortations to "secure adequate living standards" or "reducing economic inequality" presented as "policy" solutions. Paraphrasing Krieger (2001), what is needed is a simultaneous analysis of the biologic expressions of social relations with an analysis of how social relations influence our most basic understandings of biology. *What* causes the population patterns of health and *who* is responsible become the central questions (Krieger, 2001).

SUMMARY OF FINDINGS AND INTERVENTIONS

Table 2.5 describes interventions to address four key problems/ interventions in which external, structural, and community determinants are addressed as strategies to improve Latinos' occupational health (Lahiri et al.,

TABLE 2.5

Examples of Problems and Interventions at the Structural Community
Level to Improve Latino Occupational Health

	Nature of problem	Nature of interventions	Policy intervention targets	Examples of cases
1	Exposure to hazards	Collective interventions/ regulations in workplace safety and health	Structural: Political, legislative Community: Unionization, participate in work organization	Toxic use reduction regulations, substitution for safer materials, demand engineering controls of hazards
2	Lack of access to health care	Extension of health service access to a wider range of employment states	Structural: Propose legislation for universal insurance Community: Network with supporters, collective bargaining	Mobilize community for legislation on insurance health coverage, political coalition formation with unions and community organizations
3	Insufficient income (i.e., insufficient consumption) related to unemployment and underemployment	Job creation or improvement of job compensation	Structural: Political work to increase wages Community: Open new lines of work for nonnative workers	Campaigns to increase minimum wage to apply to all workers, organize recent immigrants and day laborers
4	Vulnerable population (child labor, female workers, illiterate and unskilled labor) informal sector (day labor)	Universal education, access to credit, social entrepreneurship	Structural: Literacy and H&S training, provide funds for entrepreneurship Community: Organize cooperative efforts among peers	Codify human and economic rights of day laborers, provide loans and credits for education and starting of small enterprises

Note. Other examples can be found in Hege, Vallejos, Apostolopoulos, and Lemke (2015). From "Employment Conditions as Social Determinants of Health. Part I: The External Domain," by S. Lahiri, R. Moure-Eraso, M. Flum, C. Tilly, R. Karasek, and E. Massawe, 2006, *New Solutions, 16,* p. 272. Copyright 2006 by Sage Publications. Adapted with permission.

2006). The interventions described were designed for the general working population, but they also apply quite properly to the Latino working population. Four relevant problems of the Latino community are analyzed: (a) workplace exposures, (b) lack of access to occupational health care, (c) insufficient income (underemployment), and (d) vulnerable population (informal and unskilled workers). The nature of the interventions and the policy targets (structural and community determinants) corresponding to each problem are described in columns 2 and 3. Specific examples of interventions are also listed in column 4 of the table.

Systematic implementation of these interventions would improve the health status of Latino workers in the United States. The final goal to improve Latinos' social status is achievable mostly through social structure improvement interventions similar to the ones discussed in the table.

The first step in starting a general improvement of social status could be the improvement in wages paid to Latino workers (increase in minimum wage). An increase in wages will have as consequences both the expansion of access to health services (health insurance) and the improvement of access to job training and health education. Once a relatively higher social status is achieved, individual factors can be addressed—for example, efforts to recruit Latino workers to enroll in educational programs to decrease alcohol and tobacco use.

CONCLUSION: WHAT IS TO BE DONE? REFLECTIONS ON IMPLEMENTATION OF INTERVENTIONS

Interventions at the intermediate level at the point of production seem like obvious ones to implement (Figure 2.3). For example, the substitution of toxic chemicals in industrial production (banning of asbestos) and worker participation on work organization tasks affect the problems noted in rows 1 and 2 of Table 2.5. However, these interventions do not happen as natural evolutionary developments in societal progress. They are the consequence of political actions that eventually define a social–legal framework developed by consensus. Changes will only happen if this consensus changes. The changes in employment and working conditions must be structural to ultimately affect the working conditions.

The entry points of interventions shown in Figures 2.2 and 2.3 and the examples in Table 2.5 describe specific actions on structural employment conditions that will affect the workplace and ultimately the health disparities in Latino workers. Structural problems described in rows 3 and 4 (insufficient income workers and vulnerable population, respectively) require interventions at the national level, such as the increase of minimum wage legislation, to provide mechanisms for collective organization of informal workers and temporary employment. Both of these two groups (informal and temporary workers) are classified as "precarious" employees and reflect the realities of a substantial sector of Latino workers in the United States. Four specific legislative interventions to address precarious employment structural problems were described recently by WHO (2008). They are as follows:

- to provide incentives for collective organization (unionization and collective bargaining),
- to establish regulatory controls on outsourcing and job sub-contracting,
- to promote regulations to avoid discrimination toward foreign-born workers and immigrants, and
- to create incentives and sanctions for violation of these regulations.

These interventions imply an engagement of the forces in civil society willing to challenge the current imbalance of power relationships in the United States that allow the marginalization of immigrants. These imbalances of power exist at four levels:

- power imbalance of Latino immigrants denied basic human and civil rights because of their immigration status,
- power imbalance between unions representing Latino workers and corporations that employ them,
- power imbalance of Latino immigrants within U.S. political parties, and
- power imbalance of Latino immigrants' community organizations in civil society.

Given this disparity in power, the engagement of the state as the regulator of societal inequalities is suggested as the intervention of choice by legislating the four points just discussed. Legislation is the tool available to address power imbalance. The state must exert its function to promote an equal or a more just power distribution through the implementation of social policies, such as the regulation of labor market characteristics, and serve as the purveyor of public health for all. But the government's task to promote equality is fully dependent on the political will of civil society to compel the state to act. Latino organizations as part of civil society have this task of developing that political will through political engagement of their members and by joining with organizations and institutions that support a just society.

REFERENCES

Anderson, R. N., & Smith, B. L. (2005). Deaths: Leading causes for 2002. *National Vital Statistics Reports*, 53(17), 1–89. Retrieved from http://www.cdc.gov/nchs/data/nvsr/nvsr53/nvsr53_17.pdf

Brown, M. P. (2003). An examination of occupational safety and health materials currently available in Spanish for workers as of 1999. In National Research Council, *Safety is seguridad: A workshop summary* (pp. 83–92). Washington, DC: National Academies Press.

Bureau of Labor Statistics. (2006). *Census of fatal occupational injuries.* Retrieved from http://www.bls.gov/iif/oshcfoi1.htm

Cassel, J. (1976). The contribution of the social environment to host resistance: The Fourth Wade Hampton Frost Lecture. *American Journal of Epidemiology, 104,* 107–123.

De Jong, G. F., & Madamba, A. B. (2001). A double disadvantage? Minority group, immigrant status, and underemployment in the United States. *Social Science Quarterly, 82,* 117–130. http://dx.doi.org/10.1111/0038-4941.00011

Dembe, A. (1996). *Occupational diseases.* New Haven, CT: Yale University Press.

Economic Commission for Latin America and the Caribbean. (2002). *Data and statistics.* Retrieved from http://www.cepal.org/en/

Hege, A., Vallejos, Q. M., Apostolopoulos, Y., & Lemke, M. K. (2015). Health disparities of Latino immigrant workers in the United States. *International Journal of Migration, Health and Social Care, 11,* 282–298. http://dx.doi.org/10.1108/IJMHSC-06-2014-0024

Kandula, N. R., Kersey, M., & Lurie, N. (2004). Assuring the health of immigrants: What the leading indicators tell us. *Annual Review of Public Health, 25,* 357–376.

Karasek, R., & Theorell, T. (1990). *Healthy work: Stress, productivity and the reconstruction of work life.* New York, NY: Basic Books.

Katz, M. B., & Stern, M. J. (2006). *One nation divisible: What America was and what it is becoming.* New York, NY: Russell Sage Foundation.

Krieger, N. (2001). Theories for social epidemiology in the 21st century: An ecosocial perspective. *International Journal of Epidemiology, 30,* 668–677. http://dx.doi.org/10.1093/ije/30.4.668

Lahiri, S., Moure-Eraso, R., Flum, M., Tilly, C., Karasek, R., & Massawe, E. (2006). Employment conditions as social determinants of health. Part I: The external domain. *New Solutions, 16,* 267–288. http://dx.doi.org/10.2190/U6U0-355M-3K77-P486

LaVeist, T. A. (2005). Disentangling race and socioeconomic status: A key to understanding health inequalities. *Journal of Urban Health, 82*(Suppl. 3), iii26–iii34. http://dx.doi.org/10.1093/jurban/jti061

Levenstein, C., Wooding, J., & Rosenberg, B. (2000). Occupational health, a social perspective. In B. Levy & D. Wegman (Eds.), *Occupational health: Recognizing and preventing work related disease and injury* (4th ed., pp. 27–50). New York, NY: Lippincott Williams and Wilkins.

Moure-Eraso, R. (1999). The convergence of labor and public health: A natural and critical alliance. *Journal of Public Health Policy, 20,* 310–318. http://dx.doi.org/10.2307/3343403

Moure-Eraso, R. (2006). Employment conditions: Reviewing evidence and promoting action. In Commission on Social Determinants of Health, World Health Organization, and Pan American Health Organization, *Final report: Regional consultation on the work of the Commission on Social Determinants of Health* (pp. 34–36). Retrieved from http://www2.paho.org/hq/dmdocuments/2009/ResCD47-inf1_Eng.pdf

Moure-Eraso, R., Flum, M., Lahiri, S., Tilly, C., & Massawe, E. (2006). A review of employment conditions as social determinants of health part II: The workplace. *New Solutions, 16,* 429–448. http://dx.doi.org/10.2190/R8Q2-41L5-H4W5-7838

National Research Council. (1996). *Statistics on U.S. immigration: An assessment of data needs for future research.* Washington, DC: National Academies Press.

National Research Council. (2003). *Safety is seguridad: A workshop summary.* Washington, DC: National Academies Press.

Nuwayhid, I. A. (2004). Occupational health research in developing countries: A partner for social justice. *American Journal of Public Health, 94,* 1916–1921. http://dx.doi.org/10.2105/AJPH.94.11.1916

Pew Hispanic Center. (2008, August). *Hispanics and health care in the United States: Access, information, and knowledge.* Retrieved from http://pewhispanic.org/files/reports/91.pdf

Pew Hispanic Center. (2013). *Statistical portrait of Hispanics in the United States, 2011.* Retrieved from http://www.pewhispanic.org/2013/02/15/statistical-portrait-of-hispanics-in-the-united-states-2011/

Pew Research Center. (2008, February 11). *U.S. population projections: 2005–2050.* Retrieved from http://www.pewhispanic.org/2008/02/11/us-population-projections-2005-2050/

Pew Research Center. (2013). *Population decline of unauthorized immigrants stalls, may have reversed.* Retrieved from http://www.pewhispanic.org/2013/09/23/population-decline-of-unauthorized-immigrants-stalls-may-have-reversed/

Pransky, G., Moshenberg, D., Benjamin, K., Portillo, S., Thackery, J. L., & Hill-Fotouhi, C. (2002). Occupational risks and injuries in non-agricultural immigrant Latino workers. *American Journal of Industrial Medicine, 42,* 117–123.

Richardson, S., Ruser, J., & Suarez, P. (2003). Hispanic workers in the United States: An analysis of employment distributions, fatal occupational injuries, and nonfatal occupational injuries and illnesses. In National Research Council, *Safety is seguridad* (pp. 43–82). Washington, DC: National Academies Press.

Silverstein, M., Frumkin, H., & Mirer, F. (2000). Labor unions and occupational health. In B. Levy & D. Wegman (Eds.), *Occupational health: Recognizing and preventing work related disease and injury* (4th ed., pp. 715–727). New York, NY: Lippincott Williams and Wilkins.

Tarlov, A. (1996). Social determinants of health: The sociobiology translation. In D. Blane, E. Brunner, & R. Wilkinson (Eds.), *Health and social organization* (pp. 71–93). London, England: Routledge.

Taylor, A. K., & Murray, L. (2000). Minority workers. In B. Levy & D. Wegman (Eds.), *Occupational health: Recognizing and preventing work related disease and injury* (4th ed., pp. 679–687). New York, NY: Lippincott Williams and Wilkins.

U.S. Census Bureau. (2011). *2010 census data, employment*. Retrieved from http://www.census.gov/2010census/data/

Williams, D. R. (2003). The health of men: Structured inequalities and opportunities. *American Journal of Public Health, 93*, 724–731. http://dx.doi.org/10.2105/AJPH.93.5.724

World Health Organization. (2005). *Towards a conceptual framework for analysis and action on the social determinants of health* (Discussion Paper for the Commission on Social Determinants of Health). Retrieved from http://archived.naccho.org/topics/justice/resources/upload/WHOCommissionTowardsConceptualFrame.pdf

World Health Organization. (2008). *Employment Conditions Knowledge Network (EMCONET). Final report to the WHO Commission on Social Determinants of Health: Employment conditions and health inequalities*. Retrieved from http://www.who.int/social_determinants/resources/emconet_scoping_paper.pdf

II

RESEARCH

3

CURRENT THINKING ON OCCUPATIONAL HEALTH DISPARITIES IN THE GLOBAL ECONOMY

LOIS E. TETRICK

The health gradient has established that people of low social status are less healthy than those of higher social status, and this gradient holds across all levels of the social hierarchy (Adler, 2013; Brunner & Marmot, 2006; Marmot, 2004). Therefore, it is not just those at the lowest social level who are less healthy than those at the highest level, but people in the middle are less healthy than those at the highest social level. Given that social status is associated with occupations, then one can expect to see an occupational health gradient, and in fact this was evident in the Whitehall studies of British civil servants (Brunner & Marmot, 2006).

This chapter first sets forth the data that suggest that occupations reflect social status resulting in occupational health disparities and contributing to the health gradient. Then I present recent research examining the mechanisms through which the effects of social status and health may be linked through psychosocial factors of occupations and individuals' work environment.

http://dx.doi.org/10.1037/0000021-004

Occupational Health Disparities: Improving the Well-Being of Ethnic and Racial Minority Workers, F. T. L. Leong, D. E. Eggerth, C.-H. Chang, M. A. Flynn, J. K. Ford, and R. O. Martinez (Editors)

OCCUPATIONAL GHETTOIZATION
AND OCCUPATIONAL HEALTH DISPARITIES

Differences in demographic composition across various occupational groups appear to be related to occupational health disparities. In this section I review the evidence for these differences.

Racial and Ethnic Composition of Occupations

Differences in health across racial and ethnic groups have been demonstrated around the world, not only in the United States and the United Kingdom but also in Latin America, South Africa, Australia, and elsewhere (LaVeist & Lebrun, 2010; Nazroo & Williams, 2006). What continues to be debated is whether these ethnic differences can be attributed to social and economic inequalities faced by ethnic minority groups or whether there are cultural and genetic factors accounting for these differences. Despite the complexity in teasing apart these potential contributors to ethnic differences in health (Bastos, Celeste, Faerstein, & Barros, 2010; Carlson & Chamberlain, 2004; Nazroo, Falaschetti, Pierce, & Primatesta, 2009), Karlsen and Nazroo (2010) and Nazroo and Williams (2006) concluded that the accumulating evidence suggests that differences in socioeconomic factors play a significant role in ethnic inequalities in health. Is there evidence of differences in occupations by racial/ethnic groups that might be related to occupational health disparities? Murray (2003), drawing on data from the Bureau of Labor Statistics (BLS) for 1996, reported that 50% of all garbage collectors were Black, 33% of all elevator operators were Black, and 33% of all nursing aides and orderlies were Black. In comparison, 75% of all miscellaneous wood workers, 68% of all farm product graders and sorters, 37% of all farmworkers, and 34% of all fabric machine operators were Hispanic. In contrast, 97% of all dental hygienists were White. Murray took this as evidence that there are "job ghettos," suggesting that groups of workers may be exposed to very different work environments and this might explain the occupational health gradient (Adler, 2013; Brunner & Marmot, 2006).

Almost 20 years later, has the picture changed? According to the BLS for 2010, garbage collectors and elevator operators were no longer specifically listed by race/ethnicity. Blacks were now 35% of all nursing aides and orderlies, about the same proportion as in 1996. The category of miscellaneous wood workers was no longer listed by race/ethnicity, but the proportion of all farm product graders and sorters who were Hispanic had fallen from 68% to 50%. However, the percentage of all farm workers who were Hispanic had risen from 37% to 42%. Similarly, the proportion of all fabric machine operators who were Hispanic had risen from 34% to 40%. The percentage of dental hygienists who were White had fallen from 97% to 89%. Therefore, there have been some changes in the representation of different racial/ethnic groups in different occupations, although it is clear that occupational segregation still exists.

Another indication that different groups of people may experience very different work environments emerges when examining the prevalence of different groups in management, professional, and related occupations, which was the highest paying major job category listed by the BLS (2010). Black and Hispanic workers were less likely to be in these higher paying jobs than were Asian and White workers. However, they were more likely than White and Asian workers to be employed in the lowest paying occupational groups (i.e., transportation and material moving; health care support; building and grounds cleaning; personal care and service; farming, fishing, and forestry; and food preparation and serving related).

Gender

In addition to racial/ethnic differences in occupations, there are differences in the number of men and women in various occupations. Among employed men, 48% of Asians worked in management, professional, and related occupations compared with 35% of Whites, 24% of Blacks, and 15% of Hispanics. About 40% of Black and Hispanic employed men held service jobs and sales and office jobs, whereas about 30% of Asian and White employed men were engaged in these occupations. Employed Black and Hispanic men also were more likely than other men to work in production, transportation, and material moving occupations. Nearly 50% of employed Hispanic men were employed in two groups of occupations: natural resources, construction, and maintenance; or production, transportation, and material moving. These occupations also had the highest number of reportable cases of occupational injuries and illnesses according to the BLS (2010).

The picture is similar for working women. Employed Asian women were more likely than other women to work in management, professional, and related jobs—46% of Asian women were employed in these jobs compared with 42% of White women, 34% of Black women, and 24% of Hispanic women. Sixty-five percent of Hispanic women who were working were in two job groups: service occupations and sale and office occupations. This contrasts with 59% of Black women, 53% of White women, and 47% of Asian women. These occupations do not have high rates of occupational injuries and illnesses according to the BLS (2010), but they are among the lower paid occupations.

Occupational Hazards

When looking at labor participation by industry, the BLS (2010) reported that Black men were more likely than other men to work in transportation and utilities (12% of Black men worked in this industry) and public administration (7%). Hispanic men were more heavily concentrated in construction (18%) than White men (12%), Black men (7%), and Asian men (4%). About 16% of Asian men worked in professional and business services compared with White men (12%), Black men (11%), and Hispanic men (12%). A large proportion of women in all race and ethnicity groups worked in education and health services—43% of Black women, 36% of White women, 32% of Asian women, and 31% of Hispanic women. It should be noted that education and health services had one of the highest rates of occupational injuries and illnesses according to the BLS.

The data from the United States confirm that there are disproportionate concentrations of racial and ethnic groups as well as women in various occupations and industries. Does this reflect "job ghettos" (Murray, 2003), and can these distributional asymmetries explain occupational health disparities? One way to address this question is to examine the data on occupational injuries and illnesses. Again, drawing on BLS (2011) data, there have been significant decreases in the total number of cases of occupational injuries and illnesses in construction and extraction workers, production workers, and transportation and material moving workers. However, there were increases in the incidence rate for light or delivery service truck drivers, landscapers and groundskeepers, restaurant cooks, and registered nurses. Protective service occupations had the highest proportion of injury and illness cases in each of the government sectors.

The data on occupations presented here suggest that there are differential risk factors by occupations. These occupations also differ on income and education. Occupation, income, and education are typically considered formative indicators of socioeconomic status (SES), which have been considered to contribute to the social health gradient. Individuals with high SES typically live longer, enjoy better health, and suffer less from disabilities (Adler, 2013; Marmot, Siegrist, & Theorell, 2006). What is less clear is what the mechanisms are by which occupation, income, and education result in occupational health disparities.

MECHANISMS UNDERLYING OCCUPATIONAL
HEALTH DISPARITIES

Since the days of the Whitehall studies, scholars have attempted to identify the 78 mechanisms that underlie the health gradient. Brunner and Marmot (2006) presented a framework of the social determinants of health. In this framework, they specifically identified work as reflective of social structure leading to health through both psychosocial and behavioral pathways. The literature has examined some more specific mechanisms empirically.

Subjective Social Status

One mechanism that has been suggested is subjective social status (Demakakos, Nazroo, Breeze, & Marmot, 2008). Subjective social status was defined as an individual's rating of where he or she stood relative to other people regarding having the most money, the most education, and the best jobs. In a longitudinal study of aging conducted in the United Kingdom of 3,368 men and 4,065 women aged 52 years or older, Demakakos et al. (2008) found that subjective social status was related to a number of health outcomes. Among men, subjective social status was related to self-rated health, depression, long-standing illness, and fibrinogen level, which is related to blood clotting and cardiovascular disease; however, after controlling for wealth, education, and occupational class, subjective social status was no longer related to fibrinogen, although it was still related to self-rated health, depression, and long-standing illness. The results were similar for women, with subjective social status being related to self-rated health, depression, long-standing illness, diabetes, and high-density lipoprotein cholesterol. For both men and women, the strongest relations were between subjective social status and self-rated health and depression, which may have reflected inflation by common method variance (Lance, Dawson, Birkelbach, & Hoffman, 2010).

In addition, Demakakos et al. (2008) found that subjective social status mediated, either fully or partially, the relations between education and occupational class with both self-reported and clinical health measures. However, subjective social status did not mediate the association between wealth and the outcome variables except in the case of self-reported health. Demakakos et al. concluded that these results support the notion that subjective social status reflects lifetime achievement, whereas SES reflects a more current, snapshot state.

Perceived Fairness and Trust

Why might wealth operate differently? Income tends to be related to well-being, but cross-sectional studies across countries, states, and cities have been inconsistent with respect to the relation between income inequality and well-being. Income inequality has been increasing in the developed countries about equally until the last 2 decades; however, the United States has one of the highest, if not the highest, levels of income inequality (Oishi, Kesebir, & Diener, 2011). Oishi et al. (2011) proposed two psychological mechanisms for the relation between income inequality and well-being. One of the mechanisms was that income inequality leads to perceived unfairness, especially if only the rich get richer, and perceived unfairness has consistently been linked to lower well-being. The second mechanism was that income inequality leads to distrust by dividing community members, and lack of trust leads to lower well-being.

Using longitudinal data from the General Social Survey, Oishi et al. (2011) found support for both mechanisms. Income inequality was related to subjective well-being only indirectly. Both perceived fairness and trust mediated the effect of income inequality on well-being. However, they also found that income level moderated the effects. For the richest group—the top 20% of income, income inequality was not related to either trust or perceived fairness. For individuals in the 60%–80% income group, their well-being was higher in years with greater income inequality. However, for people in the lowest income group, greater income inequality was associated with lower subjective well-being, and this relation was mediated by perceived unfairness and lack of trust.

These findings are consistent with a possible explanation of occupational health disparities in that occupations vary by income, and there are overall differences in occupations and income by racial and ethnic groups, with racial and ethnic minority groups more frequently being employed in lower paying occupations. Therefore, it might be argued that income accounts for occupational health disparities, potentially through experienced unfairness in the workplace and lack of trust.

Social Class

Kraus, Piff, and Keltner (2011) proposed that objective social status comprising education, occupational class/prestige, and wealth resulted in social class signals. By *social class signals*, they meant observable behaviors that connote social class. These included, for example, living in different neighborhoods, belonging to different social clubs, attending different educational institutions, eating different foods, enjoying different forms of recreation, wearing specific clothes, having different musical preferences, enacting different manners and customs, and having more or less nonverbal engagement. These signals then resulted in subjective social status, which resulted in psychological and behavior outcomes. Perceptions of low social status included perceptions of less personal control, heightened vigilance of the social context, and other-focused social orientation, although perceived high social status included a focus away from the social context and prioritizing one's self-interest. Kraus et al. (2011) found that lower perceived social status individuals attributed poverty and wealth to contextual forces (e.g., educational opportunity), whereas upper income individuals explained inequality in terms of dispositions (e.g., talent). Also, individuals with lower subjective social status experienced reduced personal control and, as a result, explained various personal, political, and social outcomes in contextual rather than dispositional terms, even after controlling for objective SES.

Extending their model, Kraus, Piff, and Keltner (2009) and Kraus, Côté, and Keltner (2010) have found that individuals differ on emphatic accuracy. Individuals with a high school education demonstrated greater empathic accuracy than individuals with a college education, and individuals who imagined interacting with an individual with high subjective social status actually reported lower subjective social status and were more accurate in identifying specific emotions. In addition, Piff, Stancato, Martinez, Kraus, and Keltner (2012) found that subjective social status was related to prosocial behavior. Individuals who reported lower subjective social status gave more to their partners than individuals who reported higher levels of subjective social status. They helped a distressed confederate more than did participants who reported higher subjective social status. Participants in whom lower subjective social status was induced experimentally supported higher levels of charitable donations, and lower income participants were more charitable than higher income participants.

Not only do these studies, which have attempted to address occupational health disparities, suggest implications for well-being of individuals in different occupational, racial/ethnic, and educational groups, they also suggest implications for organizational and societal outcomes. For example, income inequality and differences in subjective social status may lead to fewer prosocial behaviors such as teamwork, organizational citizenship behaviors, and organizational loyalty (Piff et al., 2012).

Internal Comparisons

Much of the research on occupational health disparities, at least as cited previously, has been conducted in the United States. There is some evidence that the findings are similar in Europe, especially the United Kingdom, although there are relatively few international comparisons in the literature.

Siddiqi and Nguyen (2010), in a comparison of data from the United States and Canada, found that racial inequities disappeared in the Canadian data after controlling for objective SES. This study also found that racial in-equities in health differed by whether individuals were foreign born or native born. In Canada, there were few racial inequities in health, and those occurred exclusively among foreign-born individuals. In contrast, in the United States, racial inequities occurred primarily among native-born individuals. Siddiqi and Nguyen interpreted their findings to indicate that racial differences in health are not a function of genetics but are context dependent. However, Siddiqi and Nguyen were criticized for dichotomizing race into White versus non-White (LaVeist & Lebrun, 2010), although they justified this decision because there were too few Blacks and Hispanics in the Canadian sample to be able to treat them as separate groups.

Another explanation for health disparities has been that lower status individuals may have less access to health care. Nazroo et al. (2009) analyzed data from the Health Survey for England. They did not find support for ethnic inequalities resulting from inequalities in access to and outcomes of health care, at least for the ill-health conditions that they examined, which were hypertension, elevated cholesterol, and diabetes. Nazroo et al. acknowledged that ethnic inequalities might exist for other conditions or in other countries with other health care systems; also they didn't specifically consider occupational characteristics.

Lifespan Trajectories

Meyer and Mutambudzi (2012) focused on racial disparities in hypertension. They argued that occupation is an indicator of SES and that occupations may be direct determinants of health because they differ in pay, societal prestige, authority, independence, stress, physical requirements, and exposure to hazardous conditions. They also pointed out that although occupation, education, and income are closely related, they are not equivalent. Using longitudinal data from participants in the National Longitudinal Survey of Youth reflecting the occupational trajectories of individuals from 20 to 32 years of age, Meyer and Mutambudzi found support for occupational characteristics' direct effect on health and that occupational characteristics mediated both the effects of race and the effects of education on hypertension. Another important finding of this study was that the occupational trajectory was more closely related to the health outcomes than the current work characteristics. This suggests that occupational health disparities arise not only from a specific job or work environment but also from the progression of occupational exposures over time.

In a similar vein, Leopold and Engelhardt (2013) examined the relations between education and physical health among people aged 50 to 80 years. Using data from the Survey of Health, Aging and Retirement in Europe, they found that physical health inequities for individuals with higher levels of education compared with individuals with lower levels of education became greater with age such that people with less education experienced comparatively lower physical health with age. However, for self-rated health and chronic diseases, the inequity between people with higher educational levels and people with lower educational levels remained constant with age, with higher educational levels associated with better health and fewer chronic diseases. Because education is related to occupation, and more specifically occupational characteristics (Meyer & Mutambudzi, 2012), then it would be reasonable to propose that occupational health disparities may progress over time based on work experiences.

Social Integration and Support

Another mechanism proposed to explain health inequalities has been social support (Brunner & Marmot, 2006; Klein, Vonneilich, Baumeister, Kohlmann, & von dem Knesebeck, 2012; Stansfeld, 2006). In a longitudinal design using data from the Study of Health in Pomerania, Klein et al. (2012) examined whether social relations mediated the effect of SES on self-rated health over a 5-year period. SES indicated by education, household income, and occupational status was related to social relations as indicated by social integration, instrumental social support, and emotional social support such that lower SES was associated with lower levels of social integration and social support. Social integration reflecting structural aspects of social support was related to self-rated health 5 years later, but the functional forms of social support (i.e., instrumental and emotional) were not as strongly associated with self-rated health as social integration was. The results of this study suggest that lack of social support and social integration can at least partially explain social inequalities in health. Klein et al.'s findings are also consistent with Brunner and Marmot's (2006) framework that includes the organization of work as part of the social environment that can affect health.

Intraorganizational Environment

Most of the studies described previously obtained data from large national and multinational studies. I found only one published study that looked at occupational health disparities in an organization. Schult, Awosika, Hodgson, and Dyrenforth (2011) reported a study that sought to obtain prevalence of health behaviors and chronic health conditions in the U.S. Veterans Health Administration in conjunction with the launch of an organization-wide wellness program. The data revealed occupational disparities in both health behaviors and chronic health conditions. Further, the prevalence of health behaviors and chronic health conditions differed by demographic characteristics within occupational groupings. These results suggest that occupational health disparities result from experiences within the workplace but may also result from experiences outside of the immediate workplace, including exposures to previous work characteristics as suggested by Meyer and Mutambudzi (2012).

Stress Processes

The studies mentioned previously also suggest that occupational health disparities may be the result of stress processes. Marmot, Siegrist, and Theorell (2006) reviewed the evidence of two theoretical models of stress (i.e., the demands-control model and the effort-reward imbalance model). Although some of the nuances of these theoretical models have not always been supported, such as the interaction between demands and control, the evidence is clear that the organization of work has clear implications for workers' health and that stress may be an important mechanism for understanding occupational health disparities.

The occupational stress literature has identified many stressors that relate to ill-health, and there have been several excellent recent reviews (e.g., Sonnentag & Frese, 2013), but few of these studies were designed to examine occupational health disparities. However, drawing from community psychology, Dunkel Schetter et al. (2013) provided an excellent account of a study that considered different types of stressors among mothers and fathers surrounding the birth of a child. They distinguished between chronic stressors (i.e., discrimination or marginalization based on race, ethnicity, or other personal characteristics; financial stress; relationship stress; and interpersonal violence) and acute stressors (i.e., life events with discrete beginning and endings).

Although this study did not specifically address occupational stress, Dunkel Schetter et al. (2013) recognized that there could be variation in stress by poverty and race/ethnicity. The results clearly supported the effects of both of these social structural factors on stress, and in several instances there was an interaction between poverty and race/ethnicity. Poverty was directly related to chronic stress, with low-income people perceiving greater stress, which is consistent with other research. Race/ethnicity directly affected chronic stress and racism without an interaction with poverty. Dunkel Schetter et al. concluded that the strongest form of the stress pathway, however, is through the interaction between poverty and race/ethnicity.

This study, although not directly assessing occupational stress, does inform the way work may be related to occupational health disparities. It suggests that there may be different types of stressors that have more impact on occupational health than others. For example, perhaps abusive supervision or job insecurity has more potent effects on some individuals' health than other stressors. It would seem possible that interpersonal stressors such as bullying, incivility, and workplace violence may have differential effects for women versus men, minorities versus nonminorities, and one ethnic group versus another and that the effects of gender, ethnicity, and race may be moderated by occupational status and income.

CONCLUSION AND FUTURE RESEARCH

To date, the research supports the existence of occupational health disparities. What remains unclear is the mechanism or the mechanisms by which these disparities exist. Are they the result of structural factors, personal characteristics, or other factors? Are there organizational interventions that can offset or eliminate these disparities? I have reviewed the existing research mentioned previously, and it suggests a number of factors that might address these effects. It appears that an integration of the literature on the organization of work (such factors as autonomy, growth and development, teamwork, social support, organizational justice, and inclusion) with the literature on occupational choice and mobility may be fruitful research programs for understanding occupational health disparities and developing interventions to reduce them.

The research has been primarily conducted using North American and European data, and much of it has been based on cross-sectional designs. Recently, there has been an increasing number of strong, longitudinal studies, and there appears to be an increase in studies of low-income individuals, which will help identify potential nonlinearities in occupational health disparities. However, we do need more studies from other countries, especially developing countries.

REFERENCES

Adler, N. E. (2013). Health disparities: Taking on the challenge. *Perspectives on Psychological Science, 8*, 679–681. http://dx.doi.org/10.1177/1745691613506909

Bastos, J. L., Celeste, R. K., Faerstein, E., & Barros, A. J. D. (2010). Racial discrimination and health: A systematic review of scales with a focus on their psychometric properties. *Social Science & Medicine, 70*, 1091–1099. http://dx.doi.org/10.1016/j.socscimed.2009.12.020

Brunner, E., & Marmot, M. (2006). Social organization, stress, and health. In M. Marmot & R. G. Wilkinson (Eds.), *Social determinants of health* (pp. 6–30). London, England: Oxford University Press.

Bureau of Labor Statistics. (2010). *Table 10. Employed persons by occupation, race, Hispanic or Latino ethnicity, and sex.* Retrieved from http://www.bls.gov/cps/aa2010/cpsaat10.pdf

Bureau of Labor Statistics. (2011). *2010 Survey of Occupational Injuries and Illnesses.* Retrieved from http://www.bls.gov/iif/oshwc/osh/os/osch0044.pdf

Carlson, E. D., & Chamberlain, R. M. (2004). The black-white perception gap and health disparities research. *Public Health Nursing, 21*, 372–379. http://dx.doi.org/10.1111/j.0737-1209.2004.21411.x

Demakakos, P., Nazroo, J., Breeze, E., & Marmot, M. (2008). Socioeconomic status and health: The role of subjective social status. *Social Science & Medicine, 67*, 330–340. http://dx.doi.org/10.1016/j.socscimed.2008.03.038

Dunkel Schetter, C., Schafer, P., Gaines Lanzi, R., Clark-Kauffman, E., Raju, T. N. K., Hillemeier, M. M., & the Community Child Health Network. (2013). Shedding light on the mechanisms underlying health disparities through community participatory methods: The stress pathway. *Perspectives on Psychological Science, 8*, 613–633. http://pps.sagepub.com/content/8/6/613

Karlsen, S., & Nazroo, J. Y. (2010). Religious and ethnic differences in health: Evidence from the Health Surveys for England 1999 and 2004. *Ethnicity & Health, 15*, 549–568. http://dx.doi.org/10.1080/13557858.2010.497204

Klein, J., Vonneilich, N., Baumeister, S. E., Kohlmann, T., & von dem Knesebeck, O. (2012). Do social relations explain health inequalities? Evidence from a longitudinal survey in a changing eastern German region. *International Journal of Public Health, 57*, 619–627. http://dx.doi.org/10.1007/s00038-012-0356-y

Kraus, M. W., Côté, S., & Keltner, D. (2010). Social class, contextualism, and empathic accuracy. *Psychological Science, 21*, 1716–1723. http://dx.doi.org/10.1177/0956797610387613

Kraus, M. W., Piff, P. K., & Keltner, D. (2009). Social class, sense of control, and social explanation. *Journal of Personality and Social Psychology, 97*, 992–1004. http://dx.doi.org/10.1037/a0016357

Kraus, M. W., Piff, P. K., & Keltner, D. (2011). Social class as culture: The convergence of resources and rank in the social realm. *Current Directions in Psychological Science, 20*, 246–250. http://dx.doi.org/10.1177/0963721411414654

Lance, C. E., Dawson, B., Birkelbach, D., & Hoffman, B. J. (2010). Method effects, measurement error, and substantive conclusions. *Organizational Research Methods, 13*, 435–455. http://dx.doi.org/10.1177/1094428109352528

LaVeist, T. A., & Lebrun, L. A. (2010). Cross-country comparisons of racial/ethnic inequalities in health. *Journal of Epidemiology and Community Health, 64*(1), 7. http://dx.doi.org/10.1136/jech.2009.092437

Leopold, L., & Engelhardt, H. (2013). Erratum to: Education and physical health trajectories in old age. Evidence from the Survey of Health, Ageing and Retirement in Europe (SHARE). *International Journal of Public Health, 58*, 329. http://dx.doi.org/10.1007/s00038-013-0453-6

Marmot, M. (2004). *Status syndrome.* London, England: Bloomsbury.

Marmot, M., Siegrist, J., & Theorell, R. (2006). Health and the psychosocial environment at work. In M. Marmot & R. G. Wilkinson (Eds.), *Social determinants of health* (pp. 97–130). London, England: Oxford University Press.

Meyer, J. D., & Mutambudzi, M. (2012). Construction of life-course occupational trajectories: Evidence for work as a mediator of racial disparities in hypertension. *Journal of Occupational and Environmental Medicine, 54*, 1201–1207. http://dx.doi.org/10.1097/JOM.0b013e31826bb6ac

Murray, L. R. (2003). Sick and tired of being sick and tired: Scientific evidence, methods, and research implications for racial and ethnic disparities in occupational health. *American Journal of Public Health, 93*, 221–226. http://dx.doi.org/10.2105/AJPH.93.2.221

Nazroo, J. Y., Falaschetti, E., Pierce, M., & Primatesta, P. (2009). Ethnic inequalities in access to and outcomes of healthcare: Analysis of the Health Survey for England. *Journal of Epidemiology and Community Health, 63*, 1022–1027. http://dx.doi.org/10.1136/jech.2009.089409

Nazroo, J. Y., & Williams, D. R. (2006). The social determination of ethnic/racial inequalities in health. In M. Marmot & R. G. Wilkinson (Eds.), *Social determinants of health* (2nd ed., pp. 238–266). Oxford, England: Oxford University Press.

Oishi, S., Kesebir, S., & Diener, E. (2011). Income inequality and happiness. *Psychological Science, 22*, 1095–1100. http://dx.doi.org/10.1177/0956797611417262

Piff, P. K., Stancato, D. M., Martinez, A. G., Kraus, M. W., & Keltner, D. (2012). Class, chaos, and the construction of community. *Journal of Personality and Social Psychology, 103*, 949–962. http://dx.doi.org/10.1037/a0029673

Schult, T. M., Awosika, E. R., Hodgson, M. J., & Dyrenforth, S. (2011). Disparities in health behaviors and chronic conditions in health care providers in the Veterans Health Administration. *Journal of Occupational and Environmental Medicine, 53*, 1134–1145.

Siddiqi, A., & Nguyen, Q. C. (2010). A cross-national comparative perspective on racial inequities in health: The USA versus Canada. *Journal of Epidemiology and Community Health, 64*, 29–35. http://dx.doi.org/10.1136/jech.2008.085068

Sonnentag, S., & Frese, M. (2013). Stress in organizations. In N. W. Schmitt, S. Highhouse, & I. B. Weiner (Eds.), *Handbook of psychology: Vol. 12. Industrial and organizational psychology* (2nd ed., pp. 560–592). Hoboken, NJ: Wiley.

Stansfeld, S. A. (2006). Social support and social cohesion. In M. Marmot & R. G. Wilkinson (Eds.), *Social determinants of health* (2nd ed., pp. 148–171). Oxford, England: Oxford University Press.

4

COMMUNITY-BASED PARTICIPATORY RESEARCH AND OCCUPATIONAL HEALTH DISPARITIES: PESTICIDE EXPOSURE AMONG IMMIGRANT FARMWORKERS

THOMAS A. ARCURY AND SARA A. QUANDT

Community-based participatory research (CBPR) has become a widely accepted approach to involve minority and vulnerable communities in health research (Arcury, Quandt, & Dearry, 2001; Brody et al., 2009; Kreuter, Kegler, Joseph, Redwood, & Hooker, 2012; Quandt, Arcury, Austin, & Cabrera, 2001; Rhodes et al., 2012; Viswanathan et al., 2004). CBPR is a format that allows research to address the actual health concerns of minority and vulnerable communities, involves community members in all components of the research process to improve the quality and relevance of the research and

PACE3: Community Participatory Approach to Measuring Farmworker Pesticide Exposures received financial support from the National Institute of Environmental Health Sciences (Grant No. R01 ES008739 and Grant No. R03 ES015803), the National Institute for Occupational Safety and Health through the Northeast Center for Agricultural and Occupational Health (Grant No. U50 OH007542), and the Wake Forest University Cross-Campus Collaborative Research Support Fund. Laboratory analysis was provided at no cost by Integrated Systems Toxicology Division, U.S. Environmental Protection Agency. The authors appreciate the years of collaboration with all of our community partners. The authors also thank Anne Kraemer Diaz for her review of the manuscript.

http://dx.doi.org/10.1037/0000021-005
Occupational Health Disparities: Improving the Well-Being of Ethnic and Racial Minority Workers, F. T. L. Leong, D. E. Eggerth, C.-H. Chang, M. A. Flynn, J. K. Ford, and R. O. Martinez (Editors)

to grow the skills of community members, and returns information from the research to the community in a format that individuals can use to improve and protect their health and leaders can use to improve policy. However, with a few exceptions, CBPR has not been used to address occupational health disparities.

Communities are social groups with shared identities, experiences, and histories, even if the social groups are not limited to a geographic locale. Occupational groups often fit this definition of community, and CBPR is an appropriate approach for research and intervention. For example, CBPR has been used for research on the occupational health of farmworkers (Coronado et al., 2011; Farquhar, Shadbeh, Samples, Ventura, & Goff, 2008; Flocks, Kelley, Economos, & McCauley, 2012; Samples et al., 2009) and with immigrant Latino and African American poultry processing workers (Lipscomb, Epling, Pompeii, & Dement, 2007; Marín et al., 2009; Quandt et al., 2006). It also has been used in the design, implementation, and evaluation of a safety-training program for Latino day laborers (Williams, Ochsner, Marshall, Kimmel, & Martino, 2010). Each of these occupational groups is a vulnerable population.

The goal of this chapter is to introduce the use of CBPR in conducting research with minority and vulnerable occupational communities. We begin by defining CBPR and discussing its characteristics and by providing conceptual and operational models of CBPR as translational science. We present a specific CBPR project, PACE3: Community Participatory Approach to Measuring Farmworker Pesticide Exposures, focused on the occupational health (pesticide exposure) of migrant and seasonal farmworkers in North Carolina to illustrate the conceptual and operational models of CBPR. We conclude with a discussion of issues to consider when developing a CBPR project that addresses occupational health disparities.

COMMUNITY-BASED PARTICIPATORY RESEARCH

Several dimensions of applying CBPR to occupational health require specification. These include defining CBPR and listing its elements; providing conceptual and operational models of CBPR as translational science; and explaining how CBPR is appropriate in addressing occupational health disparities in vulnerable populations.

Definition and Elements

CBPR is the process by which trained health scientists and community members collaborate in a joint process to critically investigate and change the environment, both physical and social, in an effort to improve people's health

(Arcury et al., 2001). CBPR is an approach to research that maintains rigorous methods while transforming the power dynamics and barriers between the researcher and the researched by emphasizing coeducation, power sharing, and knowledge sharing (Israel, Schulz, Parker, & Becker, 1998; Minkler, 2004). It has four major elements. First, it includes the participation of the people being studied. In the purest case, community members would be involved in delineating the topic that the research addresses; it is a topic that is important to the community. They would participate in the design of the research and the implementation of data collection. They would direct the analysis and reporting of study results. Second, CBPR uses the personal experiences and perceptions of community members as data. The systematic documentation of these personal experiences and perceptions often uses textual (in-depth individual interviews, focus groups) as well as statistical (e.g., survey interviews) methods. Third, the CBPR has a focus on empowerment and capacity building in which the community gains control and sovereignty as a result of their participation. Finally, a product of the research must be action by community and academic members to change the conditions causing the problems. This action may be political in working with elected officials and government workers to change policy, it may be community organizing to increase community-member involvement in implementing solutions, it may be implementing programs to provide community members with information or training, or it may be legal action or litigation to force changes on recalcitrant entities or gain remuneration for community members.

Israel et al. (2005) presented a set of principles for CBPR that are useful to consider when establishing community collaboration. They define *community* as a unit of identity reinforced through social interaction and characterized by shared values. Foremost among their principles is the understanding that CBPR requires a long-term commitment that must transcend a specific research project or research grant and that CBPR should grow through an iterative process. For example, our work with farmworkers in North Carolina began in 1995, and it has expanded for almost 2 decades to include activities beyond research. Maintaining a long-term commitment reflects two other principles: Collaborative activities should build on community resources and relationships, and they should establish equal partnerships. Collaborative programs developing from a long-term commitment should address locally relevant health problems and balance research and action. The results gained through these collaborative programs should promote reciprocal transfer of skills, with the results of these programs being actively disseminated to all partners. We add another principle to this list: CBPR conducted with vulnerable communities is a political process in which the collaborative program is addressing the needs of the vulnerable communities in the face of powerful and opposing political forces.

Conceptual and Operational Models of CBPR as Translational Science

Translational science rests on two processes. The first is making current empirically based health information available to health care providers, public health practitioners, and community members in a format that they can readily use to improve medical care, public health practice, and health self-management. The second process is providing health scientists with information that describes the real-world needs of health care providers, public health practitioners, and community members to help the scientists focus their research.

Translational science is at the heart of our conceptual model of CBPR (see Figure 4.1). This model begins with identifying community needs. Numerous processes can be used in identifying community needs. Community-based organizations, community advisory boards, and exploratory research can all present scientists with information documenting the health issues important to a community. For example, in our research on farmworker pesticide exposure, health care providers, community advocacy organizations, and farmworker community organizations all indicated that farmworkers were exposed to pesticides at work but that little information was available to document how they were exposed, the health implications of this exposure, or how to reduce this exposure.

This model proceeds to conducting research that addresses the community-identified needs. The design of the research will vary depending on the questions being asked. However, in all cases, rigorous scientific methods must be applied in this research. CBPR with vulnerable populations is always a political process; therefore, the research must be of the highest caliber to withstand the scrutiny of the politically powerful. Community members and stakeholders will be involved to different degrees with different parts of the research.

The results of the research must be "translated" or made available to the different stakeholders in a format so that each stakeholder group (audience)

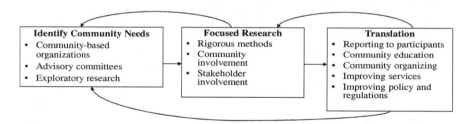

Figure 4.1. Conceptual model: Community-based participatory research (CBPR) as translational science.

can understand and use the results. This translation can be in the form of providing participants with their study results (e.g., laboratory results indicating level of exposure to a toxicant, medical diagnoses) and how they can use these study results to improve health. It can be used for community education and community organizing by providing information to all members of an affected community that they can use to improve their community. It can be used to inform the provision of services to a community or to change policies or regulations that improve the health of the community.

Connecting the three elements of the model are feedback loops. The model is not linear. Discussions of policy (translation) can inform the need for new research, as can gaps in community education. Similarly, issues related to services can be reflected in community needs. New research results can also be used in identifying community needs.

The multimode, multidomain operational model of CBPR is proactive in developing active participation from all community segments to identify community needs, conduct research, and translate research results (Arcury, Austin, Quandt, & Saavedra, 1999; see Figure 4.2). All community project participation is reflected in four domains: (a) consultation, which involves helping to delineate what should be done; (b) strategic planning,

	Community participation domains			
Examples of community participation modes	Consultation (What we should do)	Strategic planning (How we should do it)	Implementation (Do it)	Translation (Tell what we found)
Academic–CBO partnership				
Community advisory committees				
Health care provider advisory committees				
Partnership with service organizations				
Community meetings				
Training community members				
Training students				

Figure 4.2. Operational model: Multimode multidomain community-based participatory research (CBPR) model. CBO = community-based organization. From "Enhancing Community Participation in a Public Health Project: Farmworkers and Agricultural Chemicals in North Carolina," by T. A. Arcury, C. K. Austin, S. A. Quandt, and R. Saavedra, 1999, *Health Education & Behavior, 26*, p. 570. Copyright 1999 by Sage Publications. Adapted with permission.

which involves deciding how it should be done; (c) implementation, which involves completing the tasks to actually do it; and (d) dissemination, which involves sharing what was accomplished with other community residents and policymakers. We have learned that the members of vulnerable communities, because they have limited immediate economic resources, are often limited in participating even when they understand the long-term benefits of participating. If they have the opportunity for an immediate economic reward that allows them to feed their families, this takes precedent over long-term community gain. It is easier for a person with an outside income to be a volunteer; for those with a limited income or limited work opportunities, volunteering is often difficult. Therefore, this operational model allows community members to use the modes of participation in which they are comfortable within the four domains. For example, individual community members may only have the time to serve on an advisory committee involved in consultation and strategic planning that meets once per month or to attend an annual community meeting at which consultation is provided. Other community members might have the time to be active members of community-based organizations and become community investigators active in all domains of participation. Students from the community who are at all levels of education can become involved in projects and help with the implementation and translation domains. Finally, community members may be hired as project data collectors who are trained by the project and gain skills that help them with future employment.

CBPR With Vulnerable Populations

CBPR is appropriate for research and interventions addressing occupational health disparities experienced by vulnerable communities. CBPR provides a framework for conducting translational health research in vulnerable communities that allows community members the opportunity to participate in a manner that fits their situation. Through CBPR, the trust needed for environmental health research is established between community members and academic investigators. CBPR requires scientists and community members to share power, share resources, invest time, and invest effort. However, structural and cultural barriers often limit sharing power, resources, time, and effort. For example, granting agencies generally recognize one organization (most often the academic partner) as the primary grant recipient, which gives that organization control of resources. Those with more education and regular, secure employment (again, usually the representatives of the academic partner) often are seen as having more prestige and power. At the same time, community organizations can be unwilling to share the power they have in the form of community access and knowledge. The investment of time and effort requires academic partners to spend time at community venues and events; it requires community partners to learn about how research is conducted and data are interpreted.

Farmworkers are an excellent example of a vulnerable population for which CBPR is appropriate. Farmworkers experience great occupational and environmental hazards, including the physical environment (e.g., sun, heat, dust), wild plants (e.g., poison ivy) and animals (e.g., snakes), sharp tools, mechanized equipment, chemicals (e.g., pesticides, fertilizers, fuels), noise, and substandard housing (Arcury, Grzywacz, Sidebottom, & Wiggins, 2013; Arcury & Quandt, 2009). At the same time, farmworkers have little power because they are immigrants, are often unauthorized, have low incomes, have little formal education, and often do not speak English. They have limited control over the way in which their work is organized (Grzywacz et al., 2013). They have limited access to health care (Arcury & Quandt, 2007; Frank, Liebman, Ryder, Weir, & Arcury, 2013). Current occupational safety policy and regulations often exempt agriculture (Liebman et al., 2013). Therefore, research is needed to document the occupational health hazards that farmworkers face for the development of appropriate safety technology, training, and policy. Research is also required because the politically powerful deny that farmworkers experience heightened occupational health and injury risk, and refuse to consider further enforcement of existing regulations or implementation of new, stronger regulations. At the same time, the politically powerful seek to limit research so that the data needed for showing the need for greater safety technology, safety training, and safety policy are not available.

PACE3: A CBPR PROJECT ADDRESSING PESTICIDE EXPOSURE AMONG LATINO FARMWORKERS

In light of these factors, we developed and implemented PACE3: Community Participatory Approach to Measuring Farmworker Pesticide Exposures as a CBPR project to document the exposure of farmworkers to pesticides in the workplace. PACE3 was built over 10 years of community collaboration. In 1995, we began an association with the North Carolina Farmworker Health Alliance (which has since disbanded) to produce an unsuccessful proposal for research to document farmworker pesticide exposure. In 1996, we submitted a second proposal with the North Carolina Farmworkers Project (Benson, NC), which was funded; we initiated PACE1 (Reducing Farmworkers' Exposure to Agricultural Chemical, Grant No. R24 ES08739) in 1997. In 1999, we submitted another proposal in collaboration with the North Carolina Farmworkers Project, which was funded (PACE2: La Familia: Reducing Farmworker Pesticide Exposure, Grant No. R01 ES08739). Currently we are involved in PACE4: CBPR on

Pesticide Exposure & Neurological Outcomes for Latinos; PACE4 will take the partnership through 21 years.

PACE3 began in 2006 and was based on the ongoing primary partnership between Wake Forest School of Medicine and the North Carolina Farmworkers Project. The executive director of the North Carolina Farmworkers Project was a project coinvestigator. Other partners participating in data collection included Greene County Health Care, Inc., and Columbus County Community Health Center. Student Action with Farmworkers and the Farmworker Advocacy Network collaborated in the project design and in the translation of results. PACE3 included a farmworker advisory committee that met in Benson, and a health care provider advisory committee that met in Raleigh. The PACE3 structure included both informal community meetings and the work of under-graduate students (including Student Action with Farmworker interns) and graduate students.

PACE3 addressed each of the four domains of community collaboration and participation described in Figure 4.2: consultation, strategic planning, implementation, and translation. *Consultation* was based on the long-term associations of the project partners that had been initiated in 1995. This consultation reflected the continuing concerns of all parties in the exposure of farmworkers to pesticides, the limited regulations that were in place to protect farmworkers from this exposure and the limited enforcement of these regulations (Arcury, Quandt, Austin, Preisser, & Cabrera, 1999), and the lack of knowledge about pesticide exposure among farmworkers and their beliefs about this exposure (Quandt, Arcury, Austin, & Saavedra, 1998; Rao et al., 2006). At the same time, farmworker service and advocacy organiza-tion demands for greater pesticide regulation and enforcement were met with resistance from state and national regulatory agencies because of the lack of data clearly documenting that farmworkers were exposed to pesticides.

The partners were involved in the *strategic planning* that led to the grant application for which funds for PACE3 were obtained. These partners included the North Carolina Farmworkers Project and Student Action with Farmworkers, as well as Wake Forest School of Medicine. Strategic plans included specifying the specific aims and hypotheses, and designing procedures for selecting and recruiting participants and collecting data.

The farmworker and health care provider advisory committees and the community partners (North Carolina Farmworkers Project; Greene County Health Care, Inc.; Columbus County Community Health Center; and Student Action with Farmworker) all participated in the *implementation* of PACE3. Participation in implementation included input on the design of the data col-lection protocol, recruiting and hiring data collectors, providing lists of farm-worker camps and the directions to these camps, introducing data collectors to farmworkers in the camps, and participating in data collection.

PACE3 data collection was largely completed in 2007, but some additional data collection for ancillary studies was completed in 2008. The 2007 data collection design included contact with farmworkers at four points at 1-month intervals across the agricultural season (June through September). Data collection involved four components. At each contact the participants completed an interviewer administered questions that took about 45 minutes to complete at the first contact and 25 minutes to complete at the second through fourth contacts. At each contact they provide a first morning void urine sample that was processed to measure urinary pesticide metabolites and metals. At each contact they provided a finger stick blood sample that was analyzed for cholinesterase activity. (Cholinesterase is a family of enzymes critical to proper neurological function; the organophosphorus and carbamate insecticides work by binding with cholinesterase and disrupting neurological function.) At the first contact, they provided a saliva sample that was used for genetic analysis. Ancillary studies in 2008 involved three contacts at 1-month intervals with a subsample of participants who completed an interview and a finger stick blood sample at each contact, and an eye test and a venous blood draw at one contact.

We had great success in recruiting and maintaining participation of farmworkers because of the collaboration of our community partners. Farmworkers were recruited in 44 camps in 11 counties in 2007. A total of 287 farmworkers participated, with 50 completing only the first contact, 14 completing two contacts, 27 completing three contacts, and 196 completing all four contacts. The participation rate was 95.7%, and we had a total of 939 data points. In 2008, 122 farmworkers were recontacted and agreed to participate for a set of ancillary studies.

The primary findings of this project focused on farmworker pesticide exposure (Arcury et al., 2009, 2010). Analyses showed that biomarkers (urinary pesticide metabolites) for several different pesticides were common among all farmworkers. The presence of metabolites varied across the agricultural season; farmworkers were exposed to multiple pesticides, and they were exposed to individual pesticides multiple times. Farmworker pesticide exposure had implications for health, with cholinesterase depression being associated with the number of organophosphorus and carbamate pesticide metabolites detected in urine samples (Quandt, Chen, et al., 2010).

We found that field and camp sanitation requirements that would reduce pesticide exposure were widely ignored (Vallejos et al., 2011; Whalley et al., 2009). For example, one in five of the farmworkers reported not having received required pesticide safety training (EPA Worker Protection Standard: Final Rule, 1994), and an equal number reported not understanding the training that they received. One third of the farmworkers reported having no access to water for hand washing available at work, and one half reported not having soap or towels for hand washing available at work. One in five farmworkers reported that they lived in camps in which there were more than 30 residents present for each working washing machine or washtub. The number of substandard housing conditions increased across the agricultural season.

We also worked with our community partners to address several other issues of farmworker health. We found that farmworkers have high levels of arsenic and lead in their systems (Quandt, Jones, et al., 2010), they had poor vision and high rates of eye injuries (Quandt, Schulz, Talton, Verma, & Arcury, 2012), and because they are often separated from their families for 6 months of the year as a condition of their employment, they had limited knowledge of sexually transmitted disease (Rhodes et al., 2010). Other analysis investigated the genetics of pesticide metabolism and cholinesterase depression among farmworkers (Howard et al., 2010).

Four audiences were the foci for the *translation* of PACE 3 results: the actual study participants, the general farmworker community, advocates and policymakers, and environmental and occupational health scientists. Translation of study results differed for each of these audiences. The community advisory committees and community partners participated in the translation by helping to delineate the messages for each audience as well as the formats in which messages were to be delivered. Students also participated in translation.

Three approaches were taken in the translation of study results for participants. First, we prepared materials describing the pesticide urinary metabolites detected in each participant to provide these results to the participants in a manner that they could use. It is difficult to translate these results because they are complicated (results include data for 23 different metabolites with measures indicating if the metabolite was present in a urine sample in an amount above the laboratory limit of detection and the amount of the metabolite in μg/liter) and because the actual health effects of any amount of pesticide exposure is not known. Our approach was based on our earlier work in which we reported this information to the members of farmworkers families, indicated our lack of knowledge of the health implications, and provided them with safety information to reduce exposure to pesticides (Quandt et al., 2004). Second, we prepared materials describing the levels of pesticides found for all members who lived in a camp. Finally, we prepared an educational program on pesticide safety for all camp residents. Results were reported to camp residents by a member of the project team who was fluent in Spanish.

The study results were translated into a community education program on pesticide safety that was delivered to farmworker camps (Lane, Vallejos, Marín, Quandt, & Arcury, 2008). Community partners were trained to deliver the education program, which used a flipchart to present information on pesticide safety behaviors at work and at home, with brochures based on the flipchart left in the camps. Community partners also suggested that we reach a wider audience with pesticide safety using radio announcements. We developed five different radio announcements that were played for 10 weeks in 1-week rotations on two Spanish language radio stations (Lane et al., 2009). The foci of the radio announcements were as follows: (a) farmworkers should bathe immediately after work to remove pesticide residues; (b) employers are required to provide pesticide safety training to farmworkers in a language they can understand; (c) it is important for farmworkers to wash their hands during the work day to keep pesticides from entering the body, and employers are required to provide hand-washing facilities at the worksite; (d) farmworkers should store and wash their work clothes separately from other clothes to prevent contaminating nonwork clothes with pesticide residues; and (e) farmworkers should wear long sleeves, pants, and closed shoes while working to decrease exposure to pesticides. Two versions of the radio announcements were prepared, one for North Carolina with state-specific information and a general one for the United States that did not have contact information for North Carolina agencies.

The translation of PACE3 results for advocates and policymakers began with the development of policy briefs. These two-page documents summarized results reported in peer-reviewed journal articles, noted the policy implications of the results, and presented recommendations for achieving policy changes. Three policy briefs were developed from PACE3 results: Biomarkers of Farmworker Pesticide Exposure in North Carolina, Meeting the Requirements for Occupational Safety and Sanitation for Migrant Farmworkers in North Carolina, and Housing Conditions in Temporary Labor Camps for Migrant Farmworkers in North Carolina (Arcury et al., in press). Development of the policy briefs was undertaken as a collaboration of the academic investigators and the community investigators. Investigators also made presentations of study results in forums attended by advocates and policymakers, including the Governor's Pesticide Task Force in Raleigh, North Carolina (2008); 22nd East Coast Migrant Stream Forum (2009); 19th Annual Midwest Stream Farmworker Health Forum (2009); National Institute for Farm Safety (2010); and National Occupational Research Agenda (NORA) Symposium (2011).

The translation of PACE3 results to health scientists followed the traditional frameworks. Numerous presentations were made at professional conferences by PACE3 investigators and staff members. Investigators and staff members have written 23 peer-reviewed journal articles and one book chapter (not counting this chapter) that have been published or accepted for publication. An edited volume (Arcury & Quandt, 2009) draws heavily from the investigators' PACE3 experiences. Community partners were included as coauthors of PACE3 materials when it was appropriate given the requirements for coauthorship. For example, Leonardo Galván, project coordinator with the NC Farmworkers Project, was a coauthor on nine PACE3 peer-reviewed articles, and Melinda Wiggins, coinvestigator from Student Action with Farmworkers, wrote a chapter in the edited volume. The inclusion of community investigators as coauthors acknowledges their contributions to the research.

PACE3 resulted in other forms of health science translation. On the basis of study results and discussions with community partners, PACE3 provided a framework for four ancillary studies not included in the original study protocol. These ancillary studies addressed farmworker biological burden of heavy metals, farmworker cholinesterase depression, farmworker eye health and eye injuries, farmworker knowledge of sexually transmitted infection, and the genetics of pesticide metabolism. Four new research projects are based on PACE3 results. These include studies of the effects of pesticide exposure on neurological and cognitive outcomes (CBPR on Pesticide Exposure and Neurological Outcomes for Latinos: PACE4, Grant No. R01 ES008739; and Pesticide Exposure and Age-Related Changes in Cognitive Function, Grant No. R21 ES019720); a collaborative project directed at improving health science communication with community partners (A CBPR Approach to Biomedical & Behavioral Health Communication with Farmworkers, Grant No. R03 ES017364); and research on scientific integrity in CBPR research (Scientific Integrity in Community-Based Participatory Research, Grant No. R21 ES020967). Several additional project applications are planned. Finally, PACE3 promoted increased collaboration of the academic investigators with investigators at other institutions, including Virginia Tech, Duke University, and East Carolina University.

Summary

PACE3 was the product of a long-term commitment of community and academic partners working in collaboration to reduce pesticide exposure and improve health among farmworkers. It addresses a concern of farmworkers and farmworker service providers and advocates. The project recruited a large number of farmworkers and maintained their participation over several months; those participating in an ancillary study remained involved for over a year. Participants completed a diverse set of data collection activities that were often time consuming and unpleasant, in that they included participants' providing saliva, urine, and blood samples. The results have been communicated to a number of audiences—including farmworker participants, farmworker communities, advocates and policymakers, and scientists. The results were used to develop educational programs for farmworkers that have been used across North Carolina and the United States. The PACE3 partners continue to use study results to influence policy.

A variety of community members were involved in each of the domains of consultation, strategic planning, implementation, and translation. Community participation was structured so that individual involvement reflected the time and resources that community members could provide. Members of the community-based organizations had the greatest involvement, as they were paid for their time. Farmworkers who participated as members of an advisory committee had a smaller commitment, but they were provided a small honorarium and a meal for each meeting. The commitment of farmworkers who participated in community forums was very limited. Members of farmworker advocacy organizations had varying time commitments, but they were professionals committed to ensuring safety for farmworkers.

QUESTIONS TO CONSIDER WHEN DEVELOPING CBPR PROJECTS

CBPR should not be undertaken without considering its implications for community members and professional investigators. CBPR requires significant commitment from the community and professional investigators. If a CBPR partnership is successful, it can result in real and permanent change that reduces occupational risk and provides workers with health sovereignty and improved health. If a CBPR partnership fails, it can result in further harm to vulnerable workers, it can alienate potential allies, and it can harm the career of a professional investigator—particularly a junior investigator. In their review of CBPR projects for the Agency for Health Care Research and Quality, Viswanathan and colleagues (2004) provided a list of issues that should be considered in developing a CBPR partnership. This list provides a foundation for a set of five questions that community and professional investigators should consider in forming a CBPR collaboration.

Question 1: Are the Topic and Population Appropriate for CBPR?

Incorporating worker communities in the research and intervention process can benefit most projects. However, not all research in occupational health and safety requires the use of a CBPR approach. For example, much laboratory engineering research can be accomplished without the participation of worker communities. A number of organizations, such as unions, can facilitate CBPR research. However, CBPR research is most appropriate for occupational health and safety research when it is conducted with vulnerable worker communities, and these generally are not represented by organized labor. When worker communities are "hidden," lack trust in outsiders, and are drawn from marginalized populations, CBPR projects can provide the access needed to conduct valid and reliable research.

Ancillary to this main question are two additional considerations: (a) who needs the research, and (b) whether the partnership is driven by common need or by the requirements of a funding agency. If the community does not perceive the research to be needed, then the research is not needed by the community, or if the research is initiated by a professional researcher without community involvement, then a CBPR approach is not appropriate. For example, should an investigator wish to examine the health of a group of workers exposed to a chemical in the work place, a CBPR approach may not be appropriate if the workers or their advocates are not concerned about this exposure. The research itself may be extremely important, but the professional investigator may need to use approaches other than CBPR for it. Funding agencies that have become interested in CBPR to improve health equity have required that research applications use a CBPR approach. This can result in professional investigators convincing a community organization to participate in research when this research falls outside the organization's mission. The result of such partnerships is generally frustration for both the community organization and the investigator.

Question 2: Are Appropriate Community and Professional Partners Available?

Not all communities have the types of organizations present that can participate in a CBPR project. Occupational communities, particularly those composed of vulnerable workers, often have no "corporate" organizations representing them, such as unions, workers' centers, or advocacy and service organizations. Some communities lack any degree of formal organization; therefore, even knowing with whom to initiate a conversation is difficult.

Worker organizations involved in CBPR will be more successful if they have a volunteer or paid staff that is from the community they serve. Community staff members ensure that the organization reflects the actual needs and views held by community members. They should have a mission that is compatible with the goals of the research. For example, our research with farmworkers has included different community partners based on the topic being addressed. Toxic Free North Carolina has a mission to address pesticide exposure and has been a strong partner for our pesticide research. Student Action with Farmworkers has a mission to support the interaction of college students with farmworkers, and we have worked with them on educational programs. Finally, community organizations should have the resources to engage in a research project. Even organizations with paid staff often do not have the time to participate in a CBPR project and still perform their regular duties. Grant funding may not provide sufficient resources with continuity for the organization to expand its staff.

Many professional investigators are not trained or equipped to do CBPR. They do not have the temperament for CBPR. Academic investigators are often naïve about the actual commitment needed for CBPR; for example, they may not understand that community participation requires foregoing travel on fall, holiday, and spring breaks to work with the community, or they do not understand that communities do not work on a semester system and the work cannot be put on hold for summer travel, writing, or teaching. Work on CBPR projects often requires effort at times when community members are working, such as evenings and weekends.

Question 3: What Is the Structure of the Partnership?

Community and professional investigators need to consider how they structure a CBPR project to ensure it is successful. Issues include the types and number of staff members that are needed, who hires the staff members, and who is hired to staff the project. The first two issues are best addressed through collaboration in which the community and professional investigators together decide on the staffing needs of a project when the project is being designed and jointly select these staff members. For example, in designing our projects with farmworkers, the community and professional investigators designed the project together and together selected the project managers, data collectors, and community educators needed for the project. This is generally an iterative process in which the design suggests the staffing, which the investigators discuss in light of the funds that are available. Often the design and the staffing are revised to fit within the project's funding limits.

Who is hired by the project can be a cause of disagreement. Projects can provide employment for individuals from vulnerable communities with few opportunities. Projects need individuals with the skills required to collect data and present information to the community. Organizations want the members of their communities to benefit from the employment and career development opportunities that a project can offer; professional investigators are equally concerned about training their students. These issues are best addressed when the project is being designed. It is important to note that CBPR projects should include sufficient time and resources to provide training for community and student staff members.

The involvement of community members as investigators and staff requires that training be provided so all team members have a basic understanding of project design and research integrity. Professional investigators often move forward with project design based on years of training and experience. Similarly, their understanding of the need for research integrity (maintaining a protocol, IRB requirements and human subject protection, reporting results in an appropriate format) is part of professional training. Although this knowledge is taken for granted with professional investigators, it is often unfamiliar to community investigators. These issues came to light in PACE1, our first project with farmworkers. We planned a community lay health advisor program to train farmworkers about pesticide safety with an intervention group in the first year and a control group that would receive the delayed intervention in the next year (Arcury et al., 2000). However, at our first lay health advisors' training, we found representatives from control group camps. On asking our community partner about this obvious protocol violation, they stated that the training we were providing was valuable and that all farmworkers should receive it! We had not adequately provided the community investigators with an understanding of why it was important to have a control group.

Question 4: Who Has Power?

Power is not typically discussed in the province for research administration. However, power is often at the core of CBPR. CBPR is frequently undertaken because a group is vulnerable—it lacks power. Power in CBPR reflects several domains. It includes who controls the money for a project. Whether the community or professional organization receives the grant (is the prime contractor) can influence how power is shared. Often grant-reporting requirements make it difficult for a community organization to administer a federal grant; professional organizations, like universities, have entire departments dedicated to fulfilling these reporting requirements, whereas the director of a nonprofit organization may need to spend weekends completing these reports. Most nonprofit organizations do not have a negotiated overhead or indirect cost rate that provides the professional organizations with the resources to meet funder reporting requirements. When a community organization is not the primary recipient of a grant, having a subcontract with a budget can help equalize power between community and professional investigators.

Other constituents of power include ownership of data collected by a CBPR project and control of reporting of study results (who controls authorship). Data ownership provides power to the professional investigator in driving the research program, whereas data ownership by the community organization helps the organization control the release and publication of results in a manner that reflects its policy needs. Trust is important for data ownership and authorship. One approach to data ownership and publication is reaching agreement on common purposes for data. Professional investigators value publishing results in the peer-reviewed literature (Quandt, Arcury, & Pell, 2001). However, article authorship may not be valued by community investigators. All the investigators must agree on the requirement of authorship, with the requirements for community investigator authorship reflecting differences with the professional investigators in education and experience. Our experience is that we must often convince community investigators that they should be coauthors of peer-reviewed articles even if they do not value them. Authorship is important for community members in recognizing their contributions and ownership of the project results; community ownership of project results gives credibility to community investigators and can shield professional investigators from legal attack. We also work with community representatives to develop documents, such as policy briefs, that meet community and advocate needs. We have developed policy briefs and refrained from releasing them until a time when community members felt the briefs would have the greatest effect in the legislative process.

Results that could have adverse effects for the community must be considered in any plan for data ownership and release. Research might achieve negative results, that is, results that do not support or disprove the causes of occupational illness or injury proffered by the community. For example, community members may believe that worker cancers are the result of exposure to a common work chemical, but epidemiological and mechanistic research shows that this is not the case. Research may also document negative community characteristics, such as the fact that many immigrant workers lack proper documentation or that the use of sex workers leads to high rates of sexual transmitted infections among immigrant workers. Community and professional investigators need to agree about how to release these results at the start of a project, as ethics require that negative results be reported and that the community be protected.

Processes to equalize power and to make all partners responsible for a project are important for CBPR investigators. These processes should demystify research by including all partners in the strategic planning, implementation, and translation of a project. They also require that projects be designed to include resources that build community capacity (e.g., workshops, especially scientific writing workshops). Professional investigators must be committed to the partnership, ensuring that the community investigators can initiate research (frame the research questions); that community organizations receive some of the funds; and that benefits accrue to community members through the provision of information, employment, and skill development. Community members must also recognize that their knowledge of the community and their access to community members for CBPR projects constitute power, and they must be willing to share this power with the professional investigators.

Question 5: How Will Results Be Translated?

The entire exercise of CBPR with vulnerable worker communities is a sham without the translation of results to a format that provides workers greater health and safety. Therefore, translation needs to be at the core when CBPR partnerships are established and projects are designed. From its inception, we endeavored in PACE3 to translate study results to all potential audiences. We provided individual results to farmworker participants and used project results to provide useable information to all farmworkers through the creation of educational materials. Our goal is always health sovereignty, the state in which individual workers can control their own health. Providing individual results to farmworkers remains difficult, as the actual health risks from long-term exposure to low levels of pesticides are not entirely understood. We provided study results to health and service providers so that they could improve their practice. We also worked with advocates so that our science could be used to improve the policy and regulations that could reduce farmworker exposure to pesticides. Finally, we wrote our results so that other occupational health scientists could use them to further the empirical basis of protecting worker health and safety.

CBPR projects are ethically bound to translate their results, and they should endeavor to translate their results to formats that can be used by diverse audiences. They need to include the idea of translation at the stage when they are identifying community needs. They must also endeavor to improve translation methods and share these improved translation methods. New technologies are becoming available every day, and even the most vulnerable populations are gaining access to these technologies. In 2006, we argued that telephone lines should be provided for migrant farmworker camps in an effort to improve worker mental health (Grzywacz et al., 2006). In 2012, we found that almost all farmworkers owned or had access to cell phones. These new media provide greater opportunities to communicate information to vulnerable workers that they can use to protect their health.

POSTSCRIPT

We began our efforts to collaborate with farmworkers to improve occupational health in 1995. When we began this work we had no experience in CBPR. We have made impressive mistakes, but we have also had impressive success during the almost 2 decades of work. We have learned a great deal about farmworkers and those who advocate for farmworkers; farmworkers and their advocates have learned a great deal about research and its benefits.

The work required to establish, implement, and maintain a community-engaged approach to addressing the health of vulnerable worker populations, such as CBPR, can be daunting. However, the personal rewards and achievements in improving worker health can also be extraordinary. Community and professional investigators who select a community-engaged approach should not begin this process blindly. Nor should they shy from it because of the long hours and potential for failure (when she learned about our first CBPR project, PACE1, Sister Evelyn Mattern, a long-time farmworker advocate, exclaimed that the project was brave as we had such great potential to fail!). However, they should be realistic about the political nature of this work with vulnerable communities.

REFERENCES

Arcury, T. A., Austin, C. K., Quandt, S. A., & Saavedra, R. (1999). Enhancing community participation in intervention research: Farmworkers and agricultural chemicals in North Carolina. *Health Education & Behavior, 26*, 563–578. http://dx.doi.org/10.1177/109019819902600412

Arcury, T. A., Grzywacz, J. G., Isom, S., Whalley, L. E., Vallejos, Q. M., Chen, H., . . . Quandt, S. A. (2009). Seasonal variation in the measurement of urinary pesticide metabolites among Latino farmworkers in eastern North Carolina. *International Journal of Occupational and Environmental Health, 15*, 339–350. http://dx.doi.org/10.1179/oeh.2009.15.4.339

Arcury, T. A., Grzywacz, J. G., Sidebottom, J., & Wiggins, M. F. (2013). Overview of immigrant worker occupational health and safety for the agriculture, forestry, and fishing (AgFF) sector in the southeastern United States. *American Journal of Industrial Medicine, 56*, 911–924. http://dx.doi.org/10.1002/ajim.22173

Arcury, T. A., Grzywacz, J. G., Talton, J. W., Chen, H., Vallejos, Q. M., Galván, L., . . . Quandt, S. A. (2010). Repeated pesticide exposure among North Carolina migrant and seasonal farmworkers. *American Journal of Industrial Medicine, 53*, 802–813.

Arcury, T. A., & Quandt, S. A. (2007). Delivery of health services to migrant and seasonal farmworkers. *Annual Review of Public Health, 28*, 345–363. http://dx.doi.org/10.1146/annurev.publhealth.27.021405.102106

Arcury, T. A., & Quandt, S. A. (2009). The health and safety of farmworkers in the Eastern United States: A need to focus on social justice. In T. A. Arcury & S. A. Quandt (Eds.), *Latino farmworkers in the Eastern United States: Health, safety, and justice* (pp. 1–14). New York, NY: Springer. http://dx.doi.org/10.1007/978-0-387-88347-2_1

Arcury, T. A., Quandt, S. A., Austin, C. K., Preisser, J., & Cabrera, L. F. (1999). Implementation of EPA's Worker Protection Standard training for agricultural laborers: An evaluation using North Carolina data. *Public Health Reports, 114*, 459–468. Retrieved from https://www.ncbi.nlm.nih.gov/pubmed/10590768

Arcury, T. A., Quandt, S. A., Austin, C. K., Saavedra, R., Rao, P., & Cabrera, L. F. (2000). *Preventing agricultural chemical exposure: A safety program manual—participatory education with farmworkers in pesticide safety.* Winston-Salem, NC: Department of Family and Community Medicine, Wake Forest University School of Medicine.

Arcury, T. A., Quandt, S. A., & Dearry, A. (2001). Farmworker pesticide exposure and community-based participatory research: Rationale and practical applications. *Environmental Health Perspectives, 109*(Suppl. 3), 429–434. http://dx.doi.org/10.1289/ehp.01109s3429

Arcury, T. A., Wiggins, M. F., Brooke, C., Jensen, A., Summers, P., Mora, D. C., & Quandt, S. A. (in press). Using "policy briefs" to present scientific results of CBPR: Farmworkers in North Carolina. *Progress in Community Health Partnerships: Research, Education, and Action.*

Brody, J. G., Morello-Frosch, R., Zota, A., Brown, P., Pérez, C., & Rudel, R. A. (2009). Linking exposure assessment science with policy objectives for environmental justice and breast cancer advocacy: The northern California household exposure study. *American Journal of Public Health, 99*(Suppl. 3), S600–S609. http://dx.doi.org/10.2105/AJPH.2008.149088

Coronado, G. D., Holte, S., Vigoren, E., Griffith, W. C., Barr, D. B., Faustman, E., & Thompson, B. (2011). Organophosphate pesticide exposure and residential proximity to nearby fields: Evidence for the drift pathway. *Journal of Occupational and Environmental Medicine, 53,* 884–891. http://dx.doi.org/10.1097/JOM.0b013e318222f03a

EPA Worker Protection Standard: Final Rule, 40 C.F.R. § 170 (1994). Retrieved from http://www.epa.gov/pesticides/health/worker.htm

Farquhar, S., Shadbeh, N., Samples, J., Ventura, S., & Goff, N. (2008). Occupational conditions and well-being of indigenous farmworkers. *American Journal of Public Health, 98,* 1956–1959. http://dx.doi.org/10.2105/AJPH.2007.124271

Flocks, J., Kelley, M., Economos, J., & McCauley, L. (2012). Female farmworkers' perceptions of pesticide exposure and pregnancy health. *Journal of Immigrant and Minority Health, 14,* 626–632. http://dx.doi.org/10.1007/s10903-011-9554-6

Frank, A. L., Liebman, A. K., Ryder, G., Weir, M., & Arcury, T. A. (2013). Health care access and health care workforce for immigrant workers in the agriculture, forestry, and fisheries sector in the southeastern US. *American Journal of Industrial Medicine, 56,* 960–974. http://dx.doi.org/10.1002/ajim.22183

Grzywacz, J. G., Lipscomb, H. J., Casanova, V., Neis, B., Fraser, C., Monaghan, P., & Vallejos, Q. M. (2013). Organization of work in the agricultural, forestry, and fishing sector in the US southeast: Implications for immigrant workers' occupational safety and health. *American Journal of Industrial Medicine, 56,* 925–939. http://dx.doi.org/10.1002/ajim.22169

Grzywacz, J. G., Quandt, S. A., Early, J., Tapia, J., Graham, C. N., & Arcury, T. A. (2006). Leaving family for work: Ambivalence and mental health among

Mexican migrant farmworker men. *Journal of Immigrant and Minority Health*, 8, 85–97. http://dx.doi.org/10.1007/s10903-006-6344-7

Howard, T. D., Hsu, F. C., Grzywacz, J. G., Chen, H., Quandt, S. A., Vallejos, Q. M., . . . Arcury, T. A. (2010). Evaluation of candidate genes for cholinesterase activity in farmworkers exposed to organophosphorus pesticides: Association of single nucleotide polymorphisms in BCHE. *Environmental Health Perspectives*, 118, 1395–1399. http://dx.doi.org/10.1289/ehp.0901764

Israel, B. A., Parker, E. A., Rowe, Z., Salvatore, A., Minkler, M., López, J., . . . Halstead, S. (2005). Community-based participatory research: Lessons learned from the Centers for Children's Environmental Health and Disease Prevention Research. *Environmental Health Perspectives*, 113, 1463–1471. http://dx.doi.org/10.1289/ehp.7675

Israel, B. A., Schulz, A. J., Parker, E. A., & Becker, A. B. (1998). Review of community-based research: Assessing partnership approaches to improve public health. *Annual Review of Public Health*, 19, 173–202. http://dx.doi.org/10.1146/annurev.publhealth.19.1.173

Kreuter, M. W., Kegler, M. C., Joseph, K. T., Redwood, Y. A., & Hooker, M. (2012). The impact of implementing selected CBPR strategies to address disparities in urban Atlanta: A retrospective case study. *Health Education Research*, 27, 729–741. http://dx.doi.org/10.1093/her/cys053

Lane, C. M., Jr., Vallejos, Q. M., Marín, A., Quandt, S., & Arcury, T. A. (2008). *Pesticidas: No los traiga a la casa! / Don't take pesticides home with you!* Winston-Salem, NC: Department of Family and Community Medicine, Wake Forest University School of Medicine.

Lane, C. M., Jr., Vallejos, Q. M., Marín, A. J., Quandt, S. A., Grzywacz, J. G., & Galván, L., . . . Arcury, T. A. (2009). *Pesticide safety radio public service announcements*. Winston-Salem, NC: Center for Worker Health, Wake Forest University School of Medicine.

Liebman, A. K., Wiggins, M. F., Fraser, C., Levin, J., Sidebottom, J., & Arcury, T. A. (2013). Occupational health policy and immigrant workers in the agriculture, forestry, and fishing sector. *American Journal of Industrial Medicine*, 56, 975–984. http://dx.doi.org/10.1002/ajim.22190

Lipscomb, H. J., Epling, C. A., Pompeii, L. A., & Dement, J. M. (2007). Musculoskeletal symptoms among poultry processing workers and a community comparison group: Black women in low-wage jobs in the rural South. *American Journal of Industrial Medicine*, 50, 327–338. http://dx.doi.org/10.1002/ajim.20447

Marín, A. J., Grzywacz, J. G., Arcury, T. A., Carrillo, L., Coates, M. L., & Quandt, S. A. (2009). Evidence of organizational injustice in poultry processing plants: Possible effects on occupational health and safety among Latino workers in North Carolina. *American Journal of Industrial Medicine*, 52, 37–48. http://dx.doi.org/10.1002/ajim.20643

Minkler, M. (2004). Ethical challenges for the "outside" researcher in community-based participatory research. *Health Education & Behavior*, 31, 684–697. http://dx.doi.org/10.1177/1090198104269566

Quandt, S. A., Arcury, T. A., Austin, C. K., & Cabrera, L. F. (2001). Preventing occupational exposure to pesticides: Using participatory research with Latino farmworkers to develop an intervention. *Journal of Immigrant Health, 3,* 85–96. http://dx.doi.org/10.1023/A:1009513916713

Quandt, S. A., Arcury, T. A., Austin, C. K., & Saavedra, R. M. (1998). Farmworker and farmer perceptions of farmworker agricultural chemical exposure in North Carolina. *Human Organization, 57,* 359–368. http://dx.doi.org/10.17730/humo.57.3.n26161776pgg7371

Quandt, S. A., Arcury, T. A., & Pell, A. I. (2001). Something for everyone? A community and academic partnership to address farmworker pesticide exposure in North Carolina. *Environmental Health Perspectives, 109*(Suppl. 3), 435–441. http://dx.doi.org/10.1289/ehp.01109s3435

Quandt, S. A., Chen, H., Grzywacz, J. G., Vallejos, Q. M., Galván, L., & Arcury, T. A. (2010). Cholinesterase depression and its association with pesticide exposure across the agricultural season among Latino farmworkers in North Carolina. *Environmental Health Perspectives, 118,* 635–639. http://dx.doi.org/10.1289/ehp.0901492

Quandt, S. A., Doran, A. M., Rao, P., Hoppin, J. A., Snively, B. M., & Arcury, T. A. (2004). Reporting pesticide assessment results to farmworker families: Development, implementation, and evaluation of a risk communication strategy. *Environmental Health Perspectives, 112,* 636–642. http://dx.doi.org/10.1289/ehp.6754

Quandt, S. A., Grzywacz, J. G., Marín, A., Carrillo, L., Coates, M. L., Burke, B., & Arcury, T. A. (2006). Illnesses and injuries reported by Latino poultry workers in western North Carolina. *American Journal of Industrial Medicine, 49,* 343–351. http://dx.doi.org/10.1002/ajim.20299

Quandt, S. A., Jones, B. T., Talton, J. W., Whalley, L. E., Galván, L., Vallejos, Q. M., . . . Arcury, T. A. (2010). Heavy metals exposures among Mexican farmworkers in eastern North Carolina. *Environmental Research, 110,* 83–88. http://dx.doi.org/10.1016/j.envres.2009.09.007

Quandt, S. A., Schulz, M. R., Talton, J. W., Verma, A., & Arcury, T. A. (2012). Occupational eye injuries experienced by migrant farmworkers. *Journal of Agromedicine, 17,* 63–69. http://dx.doi.org/10.1080/1059924X.2012.629918

Rao, P., Gentry, A. L., Quandt, S. A., Davis, S. W., Snively, B. M., & Arcury, T. A. (2006). Pesticide safety behaviors in Latino farmworker family households. *American Journal of Industrial Medicine, 49,* 271–280. http://dx.doi.org/10.1002/ajim.20277

Rhodes, S. D., Bischoff, W. E., Burnell, J. M., Whalley, L. E., Walkup, M. P., Vallejos, Q. M., . . . Arcury, T. A. (2010). HIV and sexually transmitted disease risk among male Hispanic/Latino migrant farmworkers in the Southeast: Findings from a pilot CBPR study. *American Journal of Industrial Medicine, 53,* 976–983. http://dx.doi.org/10.1002/ajim.20807

Rhodes, S. D., Kelley, C., Simán, F., Cashman, R., Alonzo, J., McGuire, J., . . . Reboussin, B. (2012). Using community-based participatory research (CBPR) to develop a community-level HIV prevention intervention for Latinas: A local response to a global challenge. *Women's Health Issues, 22*, e293–e301. http://dx.doi.org/10.1016/j.whi.2012.02.002

Samples, J., Bergstad, E. A., Ventura, S., Sanchez, V., Farquhar, S. A., & Shadbeth, N. (2009). Pesticide exposure and occupational safety training of indigenous farmworkers in Oregon. *American Journal of Public Health, 99*(Suppl. 3), S581–S584.

Vallejos, Q. M., Quandt, S. A., Grzywacz, J. G., Isom, S., Chen, H., Galván, L., . . . Arcury, T. A. (2011). Migrant farmworkers' housing conditions across an agricultural season in North Carolina. *American Journal of Industrial Medicine, 54*, 533–544. http://dx.doi.org/10.1002/ajim.20945

Viswanathan, M., Ammerman, A., Eng, E., Gartlehner, G., Lohr, K. N., & Griffith, D., . . . Whitener, L. (2004). *Community-based participatory research: Assessing the evidence* (Evidence Report/Technology Assessment No. 99, prepared by RTI—University of North Carolina Evidence-based Practice Center under Contract No. 290-02-0016; AHRQ Publication 04-E022-2). Rockville, MD: Agency for Healthcare Research and Quality.

Whalley, L. E., Grzywacz, J. G., Quandt, S. A., Vallejos, Q. M., Walkup, M., Chen, H., . . . Arcury, T. A. (2009). Migrant farmworker field and camp safety and sanitation in eastern North Carolina. *Journal of Agromedicine, 14*, 421–436. http://dx.doi.org/10.1080/10599240903389508

Williams, Q., Jr., Ochsner, M., Marshall, E., Kimmel, L., & Martino, C. (2010). The impact of a peer-led participatory health and safety training program for Latino day laborers in construction. *Journal of Safety Research, 41*, 253–261. http://dx.doi.org/10.1016/j.jsr.2010.02.009

5

ADDRESSING OCCUPATIONAL STRESS AMONG AFRICAN AMERICANS

RASHAUN ROBERTS

According to the World Health Organization (WHO), stress is one of the top 10 social determinants of health disparities, with substantial research suggesting that greater stress is associated with increased risk for impairments in mental and physical health across populations (Baum, 2002; Chen & Miller, 2013). African Americans, who comprise roughly 12% of the workforce (Bureau of Labor Statistics [BLS], 2011), face job- and workplace-related circumstances that increase their risk of occupational stress per se. African Americans' overexposure to stressful aspects of work and the link between job stress and the stress-related illnesses that disproportionately impact them (e.g., hypertension) suggest that interventions designed to prevent or reduce occupational stress among Black Americans are needed. Although churches are often in unique positions of influence in Black communities

This chapter was authored by an employee of the United States government as part of official duty and is considered to be in the public domain. The findings and conclusions in this report are those of the author(s) and do not necessarily represent the views of the United States government, and the author's participation in the work is not meant to serve as an official endorsement.

http://dx.doi.org/10.1037/0000021-006
Occupational Health Disparities: Improving the Well-Being of Ethnic and Racial Minority Workers, F. T. L. Leong, D. E. Eggerth, C.-H. Chang, M. A. Flynn, J. K. Ford, and R. O. Martinez (Editors)

(Poussaint & Alexander, 2000), experts have not typically worked with them to design and deliver customized occupational safety and health interventions. Consequently, this chapter explores the question of whether an occupational stress intervention developed in partnership with churches might positively influence African Americans' awareness of risks to health and well-being posed by job stress and help them build skills and a sense of efficacy with respect to preventing or managing it.

AN INTRODUCTION TO OCCUPATIONAL STRESS

Stress is defined as "the adverse reaction people have to excessive pressures or other types of demand placed on them" (Health and Safety Executive, 2007, p. 7). It is the process that arises when work demands or work stressors of various types and combinations exceed the resources a person has available to him or her (Balducci, Schaufeli, & Fraccaroli, 2011). Stress is an internationally recognized health and safety risk factor (Jordan et al., 2003; National Institute for Occupational Safety and Health [NIOSH], 1999). According to the American Psychological Association (2011), more than one third (36%) of workers said that they typically feel tense or stressed out during their workday, and 20% reported that their average daily level of stress from work is an 8, 9, or 10 on a 10-point scale. In addition, about one fourth viewed their jobs as the top stressor in their lives (NIOSH, 1999). Further, up to 44% of women and 37% of men have been found to want to quit their jobs because of occupational stress (Marlin Company, 2003).

Stress has become increasingly visible in the field of occupational disease (Bellarosa & Chen, 1997). The basic rationale underpinning the concept of job stress is that the work situation has certain demands and that difficulties in meeting these demands can lead to illness, injury, and psychological distress (Edwards & Burnard, 2003; Health and Safety Executive, 2001; Jordan et al., 2003). An impressive body of empirical research supports the link between occupational stress and problems in health and safety. Researchers have found that mood and sleep disturbances, upset stomach, headaches, and disrupted familial relationships are common early manifestations of job stress (NIOSH, 1999). Studies have also found that stress at work plays an important role in high blood pressure and cholesterol levels (Goodspeed & DeLucia, 1990), cardiovascular disease (CVD; Sauter, Hurrell, & Cooper, 1999), infectious and autoimmune diseases (e.g., Brunner, 2000), anxiety and depression (e.g., Landsbergis, Schnall, Deitz, Friedman, & Pickering, 1992), and accidents and injuries (e.g., Schnall, Belkic, & Pickering, 2000). Researchers have reported that exposure to job stress may even amplify the impact of a given toxicant, producing a variety of health-damaging effects (Gee & Payne-Sturges, 2004).

Occupational stress has far-reaching consequences, not only for the health and safety of workers but also for employers. It contributes to a number of outcomes that threaten organizational success, including physical injuries at work, absenteeism, labor turnover, decreased work productivity, diminished job satisfaction (Alves, 2005), low morale, and burnout (e.g., Sutherland & Cooper, 1990). Some estimate that between 50% and 60% of lost workdays each year can be attributed to stress and that the average cost of absenteeism in a large company is more than $3.6 million per year (American Institute of Stress, 2012; Matteson & Ivancevich, 1987; Maxon, 1999). The American Institute of Stress (2012) estimated that 40% of job turnover is due to stress and that replacing an average employee costs 120% to 200% of the salary of the position affected. In general, stress-related health and safety problems result in considerable losses to industry, costing employers a total of up to $60 billion per year (Benton, 2000).

The U.S. economy at large also incurs considerable costs related to occupational stress. Econometric analyses show that, over the years, health care expenditures have increased nearly 50% for workers who perceive their jobs as stressful and nearly 200% for those reporting high levels of job stress and depression (Alves, 2005). Health care expenditures tend to be almost 50% greater for workers who report high levels of stress. According to national estimates, the total cost of job stress to the U.S. economy ranges from $250 to $300 billion annually in lowered productivity; turnover; and direct medical, legal, and insurance fees (American Institute of Stress, 2012; D. L. Jones, Tanigawa, & Weiss, 2003).

AFRICAN AMERICAN HEALTH STATUS

Given the adverse impact of occupational stress on individuals, organizations, and society, it is clear that there are enormous potential benefits to taking steps to reduce it. One population for which the development of interventions to reduce stress may be particularly crucial is African Americans. Approximately 13% of the U.S. population, or about 39 million persons, identify themselves as non-Hispanic Black or African American (U.S. Census Bureau, 2011), and as a group, they appear to be worse off than the general population on several dimensions of health. For example, rates of hypertension or high blood pressure have been inordinately high among Blacks (Fields et al., 2004). According to the Centers for Disease Control and Prevention (CDC), the age-adjusted prevalence of hypertension is 40.5% among non-Hispanic Blacks compared with 27.4% among non-Hispanic Whites (CDC, 2005). The racial/ethnic disparity in hypertension begins after puberty and persists into adulthood. By the ages of 40 to 59, roughly

50% of Black Americans are hypertensive, compared with 30% of White Americans. By age 65, 75% of Black women are hypertensive, compared with 50% of White women in the same age group (CDC, 2005).

Hypertension is a major risk factor for CVD, coronary heart disease (CHD), stroke, and other adverse health outcomes. The CVD prevalence rates for African American males and females are about 46% for each group, compared with 38% and 33% for non-Hispanic White males and females, respectively. African Americans also have an earlier onset and a higher risk of first myocardial infarction or heart attack at all ages than do their White counterparts (Clark, 2006), as well as the highest overall out-of-hospital CHD death rates of any U.S. ethnic group—particularly at younger ages (Clark & Anderson, 2001).

The prevalence rate for stroke for African American males and females is about 4% for each group, compared with about 2% and 3% for non-Hispanic males and females, respectively (Klag et al., 1996; McGruder, Malarcher, Antoine, Greenlund, & Croft, 2004). There are racial differences in the subtypes of stroke, and these racial disparities in subtype are greatest at younger ages. Young African Americans have a 2- to 3-fold greater risk of ischemic stroke than their White counterparts and are more likely to die as a result of stroke (CDC, 2001). African Americans also possess a disproportionate burden of the risk factors for stroke mortality. They have the highest age-adjusted death rate due to stroke at 65.2 per 100,000 persons, compared with 46.6 per 100,000 persons for all other races combined (CDC, 2005).

In general, National Center for Health Statistics (2007) data indicate that Blacks have the highest all-cause, age-adjusted death rate at an alarming 1016.5 per 100,000 persons. This exceeds the age-adjusted death rate of 798.8 per 100,000 persons for all races combined. The average life expectancy of African Americans is about 6 years shorter than that of White Americans, and CVD, CHD, and stroke account for a significant portion of these years. CVD accounts for 2.2 years of this reduced life expectancy, with CHD accounting for 1.7 of those years and stroke for 0.5 of those years (CDC, 2001; Astone, Ensminger, & Juon, 2002).

STRESS AND HEALTH DISPARITIES

The root causes of these health disparities are not well understood, but a variety of factors are thought to contribute to them. These include but are not limited to socioeconomic factors, geography, behavioral risk factors, lifestyle choices (e.g., smoking, physical inactivity, excess weight), and health care provider behavior. Further, many scholars believe that the disparities that affect African Americans and other minority groups ultimately reflect inequalities in many aspects of life, including in access to health care, social and economic status, educational opportunity, and environmental conditions (Diez-Roux, 2000; Diez-Roux et al., 1997).

Researchers have begun viewing stress as an important contributor to racial and ethnic health disparities (Williams, Neighbors, & Jackson, 2003) in light of the fact that stress has been long identified as an important factor in chronic disease development, maintenance, and/exacerbation and in increased susceptibility to infectious and other diseases (Cohen, Tyrrell, & Smith, 1991). Scholars have proposed that differential exposure and vulnerability to environmental, sociocultural, and psychosocial stressors of various types is at the core of health disparities. For instance, Gee and Payne-Sturges (2004) asserted that stress is a key component of differential susceptibility to illness and further explained that stressors, especially when not ameliorated by resources, may lead directly to health disparities among racial/ethnic groups.

Scholars have directly speculated that the high rates of hypertension and related illnesses that disproportionately affect African Americans are attributable to their differential exposure to psychosocial stress (Poussaint & Alexander, 2000), and there are data that support this theory. Studies have demonstrated that Blacks as a group are exposed to more chronic and insidious stressors and report more distress, disease, and dysfunction than Whites (Orr et al., 1996). Further, some research investigations have found that Blacks often report a greater number of negative life events, report greater and more frequent exposure to generic life stressors (i.e., stressors that are a usual part of modern life—financial, occupational, relationship, parental, etc.), perceive these events as more stressful, and report greater psychological distress from these stressful life experiences than their White counterparts (Orr et al., 1996).

It is fairly well established that Blacks/African Americans and other minority groups are differentially exposed to race-related stressors (e.g., racial and ethnic discrimination). These stressors appear to make an additional contribution to the level of experienced psychological distress beyond that accounted for by generic life stressors that all people experience. In addition, African Americans and other minority groups may perceive greater stigma or pressures not to report episodes of discrimination, which may only increase stress levels. Both generic and race-related stressors impact health. For example, a study examining the effects of stress on self-reported physical and mental health of 520 White Americans and 586 African Americans in Detroit found that both race-related stressors and general life stressors significantly account for racial differences in physical health status (Williams et al., 2003).

AFRICAN AMERICAN EXPOSURE
TO OCCUPATIONAL STRESSORS

An extensive literature indicates that a variety of stressors that are associated with the way jobs are designed and other working conditions contribute to problems in health and safety. For example, Karasek and Theorell (1990) proposed that workers that confront high psychological demands and low control or decision latitude in meeting those demands on the job appear to be at greater risk for cardiovascular disease than workers who are not subjected to such conditions (Johnson, Hall, & Theorell, 1989). Further, Whitehall II study researchers investigating the relationship between work-related factors and ill-health found that a variety of health outcomes were dependent on effort and reward, job demands, decision latitude, and job stability (e.g., Stansfield, Head, & Marmot, 2000).

African Americans may confront a greater number of stressors in the workplace than other racial/ethnic groups, and this may contribute to their susceptibility to illness. Some evidence lends support to this conjecture. First, it appears that as a group, Blacks are overrepresented in lower status occupations and underrepresented in higher status occupations (Darity, 2003). For example, recent national surveys indicate that Whites are more likely to hold managerial positions, whereas Blacks are more likely to be employed in service and transportation jobs (Roberts, Swanson, & Murphy, 2004). It is noteworthy that managers and other white-collar professionals are more likely to have health benefits and access to additional financial and other resources to help them manage workplace stressors, whereas this is less likely to be the case for blue-collar workers.

Blue-collar occupations have been linked to problems in health. In a ranking of jobs based on the blood pressures of incumbents, Leigh, Markowitz, Fahs, Shin, and Landrigan (1997) determined that service and transportation positions were in the top 40% in terms of having an incumbent with high blood pressure, whereas a disproportionately low number of professional and managerial incumbents had higher than average blood pressure. Leigh et al. explained that managers and professionals may have high levels of psychological demands, but they also have considerable decision latitude, which protects them from developing strain reactions, whereas service and transportation workers are not afforded this protection.

In addition to their potential overexposure to high demand/low control job conditions, Blacks must contend with an increased risk of stress due to job insecurity that involves threat of job loss and uncertainty regarding future employment. This is because they tend to be overrepresented in work involving atypical employment contracts and low job tenure. For example, Black females tend to be disproportionately employed in temporary work arrangements. They constitute 21% of the workforce provided by temporary help firms, which is almost twice their representation in the traditional workforce (DiNatale, 2001).

Another indication that African Americans are differentially exposed to job insecurity is high rates of joblessness. Layoffs and discharges are higher for Black males than White males (Elvira & Zatzick, 2002; Holzer, 1998). Also, the unemployment rate for African Americans has historically been higher than the national average. In 2010, the average unemployment rate for Blacks was 16%, compared with 8.7% for Whites (BLS, 2011). Further, 48.4% of all unemployed Blacks were unemployed 27 weeks or longer in 2010, compared with 41.9% of unemployed Whites (BLS, 2011). The unemployment rate for African Americans remained high in 2011. In mid-2011, their unemployment rate was 16.2%, only 0.3 percentage points down from its peak of 16.5% in 2010 (BLS, 2011).

Although the impact of job insecurity on African Americans has rarely been studied, empirical studies have suggested that precarious forms of employment are associated with poor health and high levels of stress-related tension and exhaustion (Vosko, Zukewich, & Cranford, 2003). Threat of job loss has also been associated with increases in self-reported morbidity, serum cholesterol, depression, anxiety (Ferrie, Shipley, Marmot, Stansfeld, & Davey Smith, 1998; Kivimäki, Vahtera, Pentti, & Ferrie, 2000), and accidents (Probst, Graso, Estrada, & Greer, 2013; Probst & Hagger, 2014).

In addition to their overexposure to the stressors mentioned previously, Blacks might be more likely than other groups to contend with racial/ethnic discrimination in the workplace. *Discrimination* is defined as an adverse distinction made with regard to a person or group (Krieger, 1999). These distinctions are manifested in judgment and/or action and result in structured opportunity and assignment of value that unfairly disadvantage some groups while unfairly advantaging others (Krieger & Sidney, 1996). Discrimination can appear at the interpersonal and institutional levels. Interpersonal discrimination may have its roots in stereotypes and pigeonholing attitudes and assumptions, making ethnic slurs or ethnic jokes. At the institutional level, discrimination can block opportunities for certain groups and limit their access to resources (Krieger & Sidney, 1996). It is important to note that racial harassment is a form of discrimination that involves creation of a hostile work environment on the basis of race. It includes verbal abuse such as name-calling, slurs, epithets, threats, derogatory comments, and other unwelcome remarks.

Evidence indicates that Blacks encounter racial/ethnic discrimination and harassment in the workplace. The General Social Survey found that of all employed adults 18 years and older, 19.4% of Blacks, compared with only 2.1% of Whites, responded affirmatively when asked if they felt "in any way" discriminated against on their job because of race or ethnic origin (Roberts et al., 2004). In one study of racial bias in the workplace, researchers found that 60% of African American respondents reported that they hear racial and ethnic jokes in the workplace, which indicates a very real presence or perception of negative racial overtones in the workplace. Additionally, studies have shown that African American women encounter both sexual and racial harassment and tend to leave workplace cultures that they perceive to be negative and oppressive.

Exposure to racial/ethnic discrimination and harassment impacts individuals in a variety of ways that in turn affects health, safety, and well-being. Those who are exposed may respond with anger, rage, hostility, resentment, bitterness, and aggression (Keashly, 1998). Some may displace their feelings of frustration onto others and may have problems in their family and personal lives. Feelings resulting from psychological and emotional abuse in the workplace include confusion; depression; feelings of helplessness, hopelessness, and despair; and an attitude of distrust and paranoia toward the hostile environment. Research has suggested that workplace environment characterized by hostility based on race/ethnicity contributes to poor mental health of employees. Studies have previously reported that stress engendered by racial discrimination in general is associated with high blood pressure (Krieger & Sidney, 1996), mental health problems (Gee, 2002; Kessler, Mickelson, & Williams, 1999), and alcohol consumption (Yen & Syme, 1999).

LIMITATIONS OF EMPLOYER-SPONSORED STRESS INTERVENTIONS

African Americans' overexposure to stressful aspects of work and the linkage between job stress and illnesses that undermine their overall health and safety status suggest that customized interventions designed to prevent or reduce job stress among Blacks are needed. Stress management programs (SMPs) are one type of intervention. Evidence has suggested that these programs can result in reduction of physiological arousal level and stress indicator variables such as anxiety, as well as in increased emotional stability and fewer somatic complaints (e.g., Bunce, 1997; van der Klink, Blonk, Schene, & van Dijk, 2001). SMPs typically consist of three core components: psychoeducation, skill-building in stress arousal reduction, and employee support and active problem solving (Girdano, 1986; Lamontagne, Keegel, Louie, Ostry, & Landsbergis, 2007; Murphy, 1984, 1985; Raeburn, Atkinson, Dubignon, McPherson, & Elkind, 1993).

Psychoeducation is an evidenced-based practice shown to be effective in addressing a variety of health problems (U.S. Department of Health and

Human Services, 2002), and it involves providing instruction about a given problem. It may include providing education about occupational stress and its health consequences using one or more stress models as a teaching tool. Further, interactive exercises may be used to foster (stress) symptom recognition and recognition of occupational stress triggers. In addition, education about the role that nutrition, physical fitness, and other key lifestyle factors that can build resistance to stress may be provided. Finally, participants may be made aware of accessible occupational safety and health resources that may be drawn on for assistance in addressing various occupational safety and health problems in the workplace.

The second core component of an SMP may involve helping participants build skills to reduce stress arousal. Health psychologists are in agreement that stress is lessened in situations where there is a sense of personal control and efficacy (Bandura, 1977; Roddenberry & Renk, 2010). Breathing and relaxation techniques foster this sense because they enable individuals to actively reduce body arousal under or in anticipation of stressful conditions. In an SMP, participants may be taught the mechanics of relaxation, and multiple practice sessions may be provided to build relaxation skills.

In addition to relaxation, participants may be taught how to change responses to stressors from a cognitive perspective. For example, cognitive rehearsal involves helping people respond adaptively to stressors by anticipating them before they happen and rehearsing ways to respond to them adaptively (Matteson & Ivancevich, 1987). This and similar techniques help reduce stress arousal, develop a capacity to effectively manage stressors, build resistance to stress-related situations, and increase well-being.

The third core component of a generic SMP is support and active problem solving. Stress appears to be buffered in situations where perceived social support is present (Baqutayan, 2011; Cohen & Wills, 1985; J. Jones, 2003). Social support can extend individual resources by allowing reciprocal receiving and giving of emotional and tangible assistance. Consequently, this portion of the intervention allows participants to discuss various stressors in the workplace, receive and give support, and problem solve around addressing the sources of stress. Participants may be taught specific brainstorming and creativity techniques that may help them generate innovative ways of changing or responding to identified workplace stressors. Following the brainstorming, participants may be coached to develop action plans detailing when, where, and how the ideas generated will be implemented. The formulation of such plans typically makes it easier for people to follow through on their intended actions. In addition to providing support and a stimulating, interactive environment for problem solving, this SMP component may provide an excellent opportunity for reinforcement of information and skills taught throughout the program.

Although companies are increasingly offering these types of SMPs, they are generally not tailored to the demographic characteristics of workers (e.g., Lambert, 2001; Tsui & Milkovich, 1987). Program customization appears to be needed, as variations in program and policy utilization according to certain characteristics exist. For example, a study of the company Johnson & Johnson found that its employees from higher income households were more likely than employees from lower income households to have used virtually all family-responsive programs and policies offered by the company (Families and Work Institute, 1993). In a similar case study, Lambert (2001) found that a greater proportion of managers/supervisors (73.4%) used workplace programs and policies than operatives/laborers (30.7%).

This pattern of variability in program and policy utilization may emerge because limited income restricts workers' access to benefits in cases where workers must share cost. Job status may also be related to benefit use because of differences in corresponding job conditions. Higher status workers are likely to have more flexible jobs and to be better able to take advantage of programs operating at the worksite or off-site.

COMMUNITY-BASED STRESS INTERVENTIONS AS AN ALTERNATIVE

As discussed, African Americans may be one of the least advantaged racial/ethnic groups in the workplace because of their overcrowding into lower status occupations, overrepresentation in temporary work arrangements, and so forth. Consequently, this may significantly restrict their access to occupational SMPs that may be available through employers. Another issue is that for African Americans and other groups, perceptions of programs and program utilization are likely to depend on cultural background, preferences, and beliefs (Cervantes, 1992; James, Pobee, Oxidine, Brown, & Joshi, 2012; Lettlow, 2008). Given these considerations, culturally appropriate occupational stress management and prevention programs designed for and clearly accessible to African Americans are needed.

Prior to designing such interventions, researchers and practitioners should first develop a full understanding of the African American community's strengths. There are a number of strengths in the African American community that have enabled families and communities to overcome the various challenges in the past and those that are present in today's society (Hill, 2003) that are relevant to the design of health interventions. These strengths include, but are not limited to, a high achievement orientation, strong kinship (i.e., strong relationships with immediate and extended family and friends), social participation and volunteerism, strong work orientation, high levels of religious involvement, and strong religious values and family support (Walker, 2007). Designing effective interventions entails empowering and mobilizing Black communities to increase their knowledge of these and other strengths, natural supports, and resources. It also requires increasing their capacity to promote, develop, and implement their own interventions for improving health in collaboration with community-based organizations that have a vested interest and sense of responsibility in improving the health, safety, and well-being of African Americans (Briscoe, 2009).

One such community-based organization is the Black church, which has been the most important social institution in the Black community (Williams, Neighbors, & Jackson, 2003). Historically, it has responded directly to the interests and needs of African Americans and has been a support system critical to Black survival (Poussaint & Alexander, 2000). Churches frequently offered the only respite from the continuous repression of slavery and afforded the only places where members would exercise leadership. Not only have African American churches provided for spiritual and physical needs, they have also served as centers of political organization for the wider Black community. The church has also been where many Blacks learn important aspects of socialization.

The church continues to be important to Black life and Black communities. The value of religion, reading religious materials, listening to religious programs, music, prayer, and other forms of nonorganized religious participation are part of the fabric in the life and culture of Blacks/African Americans in this country. Further, according to the Pew Forum's U.S. Religious Landscape Survey, conducted in 2007 and released in 2008 (Pew Research Center, 2009), African Americans attend church more regularly than do Whites, and the typical African American church has average attendance that is about 50% greater than that of the typical White church. Estimates of regular church attendance among African Americans range as high as 80% (Strawbridge, Cohen, Shema, & Kaplan, 1997). Church attendance appeared to have the greatest health benefit for the most vulnerable individuals. Church attendance may provide social support that facilitates and reinforces positive health-seeking behaviors.

With their long tradition of informing, organizing, and mobilizing, churches are in an ideal position to chart a new course of health, well-being, and safety for African Americans. The nation's Black churches play primary roles as community employers, educators, and caregivers. Particularly in rural communities or communities with few services, churches play a special role, often serving as the provider of various services. Clergies deal with marital and family problems, drug and alcohol problems, and financial problems—all of which directly affect the health of their parishioners. Churches have steadily expanded their role in building a community-based infrastructure of supportive and health-related services for the African American community. Black churches sometimes function as centers for health screening, promotion, and counseling. Also, the church may serve as a site of heath care serve delivery and provide information on available services.

It appears that the Black church can provide practical and pragmatic answers to health and other problems among African Americans (Poussaint & Alexander, 2000). Some agencies have recognized the church's potential and efforts in addressing health and safety in African American communities. For example, the CDC has a rich history of working with churches and has been involved in funding participatory research that supports health promotion activities and examines health services and interventions provided by or through churches and other community-based organizations (CDC, 2005).

Given the church's potential for and efforts in addressing health and safety in the African American community, occupational safety and health professionals, regardless of race and religious affiliation, should also consider partnering with churches in responding to the health and safety needs of African Americans. Although an important limitation to partnering with churches (vs. employers) to address these needs is that workplace and job stressors cannot directly be addressed, this approach still has significant value. By working with churches, occupational safety and health professionals can reach a significant proportion of the African American population through the large number of African Americans who hold church membership, as well as churches' community outreach with the unchurched. In addition, this type of collaboration can ensure that messages are communicated in a culturally appropriate manner.

If occupational stress interventions were designed and delivered in partnership with churches, the likelihood of the success of these interventions would be promising. It appears that community-based health interventions that are delivered in partnership with churches in general are effective. Duan, Fox, Derose, and Carson (2000) and Derose, Fox, Reigadas, and Hawes-Dawson (2000) conducted research on a Los Angeles–based population of Latinos and African Americans and found that a church-based telephone counseling intervention helped maintain mammography adherence among baseline-adherent participants and reduced the nonadherence rate from 23% to 16%. Further, Johnson (2002) conducted an extensive literature review of community-based interventions and concluded that these interventions are associated with improved outcomes and are cost-effective and feasible to implement.

CONCLUSION

The workplace is an important setting to include in dialogues that are relevant to understanding and eliminating health disparities. Blacks/African Americans face a number of stress-related health challenges to which occupational stress may be a key contributor. However, much of the knowledge that has been acquired about workplace conditions that are related to stress and adverse health and safety outcomes has been acquired from empirical investigations conducted with few large African American samples. Thus, little to date is known about how and to what extent African Americans are exposed to, how they respond to, and how they are affected by generic stressors that all workers experience irrespective of race and ethnicity (e.g., job demands and control). In addition, although some research efforts have attempted to study the impact of workplace racial and ethnic discrimination on African Americans and other minority groups, many of these efforts have focused on the impact of this particular race-related stressor on outcomes like job quality and job satisfaction rather than on more direct occupational safety and health outcomes. Thus, additional studies of discrimination, as well as of other race-related stressors that are encountered by African Americans, are needed. In summary, future studies should take a fuller approach to understanding how the workplace psychosocial environment influences the health and safety status of African American workers. These research efforts should investigate protective and resilience factors.

A combination of strength-based, community-based, and collaborative approaches can contribute to the development of occupational safety and health interventions that are culturally acceptable, relevant, and effective. It is clear that there are numerous strengths within the Black/African American community that have historically enabled them to overcome many social and other difficulties. Community-based organizations, including the Black church, have contributed to this resilience. However, despite the potential advantages associated with partnering with churches to design and deliver health messages or interventions, occupational safety and health professionals appear to have rarely worked with them to design, deliver, and evaluate community-based occupational stress interventions. Increased occupational safety and health efforts are needed in this area.

REFERENCES

Alves, S. L. (2005). A study of occupational stress, scope of practice, and collaboration in nurse anesthetists practicing in anesthesia care team settings. *American Association of Nurse Anesthetists Journal, 73,* 443–452.

American Institute of Stress. (2012). *Job stress*. Retrieved from http://www.stress.org/workplace-stress/

American Psychological Association. (2011). Stressed in America. *Monitor on Psychology, 42*(1), 60.

Astone, N. M., Ensminger, M., & Juon, H. S. (2002). Early adult characteristics and mortality among inner-city African American women. *American Journal of Public Health, 92*, 640–645. http://dx.doi.org/10.2105/AJPH.92.4.640

Balducci, C., Schaufeli, W. B., & Fraccaroli, F. (2011). The job demands–resources model and counterproductive work behaviour: The role of job-related affect. *European Journal of Work and Organizational Psychology, 20*, 467–496.

Bandura, A. (1977). Self-efficacy: Toward a unifying theory of behavioral change. *Psychological Review, 84*, 191–215. http://dx.doi.org/10.1037/0033-295X.84.2.191

Baqutayan, S. (2011). Stress and social support. *Indian Journal of Psychological Medicine, 33*, 29–34. http://dx.doi.org/10.4103/0253-7176.85392

Baum, C. M. (2002). Creating partnerships: Constructing our future. *Australian Occupational Therapy Journal, 49*, 58–62. http://dx.doi.org/10.1046/j.1440-1630.2002.00318.x

Bellarosa, C., & Chen, P. Y. (1997). The effectiveness and practicality of occupational stress management interventions: A survey of subject matter expert opinions. *Journal of Occupational Health Psychology, 2*, 247–262. http://dx.doi.org/10.1037/1076-8998.2.3.247

Benton, J. C. (2000). Washington's repetitive stress over ergonomics rules. *CQ Weekly, 58*, 401–406.

Briscoe, F. M. (2009). "They make you invisible": Negotiating power at the academic intersections of ethnicity, gender and class. *Equity & Excellence in Education, 42*, 233–248. http://dx.doi.org/10.1080/10665680902794027

Brunner, E. J. (2000). Toward a new social biology. In L. F. Berkman & I. Kawachi (Eds.), *Social Epidemiology* (pp. 306–331). New York, NY: Oxford University Press.

Bunce, D. (1997). What factors are associated with the outcome of individual-focused worksite stress management interventions? *Journal of Occupational and Organizational Psychology, 70*, 1–17. http://dx.doi.org/10.1111/j.2044-8325.1997.tb00627.x

Bureau of Labor Statistics. (2011, July 11). *The black labor force in the recovery*. Available at https://www.dol.gov/_sec/media/reports/BlackLaborForce2011/BlackLaborForce.pdf

Centers for Disease Control and Prevention. (2001). Prevalence of disabilities and associated health conditions among adults—United States, 1999. *Morbidity and Mortality Weekly Report, 50*, 120–125.

Centers for Disease Control and Prevention. (2005). Racial/ethnic disparities in prevalence, treatment, and control of hypertension—United States, 1999–2002. *Morbidity and Mortality Weekly Report, 54*, 7–9.

Cervantes, R. (1992). Occupational and economic stressors among immigrant and United States-born Hispanics. In S. Knouse, P. Rosenfeld, & A. Culbertson

(Eds.), *Hispanics in the workplace* (pp. 120–134). Newbury Park, CA: Sage. http://dx.doi.org/10.4135/9781483325996.n7

Chen, E., & Miller, G. E. (2013). Socioeconomic status and health: Mediating and moderating factors. *Annual Review of Clinical Psychology, 9,* 723–749. http://dx.doi.org/10.1146/annurev-clinpsy-050212-185634

Clark, R. (2006). Perceived racism and vascular reactivity in black college women: Moderating effects of seeking social support. *Health Psychology, 25,* 20–25.

Clark, R., & Anderson, N. B. (2001). Efficacy of racism-specific coping styles as predictors of cardiovascular functioning. *Ethnicity & Disease, 11,* 286–295.

Cohen, S., Tyrrell, D. A., & Smith, A. P. (1991). Psychological stress and susceptibility to the common cold. *The New England Journal of Medicine, 325,* 606–612. http://dx.doi.org/10.1056/NEJM199108293250903

Cohen, S., & Wills, T. A. (1985). Stress, social support, and the buffering hypothesis. *Psychological Bulletin, 98,* 310–357. http://dx.doi.org/10.1037/0033-2909.98.2.310

Darity, W. A., Jr. (2003). Employment discrimination, segregation, and health. *American Journal of Public Health, 93,* 226–231. http://dx.doi.org/10.2105/AJPH.93.2.226

Derose, K. P., Fox, S. A., Reigadas, E., & Hawes-Dawson, J. (2000). Church-based telephone mammography counseling with peer counselors. *Journal of Health Communication, 5,* 175–188. http://dx.doi.org/10.1080/108107300406884

Diez-Roux, A. V., Nieto, F. J., Muntaner, C., Tyroler, H. A., Comstock, G. W., Shahar, E., . . . Szklo, M. (1997). Neighborhood environments and coronary heart disease: A multilevel analysis. *American Journal of Epidemiology, 146,* 48–63. http://dx.doi.org/10.1093/oxfordjournals.aje.a009191

Diez-Roux, A. V. (2000). Multilevel analysis in public health research. *Annual Review of Public Health, 21,* 171–192. http://dx.doi.org/10.1146/annurev.publhealth.21.1.171

DiNatale, M. (2001). Characteristics of and preference for alternative work arrangements, 1999. *Monthly Labor Review, 124*(3), 28–49.

Duan, N., Fox, S. A., Derose, K. P., & Carson, S. (2000). Maintaining mammography adherence through telephone counseling in a church-based trial. *American Journal of Public Health, 90,* 1468–1471. http://dx.doi.org/10.2105/AJPH.90.9.1468

Edwards, D., & Burnard, P. (2003). A systematic review of stress and stress management interventions for mental health nurses. *Journal of Advanced Nursing, 42,* 169–200. http://dx.doi.org/10.1046/j.1365-2648.2003.02600.x

Elvira, M. M., & Zatzick, C. D. (2002). Who's displaced first? The role of race in layoff decisions. *Industrial Relations, 41,* 329–361. http://dx.doi.org/10.1111/1468-232X.00248

Families and Work Institute. (1993). *An evaluation of Johnson & Johnson's work–family initiative.* New York, NY: Author.

Ferrie, J. E., Shipley, M. J., Marmot, M. G., Stansfeld, S., & Davey Smith, G. (1998). The health effects of major organisational change and job insecurity. *Social Science & Medicine, 46,* 243–254. http://dx.doi.org/10.1016/S0277-9536(97)00158-5

Fields, L. E., Burt, V. L., Cutler, J. A., Hughes, J., Roccella, E. J., & Sorlie, P. (2004). The burden of adult hypertension in the United States 1999 to 2000: A rising tide. *Hypertension, 44*, 398–404. http://dx.doi.org/10.1161/ 01.HYP.0000142248.54761.56

Gee, G. C. (2002). A multilevel analysis of the relationship between institutional and individual racial discrimination and health status. *American Journal of Public Health, 92*, 615–623. http://dx.doi.org/10.2105/AJPH.92.4.615

Gee, G. C., & Payne-Sturges, D. C. (2004). Environmental health disparities: A framework integrating psychosocial and environmental concepts. *Environmental Health Perspectives, 112*, 1645–1653. http://dx.doi.org/10.1289/ehp.7074

Girdano, D. (1986). *Occupational health promotion.* New York, NY: Macmillan.

Goodspeed, R. B., & DeLucia, A. G. (1990). Stress reduction at the worksite: An evaluation of two methods. *American Journal of Health Promotion, 4*, 333–337. http://dx.doi.org/10.4278/0890-1171-4.5.333

Health and Safety Executive. (2001). *Tackling work-related stress.* London, England: HSE Books.

Health and Safety Executive. (2007). *Managing the causes of work-related stress: A step-by-step approach using the Management Standards* (2nd ed.). Norwich, England: Her Majesty's Stationery Office.

Hill, R. B. (2003). *The strengths of black families* (2nd ed.). Lanham, MD: University Press of America.

Holzer, H. (1998, October). *Racial differences in labor market outcomes among men.* Paper presented at the Research Conference on Racial Trends in the United States, Washington, DC.

James, D. C., Pobee, J. W., Oxidine, D., Brown, L., & Joshi, G. (2012). Using the health belief model to develop culturally appropriate weight-management materials for African-American women. *Journal of the Academy of Nutrition & Dietetics, 112*, 664–670. http://dx.doi.org/10.1016/j.jand.2012.02.003

Johnson, B. R. (2002). *Objective hope: Assessing the effectiveness of faith-based organizations: A review of the literature.* New York, NY: Center for Research on Religion and Urban Civil Society.

Johnson, J. V., Hall, E. M., & Theorell, T. (1989). Combined effects of job strain and social isolation on cardiovascular disease morbidity and mortality in a random sample of the Swedish male working population. *Scandinavian Journal of Work, Environment & Health, 15*, 271–279. http://dx.doi.org/10.5271/ sjweh.1852

Jones, D. L., Tanigawa, T., & Weiss, S. M. (2003). Stress management and workplace disability in the US, Europe and Japan. *Journal of Occupational Health, 45*, 1–7. http://dx.doi.org/10.1539/joh.45.1

Jones, J. (2003). Stress responses, pressure ulcer development and adaptation. *British Journal of Nursing, 12*(Suppl. 2), S17–S24. http://dx.doi.org/10.12968/ bjon.2003.12.Sup2.11321

Jordan, J., Gurr, E., Tinline, G., Giga, S., Faragher, B., & Cooper, C. (2003). *Beacons of excellence in stress prevention* (Health and Safety Executive Research Report 133). Sudbury, England: HSE Books.

Karasek, R., & Theorell, T. (1990). *Healthy work.* New York, NY: Basic Books.

Keashly, L. (1998). Emotional abuse in workplace: Conceptual and empirical issues. *Journal of Emotional Abuse, 1,* 85–117. http://dx.doi.org/10.1300/J135v01n01_05

Kessler, R. C., Mickelson, K. D., & Williams, D. R. (1999). The prevalence, distribution, and mental health correlates of perceived discrimination in the United States. *Journal of Health and Social Behavior, 40,* 208–230. http://dx.doi.org/10.2307/2676349

Kivimäki, M., Vahtera, J., Pentti, J., & Ferrie, J. E. (2000). Factors underlying the effect of organisational downsizing on health of employees: Longitudinal cohort study [Abstract]. *BMJ, 320,* 971–975. http://dx.doi.org/10.1136/bmj.320.7240.971

Klag, M. J., Whelton, P. K., Randall, B. L., Neaton, J. D., Brancati, F. L., Ford, C. E., ... Stamler, J. (1996). Blood pressure and end-stage renal disease in men. *The New England Journal of Medicine, 334,* 13–18. http://dx.doi.org/10.1056/NEJM199601043340103

Krieger, N. (1999). Embodying inequality: A review of concepts, measures, and methods for studying health consequences of discrimination. *International Journal of Health Services, 29,* 295–352.

Krieger, N., & Sidney, S. (1996). Racial discrimination and blood pressure: The CARDIA Study of young black and white adults. *American Journal of Public Health, 86,* 1370–1378. http://dx.doi.org/10.2105/AJPH.86.10.1370

Lambert, S. J. (2001). Workers' use of supportive workplace policies: Variations by gender, race and class-related characteristics. In A. Daly (Ed.), *Workplace diversity issues and perspectives* (pp. 297–313). Washington, DC: National Association of Social Workers.

Lamontagne, A. D., Keegel, T., Louie, A. M., Ostry, A., & Landsbergis, P. A. (2007). A systematic review of the job-stress intervention evaluation literature, 1990–2005. *International Journal of Occupational and Environmental Health, 13,* 268–280. http://dx.doi.org/10.1179/oeh.2007.13.3.268

Landsbergis, P. A., Schnall, P. L., Deitz, D., Friedman, R., & Pickering, T. (1992). The patterning of psychological attributes and distress by "job strain" and social support in a sample of working men. *Journal of Behavioral Medicine, 15,* 379–405. http://dx.doi.org/10.1007/BF00844730

Leigh, J. P., Markowitz, S. B., Fahs, M., Shin, C., & Landrigan, P. J. (1997). Occupational injury and illness in the United States. Estimates of costs, morbidity, and mortality. *Archives of Internal Medicine, 157,* 1557–1568. http://dx.doi.org/10.1001/archinte.1997.00440350063006

Lettlow, H. A. (2008). Engaging culturally competent, community-based programs in reducing tobacco-related health disparities. *American Journal of Public Health, 98,* 1936–1939. http://dx.doi.org/10.2105/AJPH.2008.147314

Marlin Company. (2003). *Attitudes in the American workplace IX*. North Haven, CT: Author.

Matteson, M., & Ivancevich, J. (1987). *Controlling work stress*. London, England: Jossey-Bass.

Maxon, R. (1999). Stress in the workplace: A costly epidemic. *FDU Magazine* (Summer). http://www.fdu.edu/newspubs/magazine/99su/stress.html

McGruder, H. F., Malarcher, A. M., Antoine, T. L., Greenlund, K. J., & Croft, J. B. (2004). Racial and ethnic disparities in cardiovascular risk factors among stroke survivors: United States 1999 to 2001. *Stroke, 35*, 1557–1561. http://dx.doi.org/10.1161/01.STR.0000130427.84114.50

Murphy, L. R. (1984). Occupational stress management: A review and appraisal. *Journal of Occupational Psychology, 57*, 1–15. http://dx.doi.org/10.1111/j.2044-8325.1984.tb00143.x

Murphy, L. R. (1985). Evaluation of worksite stress management. *Corporate Commentary, 1*, 24–31.

National Center for Health Statistics. (2007). *Health, United States, 2006: With chartbook on the trends in the health of Americans*. Hyattsville, MD: Author. Retrieved from http://www.cdc.gov/nchs/data/hus/hus06.pdf

National Institute for Occupational Safety and Health. (1999). *Stress at work* (Publication No. 99-101). Atlanta, GA: Author.

Orr, S. T., James, S. A., Miller, C. A., Barakat, B., Daikoku, N., Pupkin, M., . . . Huggins, G. (1996). Psychosocial stressors and low birthweight in an urban population. *American Journal of Preventive Medicine, 12*, 459–466.

Pew Research Center. (2009). *A religious portrait of African Americans*. Retrieved from http://www.pewforum.org/2009/01/30/a-religious-portrait-of-african-americans/

Poussaint, A. F., & Alexander, A. (2000). *Lay my burden down: Suicide and the mental health crisis among African-Americans*. Boston, MA: Beacon Press.

Probst, T. M., Graso, M., Estrada, A. X., & Greer, S. (2013). Consideration of future safety consequences: A new predictor of employee safety. *Accident Analysis and Prevention, 55*, 124–134. http://dx.doi.org/10.1016/j.aap.2013.02.023

Probst, T. M., & Hagger, M. S. (2014). Standing on the shoulders of a giant: A reflection on the past and future of *Stress and Health*. *Stress and Health, 30*, 1–2. http://dx.doi.org/10.1002/smi.2561

Raeburn, J. M., Atkinson, J. M., Dubignon, J. M., McPherson, M., & Elkind, G. S. (1993). "Unstress": A low-cost community psychology approach to stress-management: An evaluated case study from New Zealand. *Journal of Community Psychology, 21*, 113–123. http://dx.doi.org/10.1002/1520-6629(199304)21:2<113::AID-JCOP2290210204>3.0.CO;2-R

Roberts, R. K., Swanson, N. S., & Murphy, L. R. (2004). Discrimination and occupational mental health. *Journal of Mental Health, 13*, 129–142. http://dx.doi.org/10.1080/09638230410001669264

Roddenberry, A., & Renk, K. (2010). Locus of control and self-efficacy: Potential mediators of stress, illness, and utilization of health services in college students. *Child Psychiatry & Human Development, 41*, 353–370.

Sauter, S. L., Hurrell, J. J., & Cooper, C. L. (1999). *Job control and worker health.* Chichester, England: Wiley.

Schnall, P., Belkic, K., & Pickering, T. G. (2000). Assessment of the cardiovascular system at the workplace. *Occupational Medicine, 15*, 189–212.

Stansfield, S., Head, J., & Marmot, M. (2000). *Work related factors and ill health: The Whitehall II study* (Health and Safety Executive Contract Research Report No. 266/2000). Sudbury, England: HSE Books.

Strawbridge, W. J., Cohen, R. D., Shema, S. J., & Kaplan, G. A. (1997). Frequent attendance at religious services and mortality over 28 years. *American Journal of Public Health, 87*, 957–961. http://dx.doi.org/10.2105/AJPH.87.6.957

Sutherland, V., & Cooper, C. (1990). *Understanding stress: A psychological perspective for health professionals.* London, England: Chapman & Hall.

Tsui, A., & Milkovich, G. (1987). Personnel department activities: Constituency perspectives and preferences. *Personnel Psychology, 40*, 519–537. http://dx.doi.org/10.1111/j.1744-6570.1987.tb00613.x

U.S. Census Bureau. (2011, March). *Overview of race and Hispanic origin: 2010* (2010 Census Briefs). Retrieved from http://www.census.gov/prod/cen2010/briefs/c2010br-02.pdf

U.S. Department of Health and Human Services. (2002). The changing organization of work and the safety and health of working people [DHHS (National Institute for Occupational Safety and Health)] Publication No. 2002-116.

van der Klink, J. J. L., Blonk, R. W. B., Schene, A. H., & van Dijk, F. J. H. (2001). The benefits of interventions for work-related stress. *American Journal of Public Health, 91*, 270–276. http://dx.doi.org/10.2105/AJPH.91.2.270

Vosko, L. F., Zukewich, N., & Cranford, C. (2003). Precarious jobs: A new typology of employment. *Perspectives on Labour and Income, 15*(4). Retrieved from http://search.proquest.com/docview/213992756?accountid=26724

Walker, R. L. (2007). Acculturation and acculturative stress as indicators for suicide risk among African Americans. *American Journal of Orthopsychiatry, 77*, 386–391. http://dx.doi.org/10.1037/0002-9432.77.3.386

Williams, D. R., Neighbors, H. W., & Jackson, J. S. (2003). Racial/ethnic discrimination and health: Findings from community studies. *American Journal of Public Health, 93*, 200–208. http://dx.doi.org/10.2105/AJPH.93.2.200

Yen, I. H., & Syme, S. L. (1999). The social environment and health: A discussion of the epidemiologic literature. *Annual Review of Public Health, 20*, 287–308. http://dx.doi.org/10.1146/annurev.publhealth.20.1.287

6

OCCUPATIONAL HEALTH DISPARITIES AMONG ASIAN AMERICANS: REVIEW AND RECOMMENDATIONS

FREDERICK T. L. LEONG, CHU-HSIANG (DAISY) CHANG, AND STANTON MAK

Asian Americans are one of the fastest growing immigrant populations in the United States. According to Lee (2009), factors such as race, foreign-born status, lack of proficiency in English, ethnicity, and unfamiliarity with mainstream American culture continue to contribute to this group's segregation into low-wage and low-skilled jobs with a wide range of serious occupational health and safety hazards. This chapter provides an updated review of occupational health disparities among Asian Americans. It begins with a brief history and overview of the demographics of Asian Americans followed by a proposed conceptual framework for studying occupational health problems within this ethnic minority group. The main section consists of the current occupational health challenges facing Asian Americans, and the chapter ends with research and policy recommendations.

http://dx.doi.org/10.1037/0000021-007

Occupational Health Disparities: Improving the Well-Being of Ethnic and Racial Minority Workers, F. T. L. Leong, D. E. Eggerth, C.-H. Chang, M. A. Flynn, J. K. Ford, and R. O. Martinez (Editors)

BRIEF HISTORY AND DEMOGRAPHICS OF ASIAN AMERICANS

The groups that define the term *Asian American* are remarkably diverse in terms of culture, language, and socioeconomic background. Nevertheless, these diverse groups have in common a history of exclusion and inequity in America. The first large wave of Asian immigrants arrived from China in the middle of the 19th century (Takaki, 1989). The Industrial Revolution fueled a need for cheap foreign labor to be exploited, and the Chinese were initially welcomed to meet that demand. For example, during the building of the Transcontinental Railroad, Chinese workers were brought in as contract workers to perform the most dangerous jobs, including handling dynamite while hanging in wooden baskets over high cliffs (Lee, 2009). However, as more Chinese occupied jobs and created competition in the job market, nativism and violence against the Chinese increased across the United States. Decades of anti-Chinese sentiment eventually culminated in the passing of the Chinese Exclusion Act of 1882, banning all immigration to the United States from China and denying naturalization to all Chinese residents in the United States (I. Chan, 2003).

Other Asian American groups that followed experienced similar social and economic hardships. The Japanese began to arrive in large numbers during the late 19th century, and many worked in California's agricultural economy. There, they experienced institutionalized discrimination when the passage of the alien land laws barred them from purchasing agricultural land and also when the entire Japanese population on the West Coast was forcibly incarcerated following Japan's attack on Pearl Harbor (S. Chan, 1991). Even after the war, Japanese Americans continued to struggle with poverty because the federal government confiscated their personal properties. Likewise, Filipinos who immigrated to America in the early 20th century worked in many industries, such as canneries and farms (S. Chan, 1991). Like the Asian immigrants that came before them, Filipino laborers commonly worked under brutal conditions while being paid less than their White counterparts. Economic hardships caused by the Great Depression, in combination with fears of interracial marriage, fueled anti-Filipino sentiments among the general public and resulted in rampant discrimination from the locals.

It was not until the civil rights movement of the 1960s that local anti-Asian laws were repealed, marking the reversal of many governmental policies that discriminated against Asian Americans in areas such as property ownership, employment, and marriage (Takaki, 1989). The civil rights movement and the changing racial attitudes in America also culminated with the passage of the Immigration Act of 1965, which lifted discriminatory restrictions on immigrating to the United States on the basis of national origin. This represented a watershed moment in Asian American history, as it resulted in renewed immigration from Asia and growth of the Asian American community.

Today, Asian Americans are the fastest growing ethnic group in America. Between 2000 and 2010, this racial group grew an astonishing 43% (Hoeffel, Rastogi, Kim, & Shahid, 2012). The total population of Asian Americans reached 18.2 million in 2011 and made up 5.8% of the total U.S. population (Pew Research Center, 2012). The six largest Asian American ethnicities were Chinese, Filipino, Indian, Vietnamese, Korean, and Japanese. Together, they made up 85% of the total Asian population in the United States (U.S. Census Bureau, 2011a). Much of this growth has come from immigration; 59% of Asian Americans are foreign born, compared with 13% of the U.S. population overall (Pew Research Center, 2012).

Aggregated statistics show that Asian Americans as a whole have achieved socioeconomic success. For example, the median household income for Asian Americans in 2010 was $66,000 versus $49,800 among the general U.S. population (Pew Research Center, 2012). Self-employment is also high among Asian Americans. According to the most recent Census Bureau Survey of Business Owners, Asian American businesses grew by over 40% between 2002 and 2007, more than double the national average (U.S. Department of Labor, 2011). Fifty percent of Asian Americans who were 25 years and older had a bachelor's degree or higher in 2011, compared with 28.5% of all Americans 25 years and older (U.S. Census Bureau, 2011b). The high level of educational attainment of Asian Americans is also reflected by their high achievement in employment. Data from 2011 show that 50% of Asian Americans occupied management, professional, and related occupations, compared with approximately 40% for all employed Americans (Pew Research Center, 2012). Additionally, 17% worked in service occupations; 22% in sales and office occupations; and 10% in production, transportation, and material moving occupations. Asian Americans are also concentrated in the fields of science and engineering, compared with the U.S. population overall (14% vs. 5%).

However, this ethnic gloss of Asian Americans hides serious social and economic problems that continue to plague members of many Asian American communities (Trimble & Dickson, 2005). Indeed, disaggregated data reveal that many Asian subgroups continue to struggle with low socioeconomic status (Rho, Schmitt, Woo, Lin, & Wong, 2011). For example, though Asian Americans experienced a low unemployment rate relative to the U.S. population overall in 2010 (6% for Asian Americans adults, compared with 7% for U.S. adults overall), the unemployment rates for various subgroups varied considerably, from as low as 4.6% for Japanese to as high as 12% for Native Hawaiian and Pacific Islanders (U.S. Department of Labor, 2011). Likewise, aggregated data suggest that Asian American adults were less likely than U.S.

adults overall to be poor in 2010 (11.9% for Asian Americans, compared with 12.8% for the U.S. overall; Pew Research Center, 2012). However, rates of poverty varied widely by subgroup, from as low as 6.2% for Filipino adults to as high as 15.1% for Korean adults.

A MODEL FOR UNDERSTANDING OCCUPATIONAL HEALTH DISPARITIES AMONG ASIAN AMERICANS

To organize the extant literature concerning occupational health disparities among Asian Americans and provide a research road map, we propose a process model that summarizes key contributors and mechanisms underlying different indicators of occupational health disparities (see Figure 6.1). This model integrates both the system perspective (Katz & Kahn, 1978) from the organizational behavior literature and the stress–exposure disease framework (Gee & Payne-Sturges, 2004) from the environmental health literature, and has several characteristics. First, it is multilevel in nature, such that it recognizes the characteristics of the environment or the exposure risks and the characteristics of the individual workers as possible factors contributing to occupational health disparities (Gee & Payne-Sturges, 2004). In particular, we identify both physical and psychosocial environmental characteristics as potential risk factors contributing to occupational disparities among Asian Americas. Moreover, characteristics of both the workplace (e.g., organizational policies and procedures) and the general environment (e.g., community features, local and national labor laws) in which Asian Americans tend to dwell are considered in our model, reflecting the open-system perspective (Katz & Kahn, 1978). In addition to the physical and psychosocial risk factors on and off work, our model also includes a number of individual attributes that may influence Asian Americans' occupational disparities. Asian American employees' general health status, knowledge of the general health care system and the system associated with occupational health and safety, and attributes associated with their immigration status (e.g., language skills, acculturation levels) are likely to influence their occupational health disparities. These individual characteristics are in and of themselves important, and they may also interact with the environmental risk factors and jointly affect the occupational health and safety among Asian American workers.

A second feature of our proposed model is that it incorporates multiple process-oriented variables to better characterize how exposure to risk factors leads to health effects. Specifically, we highlight three mechanisms underlying the linkages between exposures with health disparities. The first category, biophysiological processes, refers to biological and physiological reactions or strains caused by environmental risk factors or individual risk attributes. For

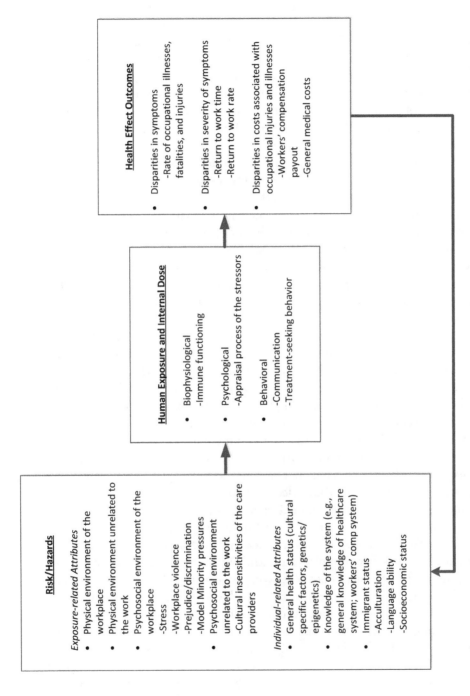

Figure 6.1. A schematic, process-oriented model of factors contributing to occupational health disparities among Asian Americans.

example, exposure to strenuous physical demands at work (e.g., repeated lifting of heavy materials) may cause biomechanical strains (e.g., fatigued muscles) and eventually lead to damage in employees' musculoskeletal structure (Sauter & Swanson, 1996). Similarly, exposure to psychosocial stressors may cause disruption in workers' immune systems, causing them to be more susceptible to other diseases (Sapolsky, 2004). In terms of individual attributes and biophysiological processes, research on epigenetics has suggested that expression of certain genes may alter the insulin secretion, thereby increasing East Asians' susceptibility to developing Type 2 diabetes (McCarthy, 2008; Unoki et al., 2008).

Asian American workers' psychological processes, such as their appraisal of the stressors and the availability of coping resources, and attributions made about the environmental events and their own symptoms, may also influence how exposure relates to health outcomes. Individuals who perceive the risk factors as less threatening or have more optimistic outlook for their abilities to cope with the environmental demands are likely to respond more positively to the exposure (Lazarus & Folkman, 1984). Having positive affectivity, high self-evaluations, and an internal locus of control may also buffer individuals from exposure to environmental risks (Kammeyer-Mueller, Judge, & Scott, 2009).

Finally, behavioral reactions to exposure risks and individual characteristics capture another mechanism underlying Asian American workers' occupational health disparities. For example, employees who are exposed to heavy physical demands at work may suffer fewer musculoskeletal damages if they can recognize the early symptoms (e.g., minor pain and discomfort), voice their concerns for better ergonomic work designs to reduce the biomechanical load, and seek treatment immediately (Sauter & Swanson, 1996). Unfortunately, for some Asian Americans, these behavioral responses to exposure risks may be hampered by their individual attributes, such as lack of language proficiency or knowledge about the health care systems. As a result, they may suffer more musculoskeletal injuries.

Similar to the exposure risks and individual attributes, we argue that these intermediate processes may interact with one another to produce negative health effects. For example, Sauter and Swanson's (1996) ecological model highlights the interplay between psychological reactions to stressors and biophysiological reactions to physical workload in determining the severity of musculoskeletal injuries among employees. Indeed, Eatough, Way, and Chang (2012) found that negative psychological strains explained employees' work-related musculoskeletal pain above and beyond their physical workload. Similarly, Chang, Eatough, and Jaiprashad (2010) found that employees' psychological assessment of their work environment (e.g., job satisfaction) was related to their treatment-seeking behaviors for work-related musculoskeletal symptoms. Taken together, our proposed model describes a complex system with multiple interactive mechanisms that explain the linkages between environmental and individual characteristics with health disparity outcomes.

A third feature of our proposed model is that we conceptualize occupational health disparities as a multidimensional construct. Prior research on occupational health disparities has typically focused on disparities in symptoms, such as identifying different rates of developing various occupational fatalities, injuries, and illnesses among Asian Americans compared with other racial and ethnic groups (e.g., *The Asian-American Labor Force in the Recovery*; U.S. Department of Labor, 2011). Our proposed model moves beyond the symptom-based conceptualization of occupational health disparities and broadens the criterion space. The model includes additional health outcomes, such as the severity of the symptoms and the resulting differences in missing workdays and return to work time and rate (e.g., Strong & Zimmerman, 2005), as well as the costs associated with occupational injuries and illnesses, as indicators of occupational health disparities. Inclusion of these additional indicators of disparities is important as they represent alternative targets for interventions, particularly tertiary ones, to address the issues related to occupational health and safety among Asian American workers.

Finally, consistent with the system perspective (Katz & Kahn, 1978), our proposed model includes a feedback loop from the health effects to the environmental exposure risks and individual attributes. This feedback loop is important, as the typical studies on occupational health disparities tend to stop at characterizing the health effect outcomes across different groups, with little attention paid to the long-term consequences of these different health effects on both the target group and other related populations. For example, workers' occupational illnesses and injuries may lead to changes in their socioeconomic status and behavioral patterns, resulting in important implications for themselves and their spouses and dependent children (He, Hu, Yu, Gu, & Liang, 2010; Mobed, Gold, & Schenker, 1992). These implications may have long-term effects on the occupational health and safety of the next generation.

OCCUPATIONAL HEALTH DISPARITIES AMONG ASIAN AMERICANS

In the following sections, we review the literature concerning occupational health disparities among Asian Americans. Our review is organized on the basis of the proposed model. We first present evidence for occupational health disparities among Asian American workers. Next, we summarize literature concerning the environmental risk factors, individual attributes, and their interplay in relating to the health outcomes. Finally, we discuss research recommendations and policy implications based on our proposed framework.

Occupational Illnesses and Injuries Among Asian Americans

The rate and type of occupational safety and health risks that are faced differ depending on the Asian American subgroup. Certain ethnic groups are more likely to be exposed to jobs that are at high risk for fatal injuries (e.g., small, late-night retail workers, taxi drivers, commercial fishers), nonfatal injuries (restaurant workers, hotel housekeeping workers, home care, nursing), or chemical exposures (dry cleaning operators, nail salon workers; U.S. Department of Labor, 2011). In 2012, 147 Asian American and seven Native Hawaiian or Pacific Islander workers suffered occupational fatalities, accounting for 3.3% of all fatal occupational injuries in the United States (Bureau of Labor Statistics [BLS], 2013a). These statistics suggest a lower rate of occupational fatalities compared with the general population. However, compared with the general population, causes of workplace fatalities among Asian Americans were slightly different. Among the general population, transportation incidents were the leading cause of workplace fatalities in 2012 (41%) and include incidents on highways and nonhighways, as well as those involving air, rail, and water transportation. However, the most common cause of workplace fatalities among Asian Americans was assaults and violent acts (48%). These incidents include violence by other persons, self-inflicted injuries, and attacks by animals. Assault and violent acts constituted the second highest percentage of fatal occupational injuries for the general population (17%), whereas for Asians it was transportation incidents (19%).

According to data for 2012, Asian American and Native Hawaiian and Pacific Islander workers reported a total of 19,270 nonfatal occupational injuries that required days away from work, accounting for 1.7% of all reported injuries (BLS, 2013b). Also, the number of reported injuries varies by industry (BLS, 2013c). The education and health services industry had the most nonfatal injuries for Asian Americans (3,340 incidents). This was followed by transportation and utilities (3,060) and leisure and hospitality (2,680). In comparison, the industry sector with the most nonfatal occupational injuries for the general population was transportation and utilities, followed by education and health services, and manufacturing.

Exposure to Environmental Risk Factors Among Asian Americans

A significant source of health disparities among Asian Americans comes from their occupations. Throughout American history, minority and immigrant workers have faced significant health and safety hazards because they have been hired disproportionately into physically demanding and hazardous occupations, as well as from encountering poor environmental conditions in their homes and communities (Frumkin, Walker, & Friedman-Jiménez, 1999). When Asian immigrants arrived in the United States during the mid-1800s, they encountered the same obstacles that other immigrants faced and found themselves in grueling and dangerous jobs (Lee, 2009). Even today, many Asians are in low-wage and low-skilled work that is replete with workplace health and safety hazards (S. Chan, 1991), including ergonomic, chemical, physical, safety, and psychosocial hazards.

Ergonomic Risk Factors

Ergonomic hazards are risk factors caused by poor design of the workplace and equipment, resulting in musculoskeletal damages to the muscles and joints of the workers (Lee, 2009). Ergonomic risk factors are becoming the fastest growing occupational concerns (Lee, 2009) and include repeating the same motion throughout the day; performing work in an awkward position; frequent forceful exertions to push, pull, or lift; sustained pressure against a hard surface or edge; and vibration from tools.

For example, Azaroff, Levenstein, and Wegman (2003) surveyed Cambodian and Lao workers in Lowell, Massachusetts. They found that their participants were employed at a disproportionately higher rate in the manufacturing sector (25%) compared with the general resident population in Lowell (4.5%). Southeast Asian workers in their sample also reported high rates of exposure to ergonomic risks, such as overexertion and strenuous movements. Burgel, Lashuay, Israel, and Harrison (2004) surveyed Chinese immigrant workers in the garment industry in Oakland, California. Almost all of their 100 participants reported musculoskeletal pain and discomfort, particularly in the areas of neck and shoulders, back, and upper extremities (elbows and wrists). These musculoskeletal injuries are likely associated with the nature of garment work, which involves highly repetitive tasks and sustained awkward postures. Finally, in a qualitative interview with Chinese workers in the restaurant industry, Tsai (2009) found that musculoskeletal pain and discomfort was the most commonly mentioned occupational illness, especially in the areas of shoulders, back, fingers, knees, and feet. Instances such as heavy workload during the busy hours, long work hours, and exertions from lifting were reported as primary sources that cause discomfort.

Chemical Risk Factors

Asian American workers also encounter many sources of chemical exposure in the workplace. Chemical agents in the workplace interact with body tissues and cells, potentially having deleterious effects on human health. They may cause damage wherever they directly contact the body, such as on the skin, eyes, nose, or throat. Exposure can also occur by breathing or ingesting a chemical. Once inside, chemicals may enter the bloodstream and can cause serious damage to internal organs such as the liver, kidney, heart, nervous system, brain, and reproductive organs (Lee, 2009).

Cambodia and Lao immigrant workers in Azaroff et al.'s (2003) study reported higher rates of exposure to chemical hazards in the survey compared with the official records they obtained from workers' compensation system or hospital records. Nine percent of injuries were attributed to solvents, dusts, and fumes in the survey, and 4% were attributed to biological or chemical exposure. However, chemical exposure cases were nearly absent in the workers' compensation system and hospital data. Participants also reported higher rates of dermatitis resulting from chemical exposure compared with other sources of records. Dermatitis constituted 6% of work-related illnesses and injuries, but only 13% of survey respondents who reported dermatitis sought medical care for the condition. In addition, Chinese immigrant restaurant workers frequently use high levels of bleach with limited safety precautions for cleaning floors, towels, and kitchen counters in restaurants (Tsai & Salazar, 2007). Another study showed that Asian American workers in nail salons are exposed to hazardous solvents, with approximately one third of the sample reporting that they had experienced skin problems in the past 6 months resulting from chemical exposures (Roelofs, Azaroff, Holcroft, Nguyen, & Doan, 2008).

Exposure to chemical hazards may have serious side or long-term effects beyond the immediate damages to the body parts that were directly in contact with the agents. Asian American restaurant workers in New York City have reported developing lung disorders because of repeated inhalation of toxic fumes and dust caused by chemicals, hot cooking fumes, smoking, and secondhand smoke (Restaurant Opportunities Center of New York, 2005). Similarly, 48% of Asian garment workers developed breathing difficulties because of prolonged exposure to fabric dust (Burgel et al., 2004). Chappell (2005a, 2005b) reported that 38% of female Asian Americans and Pacific Islanders who worked in semiconductor production had miscarriages because of their exposure to chemicals and heavy metal. Moreover, long-term exposure to these solvents may lead to risks for cancer and reproductive health issues among Asian female workers (Chappell, 2005b).

Safety Hazards

Many Asian American workers are exposed to safety hazards beyond ergonomic and chemical risk factors. Safety hazards are dangers arising from the job's physical space and can include hot surfaces, slippery floors, working at heights, fire and electrical hazards, sharp objects, poor lighting, and physical assault (Lee, 2009). Asian American workers are at high risk for traumatic injuries from sources such as slips, trips, falls, burns, fire, and violence (Sincavage, 2005). A study of Asian American restaurant workers in New York City revealed that 38% of workers had been burned, 46% had been cut, and 19% had slipped and become injured (Restaurant Opportunities Center of New York, 2005). Moreover, other physical hazards, such as radiation and noise, are a source of work hazard that Asian American workers routinely face, resulting in illnesses such as radiation poisoning, cancer, heat stress, hypothermia, and hearing loss (Lee, 2009). Racial and ethnic minority workers have also been found to have increased lead levels in their blood as a result of occupational lead exposure (Sakamoto, Vaughan, & Tobias, 2001).

Other workplace hazards that Asian Americans face include the increased risk for encountering workplace violence. Workplace violence can range from harassment and verbal abuse to physical assaults and violent acts. Exposure to workplace violence results in stress, psychological trauma, physical injuries, and even death. Sources of violence include customers, coworkers, or individuals who bully or sexually harass their coworkers (Lee, 2009). In one study, approximately one third of Asian American textile workers reported that their bosses yelled at them or their coworkers at least once a week (Burgel et al., 2004). Asian American workers participating in the underground economy are especially at risk for encountering workplace violence. Nemoto, Operario, Takenaka, Iwamoto, and Le (2003) explored factors that influence HIV-related risk behaviors among Asian women who work at massage parlors in San Francisco. It was found that women who worked an average of 10.5 hours a day had sex with up to 11 clients a day, and with an average of 27 clients a week, to make more money. In addition, 62% of the women suffered physical abuse from clients, and 45% experienced threats of violence. Of the women who sought a doctor or nurse in the past 6 months, 94% were diagnosed with a sexually transmitted disease. However, the massage parlors did not have clear policies for condom use because parlor owners and managers feared that formal business policies would draw attention to the illegal prostitution. As a result, male clients often did not use a condom, especially if they were repeat customers or if they used coercive tactics, such as negotiating with more money or threatening to not return (Nemoto, Iwamoto, Oh, Wong, & Nguyen, 2005).

For Asian Americans, assaults and violent acts are the most common causes of fatal work injuries and are a significant source of occupational health disparity. In 2012, 48% of all fatal work injuries sustained by Asian Americans were caused by assaults and violent acts (BLS, 2013a). This was a significantly higher rate than that of other races: Assaults and violent acts accounted for 27% of fatal work injuries for Blacks, 11% for Latinos/

Hispanics, and 16% for Whites. Even though Asian workers were the victims in only 3% of the total workplace fatalities in 2012, they incurred 8.6% of the workplace assaults or violent acts. Injuries from violence account for nearly 50% of all job-related deaths among retail workers and workers in the transportation and service sectors, where Asian Americans are heavily represented (Lee, 2009). Indeed, taxi and delivery drivers are 60 times more likely than other workers to be murdered while on the job (U.S. Department of Labor, 2000), and Asian Americans are disproportionately represented in taxi driving in some areas of the country. For example, approximately 60% of New York City taxi drivers are of South Asian origin (Fine, 2006).

Psychosocial Risk Factors

In addition to exposure to the physical environment, many Asian Americans are at risk for encountering psychosocial hazards such as poverty, extreme workload, sweatshop conditions, lack of workplace autonomy, and lack of workplace rights (Lee, 2009). Asian American garment workers often earn below the federal minimum wage. For example, Burgel et al. (2004) found that the Chinese immigrant garment workers earned an average of $6.32 per hour, which was not only below the living wage around Oakland where the study was conducted ($9.95), but also below the U.S. poverty level rate at the time ($8.50). Asian American workers work in unhealthy conditions that include unsanitary restrooms and rooms with poor ventilation (Chappell, 2005b). Moreover, Tsai and Salazar (2007) found that Chinese immigrant restaurant employees encounter a variety of psychosocial hazards at work, such as stress from having to promptly respond to many customers' concerns in English.

Indeed, work stress is a risk factor for many Asian Americans. For instance, evidence has suggested that Asian American workers have a high risk of heart disease because of job stress and limited decision-making power (Brown, James, Nordloh, & Jones, 2003). Likewise, job-related stressors are linked to poor health for immigrant Filipino workers, especially those who are recent immigrants (de Castro, Gee, & Takeuchi, 2008a).

Psychosocial hazards are faced not only by Asian American blue-collar workers but also by those in white-collar positions. Korean physicians who immigrated to the United States typically find themselves in medical specialties with lower pay and in less competitive residencies compared with Korean physicians who stay in Korea or Korean physicians who were born in the United States (Shin & Chang, 1988). Similarly, Asian American and Pacific Islander physicians were more likely to report lower job satisfaction and higher stress levels than White physicians, factors that increase their likelihood to change jobs (Glymour, Saha, Bigby, & Society of General Internal Medicine Career Satisfaction Study Group, 2004).

Finally, Asian Americans face widespread discrimination in the workplace. The Gallup Organization sampled employees' perceptions of discrimination at work and the effect those perceptions had on performance and retention, and the survey data (released in December 2005) indicated that 15% of all workers perceived that they had been subjected to some sort of discriminatory or unfair treatment (Rosenberg, 2009). Asians were the ethnic group that reported the greatest percentage of incidents of discrimination at 31%, with African Americans constituting the second largest group at 26%. Despite the large amount of perceived discrimination, the federal agency's enforcement experience shows that only about 2% of all charges in the private sector and 3.26% in the federal sector are filed by Asian Americans and Pacific Islanders. Thus, it is likely that Asian Americans and Pacific Islanders experience more discrimination in the workplace than is being reported in our charge/complaint statistics. Workplace discrimination is associated with poor health among Asian Americans (de Castro, Gee, & Takeuchi, 2008b). Additionally, perceptions that Asian Americans are not suitable to be in senior positions of leadership result in persistent glass ceilings (Sy et al., 2010).

Individual Attributes and Exposure Risks

Beyond the exposure to various environmental risk factors, the impact of exposure on Asian American workers is often exacerbated by their individual attributes, such as low proficiency in English, lack of knowledge of policies concerning workers' health and safety, and low level of acculturation. For example, Azaroff et al. (2003) suggested that the dangers of ergonomic hazards experienced by Southeast Asian workers were magnified because they did not have sufficient knowledge of safety rights and worker's compensation system. Moreover, immigrant workers were more concerned with their job security, and as such, were afraid of raising their concerns for improving occupational health and safety. Azaroff et al. found that most of the Southeast Asian immigrants lacked safety training, and less than one third knew about workers' compensation program. Similarly, Burgel and colleagues (2004) found that Asian garment workers in California frequently did not report their musculoskeletal symptoms because they were unaware of their safety rights and the availability of workers' compensation payoffs. Despite being eligible for workers' compensation, most of them refused to file claims because they were afraid of losing their jobs. In addition, immigrant Chinese female garment workers were unwilling to voice their concerns about ergonomic hazards because they did not want to attract negative attention about their symptoms and would rather simply perform regular stretching exercises to alleviate the symptoms (Burgel et al., 2004).

In sum, Asian Americans may be at a greater risk than White Americans for encountering work hazards because of frequent employment in businesses with dangerous working conditions. Low wages, along with limited access to health care and regulatory agencies, add to the problem (Lee, 2009). In addition, limited English proficiency and lack of knowledge of safety rights can be significant as individual barriers to the establishment of safe work environments (Tsai & Salazar, 2007). Next we discuss the research and policy implications on the basis of our model.

RESEARCH AND POLICY RECOMMENDATIONS

In this final section, we provide some research and policy recommendations to promote greater attention to the occupational health disparities experienced by Asian Americans. Whereas we have identified a separate set of research recommendations and a set of policy recommendations, they are interconnected because one depends on the other. For example, greater research attention will likely occur if there are significant changes to policies. At the same time, more research will generate the necessary data that will help guide the formulation of policies.

Research Recommendations

Our research recommendations are directed at providing more in-depth examination of linkages in the proposed model, increasing and improving surveillance of occupational health and safety issues, and using a disentangling approach for racial and ethnic differences.

Additional Examinations of the Linkages in the Proposed Model

As mentioned earlier, our proposed model outlined three processes linking environmental exposure and individual attributes with health outcomes among Asian Americans. Unfortunately, extant research tends to focus only on the linkages between exposure to environmental risk factors and individual attributes with health disparities. Little research has focused on exploring how environmental exposure and individual attributes unique to Asian Americans may relate to various biophysiological, psychological, and behavioral processes. Moreover, few studies have explored how these processes relate to different indicators of occupational health disparities among Asian Americans. Finally, limited research has examined the feedback loop included in the proposed model to explore the long-term implications of occupational health disparity on future exposure risks and changes in individual attributes.

We recommend that future research pay more attention to the linkages included in the proposed model, particularly with respect to the three processes—biophysiological, psychological, and behavioral—that may link exposure risks with health outcomes. Studies that identify the specific types of processes that are relevant to the occupational health disparity outcomes among Asian Americans will be valuable. Moreover, researchers should examine the mediating roles of the proposed process variables linking risk factors with Asian American's occupational health disparities. Finally, longitudinal studies that capture the long-term effects of health disparities on subsequent exposure risks and changes in individual attributes among Asian Americans will be beneficial.

Increased and Improved Surveillance

To properly address the occupational health disparities experienced by Asian Americans, we need to gather more accurate and consistent data regarding the nature and scope of the problem. This means that we need to increase and improve our surveillance of occupational health and safety issues among this population, especially vulnerable subgroups such as recent immigrants and those with lower socioeconomic status segregated into our inner cities. We recommend that this surveillance be guided by our framework, which focuses on multiple levels and incorporates multiple processes in assessing risk factors for occupational health problems among Asian Americans.

According to the Occupational Health Equity program within the National Institute for Occupational Safety and Health (NIOSH), their first strategic goal is to "improve surveillance to describe the nature, extent, and economic burden of occupational illnesses, injuries, and fatalities among priority working populations; identify priorities for research and intervention; and evaluate trends" (NIOSH, 2014). The first intermediate goal related to this first strategic goal is particularly relevant to Asian Americans: "Improve illness, injury, and exposure surveillance by using existing morbidity data or creating new databases to identify injuries, illnesses, and hazards that appear in excess within priority working populations" (NIOSH, 2014). The key is to ensure that Asian Americans are included within the priority working populations. We strongly support the application of the three components of this intermediate goal on surveillance to Asian American workers: (a) expand occupational health surveillance capacity by enhancing existing databases to provide information on occupational health disparities and economic costs among priority working populations; (b) improve survey question design and administration methods that consider language, literacy, and cultural differences among priority working populations; and (c) improve exposure surveillance methods to describe hazards in sectors where priority populations are disproportionately employed, especially among temporary or contingent workers such as day laborers.

Greater surveillance is needed on the challenges for Asian American workers in terms of work hazards, discrimination, and work stress. Specifically, we must pay attention to the hazards faced by Asian American and Pacific Islander workers in high-risk and low-wage industries, such as taxi driving, domestic work, and garment production. Also, we need better surveillance of occupational health disparities among Asian Americans and Pacific Islanders by national agencies (Leong & Mak, 2014). Preliminary data suggest that these Asian American workers should be designated as priority worker populations in need of further surveillance (Leong & Mak, 2014).

Disentangling Approach to Occupational Health Disparities Research

In a recent chapter on clinical research with culturally diverse populations, Leong and Kalibatseva (2013) observed that

> within the field of Psychology, there has been an on-going controversy regarding the use of race and ethnicity as a demographic and not a psychological variable. While having its origins in biology and genetics, some have argued that race and ethnicity is currently a political and social construction with complex ramifications. According to these scholars, using race and ethnicity as a demographic variable to serve as a proxy for such biological and genetic grouping of humans will result in overgeneralizations at best and gross misrepresentations at worst. Psychologists have therefore varied in their level of critique in using race and ethnicity as predictor variables. (p. 16)

Therefore, one of our research recommendations is to use the disentangling approach in the study of race and ethnicity in regards to occupational health disparities. According to this approach, we need to move beyond using race and ethnicity as a demographic variable and begin to undertake deep-level diversity research that delves into the psychological processes and mechanisms that may be moderating or mediating the relationship between race–ethnicity and occupational health (Leong & Kalibatseva, 2013). Based on the premise that demography is a poor proxy for psychology, the disentangling approach advocates the use of psychological variables as predictors of health outcomes (and health disparities) in addition to using race and ethnicity as predictors. According to this approach, the psychological variables should help disentangle the "black box" effects of race and ethnicity in increasing our understanding of health disparities. Specifically, the disentangling approach will help us uncover the psychological processes and mechanisms underlying the race and ethnicity effects by providing incremental validity in our prediction models.

One recent example of this disentangling approach is a study by Leong, Park, and Kalibatseva (2013) on the predictors of immigrant mental health. According to Leong et al. (2013), much of the health disparities research has historically treated immigrant status as a demographic variable and made generalizations about immigrant mental health on the basis of such demographic variables as nativity, age at immigration, and length of residence. However, sole reliance on demographic characteristics strips immigrant status of its underlying psychological mechanisms. They used a risk and protective factors paradigm based on a disentangling approach to examine if psychological correlates of immigrant status predict psychological disorders over and beyond its demographic characteristics. The objective of the study was to disentangle the psychological mechanisms underlying immigrant status by identifying a set of psychological protective and risk factors found in the extant literature to be associated with immigrant status, which in turn can be used to predict prevalence rates of mental disorders among Latino and Asian American immigrants. Their results provided some evidence of the value of using the disentangling approach in the study of immigrant mental health.

Related to the limitations of race and ethnicity as a demographic variable, a similar problem is the overgeneralizations from studies regarding certain racial and ethnic groups (such as Asian Americans), which ignore the considerable within-group heterogeneity. Although data collection on health for Asian Americans is slowly improving, published information on health and health barriers among specific Asian ethnic groups is still very limited. To increase the value of our science, there is a clear need for greater precision when we do study racial and ethnic health disparities. Where possible, studies of specific Asian American subgroups such as Chinese Americans, Japanese Americans, and Korean Americans would provide more useful and fine-grained information than studies of undifferentiated samples of Asian Americans and Pacific Islanders. In such cases, health and population data, including the category of Asian Americans, will have significant limitations—and worse yet, when the data are simply aggregated as "other." This disentangling approach is also consistent with our conceptual framework that argues for a multidimensional approach of understanding occupational health disparities among Asian Americans.

Policy Recommendations

Our major policy recommendations center on countering racial and ethnic stereotypes, understanding the politics of numbers that undermine attention to Asian American experiences, and fulfilling the need for political action and coordination to change the status quo.

Countering Stereotypes

Racial and ethnic stereotypes are often the foundations of workplace discrimination (Einarsen, Hoel, Zapf, & Cooper, 2010). According to Stangor (2000), a *stereotype* is defined as a generalized representation of the physical, psychological, and/or behavioral characteristics of a defined group of people (as cited in Leong & Grand, 2008). For Asian Americans, a significant stereotype attributed to them is the *model minority stereotype*. Leong and Grand (2008) argued that although the conceptual basis for Asian American stereotyping in the United States can be traced as far back as the Chinese Exclusion Act of 1882 (U.S. National Archives and Records Administration, 2007), the actual labeling of Asian Americans as the model minority only dates back to 1966, following an article published by William Petersen in *The New York Times Magazine*. In that editorial, Petersen praised the hard work and discipline of the Japanese people who had immigrated and built their livelihoods in the United States despite the poor treatment and unrelenting discrimination they faced. These observations by Petersen laid the foundation for their archetypal status as the model minority, which was then perpetuated by the media, general public, and policymakers alike (Leong & Grand, 2008).

Leong and Grand (2008) also tackled the question of what factors in the Asian American experience have elevated their group to the level of model minority and enabled them to hold such a position for so long. They pointed out that the convincing and frequently cited evidence for the claim lies in the statistics used to depict socioeconomic achievement of this group (Tang, 1997). For example, according to data obtained from the U.S. Census 2000, Asian Americans were tops among the five major ethnic groups (Whites, Blacks, Hispanic/Latinos, and Native Americans) in many socioeconomic achievement indicators, including rate of college degree attainment (42.9%), advanced degree attainment (6.5%), percentage of population in the labor force (65.3%), percentage holding a high skill occupation (34.6%), median socioeconomic index score (49.0), and median family income ($59,000; Le, 2007). In addition, the Asian American population tends to exhibit low rates of juvenile delinquency, criminal activity, and divorce (Sue, Sue, Sue, & Takeuchi, 1995). Leong and Grand concluded that the cumulative profile created by these numbers paints the picture of a successful, high-achieving people who are well adjusted and integrated into American industry, culture, and society.

This model minority stereotype has had a lasting impact in the workplace, with Asian Americans perceived as valuable employees because of their dedication, productivity, and ability to perform well on many different tasks (Leong & Grand, 2008). This stereotype has often resulted in backlash from coworkers who feel intimidated by the purported work ethic and ingenuity of their Asian American counterparts. It has also generated resentment of the Asian American employee, which has resulted in a great many damaging consequences ranging from subtle forms of discrimination and obstacles to career advancement to outright acts of prejudice and—in some cases—violence (Leong & Grand, 2008).

This model minority stereotype has also contributed to the dearth of health data for Asian Americans. The perpetuation of model minority myth is a systematic problem that has prevented appropriate data collection and much-needed research. The myth masks the fact that 21% of Asian Americans are uninsured, and 12.5% live below the poverty line. Many also have language barriers that along with the lack of financial resources, keep them from navigating America's convoluted health care system (National AIDS Treatment Advocacy Project, 2005).

Politics of Numbers

Policy formulation has tended to follow data and the law of numbers. However, decision makers are also influenced by the politics of numbers, namely, if a large enough group of constituents is affected by a problem and are vocal in getting the issue resolved, then attention and resources will be devoted to that problem. If, on the other hand, a problem affects only a small minority or a silent minority, then limited attention is devoted to that problem. That is the nature of the politics of numbers, which is why many racial and ethnic minority groups have had to mount advocacy campaigns so that their problems will move to the front burners of policy and lawmakers.

The politics of numbers also applies to health disparities and the surrounding policies. Resources devoted to research on various health problems and diseases are usually commensurate with how many people are affected, but there are exceptions. In the case of health disparities, the report from the Institute of Medicine titled *Unequal Treatment: Confronting Racial and Ethnic Disparities in Health Care* (Smedley, Stith, & Nelson, 2003) found that racial and ethnic minorities receive lower quality health care than Whites, even when they are insured to the same degree and when other health care access-related factors, such as the ability to pay for care, are the same. The report also noted that there is evidence suggesting that bias, prejudice, and stereotyping on the part of health care providers may contribute to differences in care. To date, very limited resources have been devoted to addressing the health disparities of Asian Americans.

In terms of occupational health disparities among Asian Americans, there is a combination of two problems, namely, that health disparities among racial and ethnic minorities have not received much attention until recently and the fact that Asian Americans are a small minority group relative to African Americans and Hispanic Americans. The latter problem has meant that relative little attention has been paid to the health disparities experienced by Asian Americans, and this pertains to occupational health disparities as well.

There are several ways in which the problem of the politics of numbers can be alleviated for us to increase our research and interventions with regard to occupational health disparities among Asian Americans. We need to educate policymakers on the occupational health disparities experienced by Asian Americans and take political action to address these problems. Both of these strategies are discussed next.

Educating Policymakers

Given the effects of the model minority myth, it is vital that we promote more educational programs in medical schools and health professions that convey the complex background of Asian Americans in relation to health disparities and thus counter the effects of this damaging stereotype. We also need educational programs and interventions to educate lawmakers and policymakers. This model minority myth is detrimental to the Asian American community because it masks important problems in the Asian American community, including occupational health disparities. In effect, the myth creates a false picture of the Asian American community as the singularly successful minority group that is not in need of research and assistance. This creates the unfortunate circumstance of there being no evidence or data collected on the general and occupational health disparities among Asian Americans. Yet, in the current zeitgeist of evidence-base practice, the availability of data is what causes institutions such as the National Institutes of Health or NIOSH or the Centers for Disease Control and Prevention to provide funds for further studies or finance intervention/prevention programs. Clearly, we are in need of an educational campaign to counter the stereotypes created by the model minority myth as much as we need the research improvements recommended previously.

Political Action and Coordination

To address the occupational health disparities experienced by Asian Americans, we need to ensure greater political action and advocacy to counter the damaging effects of the model minority myth. This requires more cooperation and coordination between different professional groups and associations that are committed to advancing Asian American health. Currently, a variety of organizations and associations exist, with overlapping goals but limited coordination and collaboration. There is the White House Asian American Initiative, but it consists of limited staff and resources. A timely development would be the formation of an Asian American Health Alliance that can harness the expertise, resources, and energies from these disparate groups in service to the improvement of the health of Asian Americans, including occupational health.

A second level of coordination involves community engagement. The success of our research and intervention is highly dependent on the coordination between these professional groups and the community stakeholders. This is also consistent with the NIOSH Occupational Health Equity program's third strategic goal, which involves "improving outreach to stakeholders to promote the elimination of occupational health disparities" (NIOSH, 2014). This requires the intermediate goal of expanding "outreach to community-based organizations, national stakeholder organizations, labor unions, and state and federal agencies interested in the health of racial and ethnic minorities and adolescent and older populations" (NIOSH, 2014).

Just as our framework can be used to guide future research on occupational health disparities research with Asian Americans, it can also play an important role in policy as well. Our conceptual framework provides a useful framework by providing a comprehensive, multilevel, and multiple-process perspective to aid in policy analysis, formulation, and implementation. Often, policy formulation can be reactive rather than proactive and strategic. Applying a framework supported by research will counter this common error and effectively and efficiently apply our knowledge base to addressing the occupational health disparities experienced by Asian Americans.

REFERENCES

Azaroff, L. S., Levenstein, C., & Wegman, D. H. (2003). Occupational health of Southeast Asian immigrants in a US city: A comparison of data sources. *American Journal of Public Health, 93*, 593–598. http://dx.doi.org/10.2105/AJPH.93.4.593

Brown, D. E., James, G. D., Nordloh, L., & Jones, A. A. (2003). Job strain and physiological stress responses in nurses and nurse's aides: Predictors of daily blood pressure variability. *Blood Pressure Monitoring, 8*, 237–242. http://dx.doi.org/10.1097/00126097-200312000-00003

Bureau of Labor Statistics. (2013a). *National census of fatal occupational injuries in 2012.* Retrieved from http://www.bls.gov/iif/oshwc/cfoi/cftb0274.pdf

Bureau of Labor Statistics. (2013b). *Nonfatal occupational injuries and illnesses requiring days away from work* (Table 7). Retrieved from http://www.bls.gov/news.release/osh2.t07.htm

Bureau of Labor Statistics. (2013c). *Nonfatal occupational injuries and illnesses requiring days away from work* (Table 8). Retrieved from http://www.bls.gov/news.release/osh2.t08.htm

Burgel, B. J., Lashuay, N., Israel, L., & Harrison, R. (2004). Garment workers in California: Health outcomes of the Asian immigrant women workers clinic. *AAOHN Journal, 52*, 465–475.

Chan, I. (2003). *The Chinese in America.* London, England: Penguin Books.

Chan, S. (1991). *Asian Americans: An interpretive history.* New York, NY: Twayne.

Chang, C.-H., Eatough, E. M., & Jaiprashad, D. (2010, April). Employee musculoskeletal symptoms and treatment-seeking: Workplace support as moderators. In M. Ford & L. Q. Yang (Co-chairs), *Beneficial forms of social support and implications for employee well-being.* Symposium presented at the 25th Annual Society for Industrial and Organizational Psychology Conference, Atlanta, GA.

Chappell, C. (2005a). Asian American garment workers: Low wages, excessive hours, and crippling injuries. In C. Chappell, *Reclaiming choice, broadening the movement: Sexual and reproductive justice and Asian Pacific American Women* (pp. 63–97). Washington, DC: National Asian Pacific American Women's Forum.

Chappell, C. (2005b). *Reclaiming choice, broadening the movement: Sexual and reproductive justice and Asian Pacific American women.* Washington, DC: National Asian Pacific American Women's Forum. Retrieved from https://napawf.org/wp-content/uploads/2009/working/pdfs/NAPAWF_Reclaiming_Choice.pdf

de Castro, A. B., Gee, G. C., & Takeuchi, D. T. (2008a). Job-related stress and chronic health conditions among Filipino immigrants. *Journal of Immigrant and Minority Health, 10,* 551–558. http://dx.doi.org/10.1007/s10903-008-9138-2

de Castro, A. B., Gee, G. C., & Takeuchi, D. T. (2008b). Workplace discrimination and health among Filipinos in the United States. *American Journal of Public Health, 98,* 520–526. http://dx.doi.org/10.2105/AJPH.2007.110163

Eatough, E. M., Way, J. D., & Chang, C.-H. (2012). Understanding the link between psychosocial work stressors and work-related musculoskeletal complaints. *Applied Ergonomics, 43,* 554–563. http://dx.doi.org/10.1016/j.apergo.2011.08.009

Einarsen, S., Hoel, H., Zapf, D., & Cooper, C. (Eds.). (2010). *Bullying and harassment in the workplace: Developments in theory, research, and practice* (2nd ed.). Boca Raton, FL: CRC Press. http://dx.doi.org/10.1201/EBK1439804896

Fine, J. (2006). *Work centers: Organizing communities at the edge of the dream.* Ithaca, NY: Cornell University Press.

Frumkin, H., Walker, E. D., & Friedman-Jiménez, G. (1999). Minority workers and communities. *Occupational Medicine, 14,* 495–517.

Gee, G. C., & Payne-Sturges, D. C. (2004). Environmental health disparities: A framework integrating psychosocial and environmental concepts. *Environmental Health Perspectives, 112,* 1645–1653. http://dx.doi.org/10.1289/ehp.7074

Glymour, M. M., Saha, S., Bigby, J., & Society of General Internal Medicine Career Satisfaction Study Group. (2004). Physician race and ethnicity, professional satisfaction, and work-related stress: Results from the Physician Worklife Study. *Journal of the National Medical Association, 96,* 1283–1289, 1294.

He, Y., Hu, J., Yu, I. T. S., Gu, W., & Liang, Y. (2010). Determinants of return to work after occupational injury. *Journal of Occupational Rehabilitation, 20,* 378–386. http://dx.doi.org/10.1007/s10926-010-9232-x

Hoeffel, E. M., Rastogi, S., Kim, M. O., & Shahid, H. (2012). *The Asian population: 2010* (Census 2010 Briefs, No. C2010BR-11). Retrieved from http://www.census.gov/prod/cen2010/briefs/c2010br-11.pdf

Kammeyer-Mueller, J. D., Judge, T. A., & Scott, B. A. (2009). The role of core self-evaluations in the coping process. *Journal of Applied Psychology, 94,* 177–195. http://dx.doi.org/10.1037/a0013214

Katz, D., & Kahn, R. L. (1978). *The social psychology of organizations* (2nd ed.). Hoboken, NJ: Wiley.

Lazarus, R. S., & Folkman, S. (1984). *Stress, appraisal, and coping.* New York, NY: Springer.

Le, C. N. (2007). *The model minority image.* Retrieved from http://www.asiannation.org/model-minority.shtml

Lee, P. T. (2009). Occupational and environmental health. In C. Trinh-Shevrin, N. S. Islam, & M. J. Rey (Eds.), *Asian American communities and health: Context, research, policy and action* (pp. 403–440). San Francisco, CA: Jossey-Bass.

Leong, F. T. L., & Grand, J. (2008). Career and work implications of the model minority myth and other stereotypes for Asian Americans. In G. Li & L. Wang (Eds.), *Model minority myths revisited: An interdisciplinary approach to demystifying Asian American education experiences* (pp. 91–115). Greenwich, CT: Information Age.

Leong, F. T. L., & Kalibatseva, Z. (2013). Clinical research with culturally diverse populations. In J. S. Comer & P. C. Kendall (Eds.), *Oxford handbook of research strategies for clinical psychology* (pp. 413–433). New York, NY: Oxford University Press. http://dx.doi.org/10.1093/oxfordhb/9780199793549.013.0021

Leong, F. T. L., & Mak, S. (2014). Occupational health disparities among Asian Americans: A critical review with recommendations. *Asian American Journal of Psychology, 5,* 44–52. http://dx.doi.org/10.1037/a0034907

Leong, F. T. L., Park, Y., & Kalibatseva, Z. (2013). Disentangling immigrant status: An exploration of psychological protective and risk factors among Latino and Asian American immigrants using the NLAAS. *American Journal of Orthopsychiatry, 83,* 361–371. http://dx.doi.org/10.1111/ajop.12020

McCarthy, M. I. (2008). Casting a wider net for diabetes susceptibility genes. *Nature Genetics, 40,* 1039–1040. http://dx.doi.org/10.1038/ng0908-1039

Mobed, K., Gold, E. B., & Schenker, M. B. (1992). Occupational health problems among migrant and seasonal farm workers. *The Western Journal of Medicine, 157,* 367–373.

National AIDS Treatment Advocacy Project. (2005, October 6). *Asian Americans and hepatitis B.* Retrieved from http://www.natap.org/2005/HBV/100605_01.htm

National Institute for Occupational Safety and Health. (2014). *Occupational health disparities. Inputs: Strategic goals.* Retrieved from https://www.cdc.gov/niosh/programs/ohd/goals.html

Nemoto, T., Iwamoto, M., Oh, H. J., Wong, S., & Nguyen, H. (2005). Risk behaviors among Asian women who work at massage parlors in San Francisco:

Perspectives from masseuses and owners/managers. *AIDS Education and Prevention, 17,* 444–456.

Nemoto, T., Operario, D., Takenaka, M., Iwamoto, M., & Le, M. N. (2003). HIV risk among Asian women working at massage parlors in San Francisco. *AIDS Education and Prevention, 15,* 245–256. http://dx.doi.org/10.1521/aeap.15.4.245.23829

Pew Research Center. (2012). *The rise of Asian Americans.* Washington, DC: Pew Social & Demographic Trends.

Restaurant Opportunities Center of New York. (2005). *Behind the kitchen door: Pervasive inequality in New York City's thriving restaurant industry.* New York, NY: Restaurant Opportunities Center of New York and New York City Restaurant Industry Coalition. Retrieved from http://rocunited.org/publications/roc-ny-behind-the-kitchen-door/

Rho, H. J., Schmitt, J., Woo, N., Lin, L., & Wong, K. (2011, July). *Diversity and change: Asian American and Pacific Island workers.* Washington, DC: Center for Economic and Policy Research. Retrieved from http://www.cepr.net/documents/publications/aapi-2011-07.pdf

Roelofs, C., Azaroff, L. S., Holcroft, C., Nguyen, H., & Doan, T. (2008). Results from a community-based occupational health survey of Vietnamese-American nail salon workers. *Journal of Immigrant and Minority Health, 10,* 353–361. http://dx.doi.org/10.1007/s10903-007-9084-4

Rosenberg, A. (2009, January 20). Asian-American employees underreport discrimination, report finds. *Government Executive.* Retrieved from http://www.govexec.com/dailyfed/0109/012009ar1.htm

Sakamoto, M., Vaughan, J., & Tobias, B. (2001). Occupational health surveillance strategies for an ethnically diverse Asian employee population. *AAOHN Journal, 49,* 235–242.

Sapolsky, R. (2004). *Why zebras don't get ulcers: The acclaimed guide to stress, stress-related diseases and coping* (3rd ed.). New York, NY: Henry Holt.

Sauter, S. L., & Swanson, N. G. (1996). An ecological model of musculoskeletal disorders in office work. In S. D. Moon & S. L. Sauter (Eds.), *Psychosocial aspects of musculoskeletal disorders in office work* (pp. 3–21). London, England: Taylor & Francis.

Shin, E. H., & Chang, K.-S. (1988). Peripherization of immigrant professionals: Korean physicians in the United States. *International Migration Review, 22,* 609–626. http://dx.doi.org/10.2307/2546348

Sincavage, J. R. (2005, October). Occupational safety and health: Fatal occupational injuries among Asian workers. *Monthly Labor Review, 128,* 49–55.

Smedley, B. D., Stith, A. Y., & Nelson, A. R. (Eds.). (2003). *Unequal treatment: Confronting racial and ethnic disparities in health care.* Washington, DC: Institute of Medicine.

Stangor, C. (Ed.). (2000). *Stereotypes and prejudice: Essential readings.* Philadelphia, PA: Psychology Press.

Strong, L. L., & Zimmerman, F. J. (2005). Occupational injury and absence from work among African American, Hispanic, and non-Hispanic White workers in the national longitudinal survey of youth. *American Journal of Public Health, 95,* 1226–1232. http://dx.doi.org/10.2105/AJPH.2004.044396

Sue, S., Sue, D. W., Sue, L., & Takeuchi, D. T. (1995). Psychopathology among Asian Americans: A model minority? *Cultural Diversity and Mental Health, 1,* 39–54.

Sy, T., Shore, L. M., Strauss, J., Shore, T. H., Tram, S., Whiteley, P., & Ikeda-Muromachi, K. (2010). Leadership perceptions as a function of race-occupation fit: The case of Asian Americans. *Journal of Applied Psychology, 95,* 902–919. http://dx.doi.org/10.1037/a0019501

Takaki, R. (1989). *Strangers from a different shore: A history of Asian Americans.* New York, NY: Little, Brown.

Tang, J. (1997). The model minority thesis revisited: (Counter)evidence from the science and engineering fields. *Journal of Applied Behavioral Science, 33,* 291–315.

Trimble, J. E., & Dickson, R. (2005). Ethnic gloss. In C. B. Fisher & R. M. Lerner (Eds.), *Encyclopedia of applied developmental science* (Vol. 1, pp. 412–415). Thousand Oaks, CA: Sage.

Tsai, J. H.-C. (2009). Chinese immigrant restaurant workers' injury and illness experiences. *Archives of Environmental & Occupational Health, 64*(2), 107–114. http://dx.doi.org/10.3200/AEOH.64.2.107-114

Tsai, J. H.-C., & Salazar, M. K. (2007). Occupational hazards and risks faced by Chinese immigrant restaurant workers. *Family & Community Health, 30*(Suppl.), S71–S79. http://dx.doi.org/10.1097/01.FCH.0000264882.73440.20

Unoki, H., Takahashi, A., Kawaguchi, T., Hara, K., Horikoshi, M., Andersen, G., . . . Maeda, S. (2008). SNPs in KCNQ1 are associated with susceptibility to type 2 diabetes in East Asian and European populations. *Nature Genetics, 40,* 1098–1102. http://dx.doi.org/10.1038/ng.208

U.S. Census Bureau. (2011a). *2011 American Community Survey, Table B02018.* Retrieved from http://factfinder2.census.gov/bkmk/table/1.0/en/ACS/11_1YR/B02018

U.S. Census Bureau. (2011b). *2011 American Community Survey, Table S0201.* Retrieved from http://factfinder2.census.gov/bkmk/table/1.0/en/ACS/11_1YR/S0201//popgroup~012

U.S. Department of Labor. (2000, May). *Risk factors and protective measures for taxi and livery drivers.* Retrieved from http://www.osha.gov/OSHAFacts/taxi-livery-drivers.pdf

U.S. Department of Labor. (2011, July 22). *The Asian-American labor force in the recovery.* Washington, DC: Author. Retrieved from http://www.dol.gov/_sec/media/reports/AsianLaborForce/AsianLaborForce.pdf

U.S. National Archives & Records Administration. (2007). *Transcript of Chinese Exclusion Act (1882).* Retrieved from http://www.ourdocuments.gov/doc.php?doc=47&page=transcript

III
INTERVENTIONS

7

DEVELOPING OCCUPATIONAL SAFETY AND HEALTH TRAINING PROGRAMS FOR IMMIGRANT WORKERS: TRANSLATING RESEARCH TO PRACTICE

SARA A. QUANDT AND THOMAS A. ARCURY

The U.S. workforce has undergone significant changes in the past several decades, as large numbers of new immigrant workers have entered the workforce. In 2010, immigrants made up 16.4% of the labor force, compared with just 6.6% thirty years earlier (Singer, 2012). Hispanics now make up about half of all foreign-born workers, and Asians account for about a quarter (Bureau of Labor Statistics [BLS], 2012). With the aging of the U.S. native-born population, immigrant workers now make up a disproportionate share of the labor force. Many of these workers are concentrated in particular industries that are considered "3-D" jobs: dirty, demeaning, and dangerous (Connell, 1993; Quandt, Arcury-Quandt, et al., 2013). These industries include agriculture, food service, personal care, hospitality, warehousing, and construction (BLS, 2012).

This research was supported in part by grants from the National Institute for Occupational Safety and Health (R25 OH008335, R25 OH007611, and R18 OH009579), the National Institute of Environmental Health Sciences (R01 ES008739), the North Carolina Department of Agriculture and Consumer Services, Syngenta, and Aventis CropScience.

http://dx.doi.org/10.1037/0000021-008
Occupational Health Disparities: Improving the Well-Being of Ethnic and Racial Minority Workers, F. T. L. Leong, D. E. Eggerth, C.-H. Chang, M. A. Flynn, J. K. Ford, and R. O. Martinez (Editors)

Within those industries, immigrants are clustered in lower skilled and more dangerous jobs (Singer, 2012). The result has been a significant change in the composition of the labor force and the health and safety training needs in these industries.

Immigrant workers make up an increasingly large proportion of work-related fatalities both internationally (Salminen, 2011) and in the United States (Loh & Richardson, 2004; Menéndez & Havea, 2011; Richardson, 2005). Immigrant workers are also overrepresented in injuries (Argeseanu Cunningham, Ruben, & Venkat Narayan, 2008; Centers for Disease Control and Prevention, 2008). Recent data on morbidity and mortality show that the industries that are becoming composed predominantly of immigrant workers experience the highest rates of work-related injury and death. For example, 7% of all fatal occupational injuries in 2010 occurred among crop production workers, and 17% occurred in construction (BLS, 2011).

Data from Europe show that once immigrant or minority workers come to predominate in a job category, that category seldom reverts to domestic or majority workers (European Agency for Safety and Health at Work, 2007; International Labour Office, 2004). Thus, there is a clear imperative for action to reduce these disparities in injury rates in these industries and with these immigrant workers.

Efforts to address occupational safety and health (OSH) can take several different approaches. The most basic is to eliminate workplace hazards, whether they are pesticides for farmworkers or the use of ladders for construction workers. Although some hazard elimination is often possible, complete elimination often is not. Therefore, engineering controls that prevent hazard exposure, such as saw guards, are the next most effective measures. In addition, regulations on supervisor and worker behaviors that reduce worker exposure can be developed—though without enforcement, they generally have little effect (Arcury, Lu, Chen, & Quandt, 2013; Robinson et al., 2011). Finally, OSH training programs can be provided. Such programs can increase workers' knowledge, improve their skills, and increase workers' self-efficacy to put the skills into practice (Robson et al., 2012).

This chapter focuses on the last approach to OSH: developing training programs. It is aimed primarily at developing training programs for those immigrant workers in manual occupations, and we argue for greater use of research-based OSH training programs for this worker population. After summarizing the characteristics of effective training programs, we discuss characteristics of immigrant workers in manual occupations that shape their training needs. We present a framework for using OSH research to develop training programs. We then discuss procedures for developing effective training activities and materials that can be used in training programs for immigrant workers.

CHARACTERISTICS OF EFFECTIVE OSH TRAINING PROGRAMS

There is no shortage of programs or materials intended for worker OSH training. For example, our team's experience reviewing programs and materials for pesticide safety for farmworkers published from 1988 to 1998 uncovered 35 items just on this limited topic (Quandt, Austin, Arcury, Summers, & Saavedra, 1999). These materials ranged in format from crude brochures to interactive computer programs to complete curricula. Most notable was the lack of provenience for many items: They gave few clues for how and where they were developed, whether they were effective, and whether they were developed to be appropriate for immigrant worker populations. Many appeared to have been developed by simply taking materials created for native-born workers, translating text into Spanish, and substituting pictures of workers with those of more Latino-appearing workers.

Training programs should be conceptualized as (a) an overall approach, based in individual-, group-, or community-level perspectives (for examples, see Glanz, Rimer, & Viswanath, 2008); (b) a method of implementation (e.g., peer educators, community organizing); and print, electronic, or other materials used in the program. To be effective, training programs should meet a minimum set of criteria (see Exhibit 7.1). They should be evidence based: The concepts underlying the training materials should reflect current scientific research. This might include research for the dominant way worker exposure to chemicals or other agents takes place or research that compares

EXHIBIT 7.1
Checklist for Recognizing Potentially Effective Occupational
Safety and Health Training Programs

- Evidence based
  - □ Consistent with valid, reliable, and current research
  - □ Efficacy and effectiveness established
- Culturally appropriate
  - □ Consistent with targeted trainees' values and beliefs
  - □ Consistent with trainees' life experiences
- Linguistically appropriate
  - □ Presented in the language used by the trainees
  - □ Uses vocabulary and idioms familiar to the trainees
- Educationally appropriate
  - □ Literacy level fits that of trainees and trainers
  - □ Aimed at adult learners, not children
- Realistic
  - □ Fits the resources available for worker training
  - □ Consistent with resources and possibilities for worker action found in the work environment

different safety practices. For example, research published in 2011 that compared different types of personal protective equipment demonstrated, for the first time, that transmission of seasonal influenza in hospital workers seems to occur as much through the eye as through inhalation (Bischoff, Reid, Russell, & Peters, 2011). Such novel results might well need to be incorporated in infection control training in health care workers. The section in this chapter titled "Developing OSH Training From the Research Base" elaborates the steps in ensuring that training reflects underlying research.

Training should be culturally and linguistically appropriate. Workers of different cultural backgrounds vary in how they understand the workings of the human body, and they often apply widely held lay beliefs about illness to those conditions identified by biomedicine. For example, researchers studying Latin American workers have noted that some, but not all, workers base their behavior around humoral medicine, which contrasts with biomedicine in assuming that hot/cold valences characterize human exposures (e.g., water, different foods), human activities such as strenuous physical exertion, and processes of illness and injury (Quandt, Arcury, Austin, & Saavedra, 1998; Rubel & Hass, 1996). Immigrant workers also recognize lay-defined illnesses that have no counterparts in biomedicine, such as *susto* and *nervios* among Mexican workers (Baer & Penzell, 1993; Weller, Baer, Garcia de Alba Garcia, & Salcedo Rocha, 2008), and they perceive some individuals as inherently resistant to harm from occupational exposure (Hunt, Ojanguren, Schwartz, & Laperin, 1999; Quandt et al., 1998). OSH training that fails to take such beliefs into account may be unsuccessful in promoting safety behaviors. Language appropriateness extends beyond a global assessment of languages spoken by a worker population. Spanish spoken in Mexico, for example, differs to a greater or lesser degree in vocabulary and pronunciation from that spoken in other Spanish-speaking countries. Even if Spanish is spoken, it may be a second language for those workers who were raised speaking indigenous Native American languages; these workers' comprehension of Spanish-language training is often limited (Farquhar et al., 2009). Workers may also use specific work-related terms that can be amalgamations of other words, such as farmworkers using the term *sprayando* when talking about spraying pesticides (Arcury, Estrada, & Quandt, 2010). Although these cultural and linguistic examples come from Hispanic populations, comparable examples undoubtedly exist with other immigrant worker groups.

Worker safety training should be educationally appropriate. The inclusion of materials that require reading should consider the literacy level of the workers who use the materials. Most immigrant worker populations in manual occupations have a broad range of educational statuses. It is not unusual to find individuals with at least some college training in these jobs. At the same time, the modal educational level is often quite low, with some individuals who have had no formal education. The challenge for training materials and programs is to be able to accommodate this broad range. In most cases, it is best to consider ways to limit the need to read or to accompany words with audio or visual cues to help the worker grasp meaning without reliance on printed words.

Adult education principles need to be used to craft training programs appropriate for nonyouth workers. These principles are sometimes discussed as *andragogy* in contrast to *pedagogy*, the approach to teaching children. Adult education principles assume that the adult learner is self-directed, with a reservoir of experience that is both a resource for further learning and problem solving and a filter through which new information is interpreted. These principles also assume that adult learning is oriented to learners' social roles (e.g., being workers or parents), not to academic pressure, and that they are oriented to immediate application of knowledge, giving workers a problem-centered orientation to their learning (Knowles, 1973, 1980). In the context of these adult-learner characteristics, training programs that involve learners as partners rather than students, that use hands-on and active learning approaches, and that encourage learners to practice a skill or apply knowledge are appropriate. Training methods such as discussion, role-playing, games, demonstrations, mapping, and case studies are geared to adult learners (Collins, 2004). Programs that include peer-to-peer training with a lay health and safety promoter generally incorporate adult-appropriate training methods (Arcury, Marín, Snively, Hernández-Pelletier, & Quandt, 2009; Forst et al., 2004; Luque et al., 2007; Migrant Health Promotion, 2009; Quandt, Grzywacz, et al., 2013).

Finally, training programs must be a realistic match for the intended application. They need to fit the resources in time, equipment, and personnel available to provide training. Their content should also be consistent with workers' ability to take action. For example, telling workers to wear personal protective equipment (PPE) if none is provided will be less effective than accompanying the message to wear PPE with messages concerning employers' legal obligations to provide PPE and suggested actions to obtain the PPE.

CHARACTERISTICS OF IMMIGRANT WORKERS THAT SHAPE THEIR TRAINING NEEDS

Current immigrant workers in manual occupations in the United States have a number of common characteristics that should be considered in developing OSH training programs. Many of them are unfamiliar with the work tasks and work environment in which they have found employment. Even if they have previously worked in the same industry in their country of origin (e.g., agriculture, construction), they may be unfamiliar with the way work is organized in the United States and with aspects of the workplace such as machinery and chemicals used. For example, a review of worker deaths in confined spaces in California highlighted cases in which recent immigrants died when they unknowingly went into situations where they were asphyxiated by chemicals (Worksafe, 2012).

Most workers new to the United States also know little of their rights, including those related to a safe workplace and to workers' compensation for injuries suffered at work. If they are noncitizens, and particularly if they are undocumented, many erroneously assume they are entitled to no protections (Flynn, Eggerth, & Jacobson, 2015).

Finally, labor unions in the United States have historically played an important role in OSH training. Yet, many immigrants work in jobs that are not unionized. These include day laborers and domestic workers employed in private households. Some areas of the country, like the South, have a limited union presence, so industries located there (e.g., poultry and meat processing) are often not unionized. Without unions, organizations providing training programs frequently lack access to the worksite and must conduct training in the community (e.g., Marín et al., 2009). Workers asked to participate in such trainings may be reluctant to do so for fear of employer retaliation.

DEVELOPING OSH TRAINING PROGRAMS FROM A RESEARCH BASE

Strategies for developing evidence-based OSH training programs are typically based on both existing research and focused research conducted in the process of program development and in target populations. The sequence of steps for program development and the integration of research is well described by Green and Kreuter's (2005) PRECEDE–PROCEED planning framework. The framework is flexible to be able to accommodate numerous theoretical approaches to changing OSH-related behavior and environment at the individual, group, or community level.

Steps in the PRECEDE phases of the framework occur before program implementation and are most crucial for training program development (see Figure 7.1). Phases 1 through 3 represent a thorough diagnosis of the OSH problem. Phase 1, social assessment, begins the process with on-the-ground research to understand the concerns of those potentially involved with implementing or receiving the training program, including workers and supervisors. Using qualitative methods such as focus groups or individual semistructured interviews can determine whether the concerns over worker OSH are shared broadly and whether workers can be engaged in the training; they can foreshadow resistance to change and help incorporate strategies necessary to overcome this.

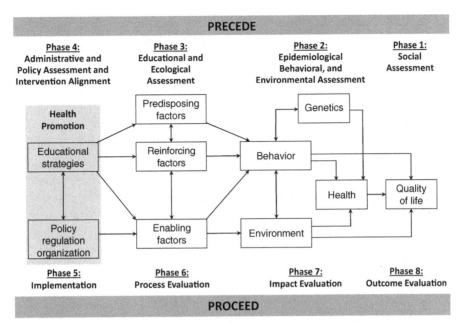

Phase 2, epidemiological, behavioral, and environmental assessment, calls for using existing, often published, research data to sharpen the focus on specific OSH issues and identify the behavioral and environmental factors most closely linked to these issues. Such factors are potential leverage points for the training program.

Phase 3, educational and ecological assessment, is the stage at which formative research is often necessary. This can be qualitative research (obtained from a combination of interview or observation), survey research, or a combination. The goal is an ethnographic understanding of the workplace, incorporating the perspectives and subjective experience of workers as well as a more objective understanding of structural factors related to OSH. It is often helpful to use this research to define the factors that must be in place for the change in behavior or environment necessary to improve OSH to occur (Green & Kreuter, 2005). *Predisposing factors* provide workers with the rationale or motivation for change. These can include beliefs, values, or existing skills. *Reinforcing factors* provide a continuing incentive for the change, including social support or the influence of peers and significant others. *Enabling factors* allow change to be realized and can include programs and services, as well as new skills for workers.

Finally, Phase 4, administrative, policy, and intervention alignment, is the stage at which data gathered in the previous phases are synthesized to create the OSH training program, or intervention. This synthesis requires two levels of alignment (Green & Kreuter, 2005). At the macrolevel, the program must consider organizational and environmental factors (e.g., worksite management and resources) that can influence achievement of the desired endpoints. At the microlevel, the program focuses on individual, peer, or group factors that can affect behavior change. The microlevel focuses quite directly on the predisposing, reinforcing, and enabling factors revealed in Phase 3.

The PRECEDE–PROCEED framework does not prescribe a particular type of program or even the type of theory underlying the program. Rather, the framework ensures that the program developed reflects data that have been systematically collected, analyzed, and considered.

Example: Developing a Comprehensive Pesticide Safety Training Program for Immigrant Farmworkers

The PACE (Preventing Agricultural Chemical Exposure) project began in 1996 as a community-based participatory research endeavor to understand and ultimately prevent exposure of Latino farmworkers to pesticides. The overall approach of the project and recent findings are described in Arcury and Quandt's Chapter 4 in this volume. Initial work in the PACE project conducted formative research on pesticide exposure and designed a safety-training program for workers. This work, described in greater detail elsewhere (Quandt, Arcury, Austin, & Cabrera, 2001), provides an example of using the PRECEDE–PROCEED planning framework to develop an OSH intervention grounded in research.

Social assessment (Phase 1) for the PACE intervention determined that health care providers and other service providers believed that pesticides were a significant health threat for farmworkers (see Figure 7.2). They cited acute poisonings, as well as concerns about the long-term health effects exposure might have for workers. Farmworkers had some concerns, though their focus was on acute exposures and their potential for lost work time due to pesticide-related illness.

Epidemiological assessment (Phase 2) found limited data for the study area (North Carolina) and more extensive data for elsewhere. These studies indicated excess morbidity and mortality for occupationally exposed workers; a time delay from exposure to health effects, including neurological, reproductive, and immunological effects; and greatest immediate effects among those who mixed and applied pesticides. The scientific literature noted that considerable pesticide exposure was due to pesticide residues remaining on plants, tools, and soil that could not be detected by sight or smell and that were absorbed through

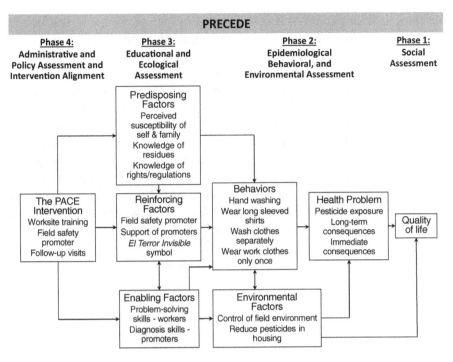

PRECEDE

| Phase 4:
Administrative and
Policy Assessment and
Intervention Alignment | Phase 3:
Educational and
Ecological
Assessment | Phase 2:
Epidemiological
Behavioral, and
Environmental Assessment | Phase 1:
Social
Assessment |

Figure 7.2. The Preventing Agricultural Chemical Exposure (PACE) model for pesticide safety intervention development. From "Preventing Occupational Exposure to Pesticides: Using Participatory Research With Latino Farmworkers to Develop an Intervention," by S. A. Quandt, T. A. Arcury, C. K. Austin, and L. F. Cabrera, 2001, *Journal of Immigrant Health, 3*, p. 92. Copyright 2001 by Plenum Publishing Group. Adapted with permission.

the skin. Behavioral and environmental assessment (Phase 2) included new research: interviews with workers, growers, and health care providers (Quandt et al., 1998). Workers expressed beliefs about pesticides that were inconsistent with scientific knowledge. They had no knowledge of pesticide residues and dermal exposure. They disliked recommended sanitation practices like wearing protective clothing and washing immediately after working because of the hot, humid working conditions and beliefs about health effects of washing that were apparently rooted in folk beliefs common in Mexico (Rubel & Hass, 1996; Weller, 1983). Growers rejected the notion that currently used pesticides were dangerous and that workers were being exposed, as workers did not mix or apply pesticides. They stated their frustration at trying to communicate with workers, few of whom spoke English, and with regulations that made them provide sanitation facilities that the workers did not seem to use.

Educational and ecological assessment (Phase 3) used interview and observational data to identify predisposing factors (lack of knowledge of residues, lack of perceived susceptibility, lack of knowledge of regulations delaying entry into pesticide-treated fields), reinforcing factors (importance of fellow workers to reinforce safety behaviors and provide positive role models), and enabling factors (need for problem solving skills to gain control of workplace pesticide exposure). On this basis, the PACE intervention program was developed (Phase 4). The intervention's target was reducing farmworker contact with pesticide residues, as the planning process had made it clear that this was likely the workers' primary source of exposure. The intervention needed to center on addressing the predisposing factors through provision of scientifically accurate information about pesticides, in ways respectful of cultural beliefs, as well as education about workers' rights and OSH regulations. Reinforcing and enabling factors called for an intervention that increased group solidarity around safety and provided skills for diagnosing and solving problems in the work environment. The actual activities are described elsewhere (Quandt et al., 2001) and were developed with the approaches described next.

DEVELOPING EFFECTIVE TRAINING ACTIVITIES AND MATERIALS

Sometimes OSH educators are tempted to start with a favorite educational medium. For example, they may have expertise in developing videos. However, decisions on training media should come after other decisions are made. The first step in materials development is to clarify the objective of the training (see Figure 7.3). Once the objective is clear, this can be broken down into behavior changes that are needed to accomplish the objective, and

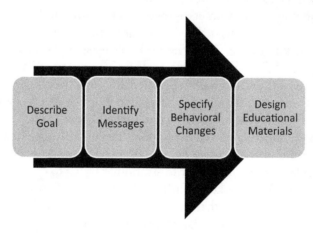

Figure 7.3. Steps for developing training materials.

messages to move from the objective to the desired changes can be drafted. Only then should specific training activities and educational materials and media be composed.

Identify the Message First

Most OSH programs will have one or more specific goals related to how worker behavior should change to achieve lower injury or disease rates. Each goal can be broken down into specific behavior changes that must occur to increase the likelihood of meeting the goal. These behavior changes can be encouraged with messages that communicate or remind the worker of the desired behavior.

Examine the "Scenario of Use" to Identify Appropriate Educational Material Formats

Educational activities for adult workers include a large number of possibilities. Hands-on, interactive activities can include role-playing, games, or quizzes; risk mapping; theater; photovoice; and storytelling. Even with the use of such activities, it is often advisable to include activities that use print or audiovisual materials. Exactly what training materials are included is best developed as part of an overall training program. Rarely does a single item stand alone. For example, a training video might need to be accompanied by a take-home item—a poster, a brochure, a hard-hat sticker—to serve as a cue to action for the worker, perhaps to call a source for additional information, to report rule violations, or to engage in a certain self-protective behavior. Initial decisions about the different training materials that are needed should take into account the overall training goals developed in a framework like PRECEDE–PROCEED and what workers need to know and do to reach those goals.

Using these goals, one can start by engaging the development team—trainers, workers, materials designers—to think about training materials' "scenario of use"—that is, think about who will use the materials, how they will interact with the materials, the context in which they will interact with the materials, and how much time they will have to interact with them (see Exhibit 7.2). For example, if training is to be delivered by a lay trainer in a community setting for a small group, this is an interactive setting. Deciding a priori that the training project should develop a comic book or *fotonovela* ignores the fact that such an item is best read individually. In such a scenario of use, games, flipchart lessons, or other means of assisting the lay leader in engaging the workers will be more appropriate. In a larger group, a video can be a useful way to present information, though it rarely can be used without

EXHIBIT 7.2
Checklist for Considering the "Scenarios of Use"
for Safety Training Materials

- Who will use the materials?
  - ☐ Workers alone
    - Age?
    - Gender?
    - Literacy level?
  - ☐ Lay trainers
  - ☐ Professional trainers
- In what context will workers interact with the materials?
  - ☐ In the workplace
  - ☐ In a community meeting
  - ☐ At home
- How will workers interact with the materials?
  - ☐ Individually
  - ☐ Small groups
  - ☐ Large groups
- How much time will be available for the interaction?
  - ☐ A brief interaction
  - ☐ All-day training session
  - ☐ Ongoing training program
- What are the cost restrictions on the training?

other more interactive training components that reinforce video content and allow workers to practice new skills.

Developing a scenario of use requires open discussion by a team including those knowledgeable about the worker population (including worker representatives), the potential trainers, and the industry for which training is to be provided. Including educational materials designers (e.g., graphic artists, videographers) can provide resources to the group, although it is important that the skills of the particular materials designers not lock in a specific format before the scenario is developed.

Example: Developing Educational Materials
for a Farmworker Pesticide Intervention

In planning an intervention to reduce pesticide exposure among migrant farmworkers and their families, formative research showed that both agricultural and residential pesticides were significant sources of exposure (Quandt et al., 2004). Because migrant farmworkers must occupy temporary housing to work, housing conditions factor in their occupational safety and health in ways different from most other worker populations. On the basis of research that showed that most farmworker housing was of poor quality (Early et al., 2006; Gentry, Grzywacz, Quandt, Davis, & Arcury, 2007), the researchers decided that encouraging farmworkers to follow pest control measures that do not require pesticides would help lower pesticide exposure while accomplishing the workers' objective of reducing the problem of insect and rodent pests. This particular component of the intervention was developed to supplement those components more directly related to agricultural work (described for the PACE project, mentioned previously).

The planned intervention drew on principles of integrated pest management (IPM), which highlights eliminating the conditions that attract pests and preventing pests from gaining access. Three messages were developed in English (with Spanish translations): Starve them out! (*¡Mátalas de hambre!*), Dry them out! (*¡Mátalas de sed!*), and Keep them out! (*¡No los dejes entrar!*). Each of these messages was linked to two behavior changes (see Figure 7.4).

Once the messages were identified, a scenario-of-use review suggested that the program to educate workers and their families would likely occur in small groups in farmworker camps. Workers would be Spanish speaking, largely from Mexico, and some would have very low literacy skills. The intervention would likely be presented by lay health promoters (*promotores de salud*) on evenings or weekends. Two media were selected: an animatic cartoon video (Lane,

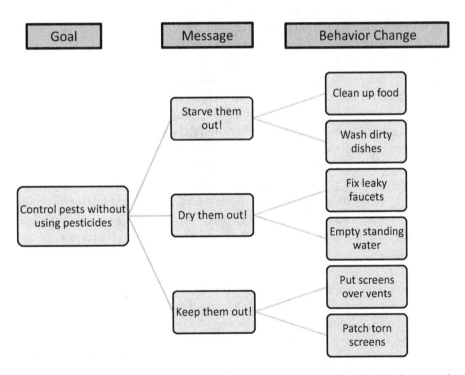

Figure 7.4. Example of plan for developing educational materials related to integrated pest management in farmworker housing.

Arcury, Quandt, & Marín, 2003a), with an accompanying print comic book (Lane, Arcury, Quandt, & Marín, 2003b). The messages and behaviors were woven into a dramatic story involving a buffoon, Pablo, who is attempting to rid his house of pests using all the wrong methods. His neighbor Maria and her friend and *promotora de salud* Selena teach him the correct ways to reduce his pesticide problems by implementing IPM techniques (see Figure 7.5). The animatic cartoon video uses brightly colored computer-generated art and professional voiceover to capture the audience's attention. The art is in a simple storyboard format with relatively little animation used at key points in the story for emphasis. Both the cartoon video and the comic book use repetition, sound effects (aural or pictured), and humor to teach and reinforce the messages and their corresponding behaviors.

Assess the Suitability of OSH Materials for Immigrant Workers

Immigrant workers vary widely in their educational experience, so materials suitable for low-literacy learners are appropriate. In developing new materials or choosing from existing ones, evaluation of materials before putting them to use is imperative. Getting feedback from workers, whether in informal one-on-one encounters or in focus groups, can help one gauge the appropriateness of the materials. Techniques such as "think aloud" can be used to judge workers' comprehension of print materials. Getting feedback on details such as color, facial expressions, skin color, and accuracy of worksite depictions can prove useful in finalizing materials (e.g., see flipchart pages in Grzywacz et al., 2009). Obtaining feedback on drafts early in the process can help avoid the need for costly revisions when materials have been finalized.

No matter the format of the OSH materials being assessed, a standard set of factors can be reviewed. Doak, Doak, and Root (1996) suggested a standardized suitability assessment of five criteria (see Exhibit 7.3): content, literacy demand, graphics and layout, stimulation and motivation, and cultural appropriateness. Reviewing these criteria throughout the development of materials can keep the process on track and produce training materials that are appealing to workers and effective in improving their OSH-related knowledge and behavior.

FINAL THOUGHTS: RESEARCH TO PRACTICE IN OSH TRAINING

The characteristics of immigrant workers and the worksites in which they are employed shape their OSH training needs. Existing OSH education and training programs vary in quality and appropriateness, and many are not evidence based. Creating OSH programs and materials requires consideration

Figure 7.5. Comic book cover for *Dígale Adios a Las Plagas* by C. M. Lane Jr., T. A. Arcury, S. A. Quandt, and A. Marín, 2003b, Winston-Salem, NC: Department of Family and Community Medicine, Wake Forest University School of Medicine. Copyright 2003 by C. M. Lane Jr., T. A. Arcury, S. A. Quandt, and A. Marín. Reprinted with permission.

EXHIBIT 7.3
Checklist for Evaluating Training Materials for Low Literacy Workers

- Content
  - □ Purpose is evident
  - □ Content focuses on "behaviors"
  - □ Scope is limited
  - □ Includes a summary or review
- Literacy demand
  - □ Uses common words
  - □ Simple writing style, active voice
  - □ Reading level is low
- Graphics and layout
  - □ Uncluttered
  - □ Only relevant illustrations
- Stimulation and motivation
  - □ Behaviors modeled and specific
  - □ Interaction used
  - □ Motivation: self-efficacy
- Cultural appropriateness
  - □ Match the language and experience of the audience
  - □ Use cultural images and examples

Note. From *Teaching Patients With Low Literacy Skills* (2nd ed., p. 51), by C. C. Doak, L. G. Doak, and J. H. Root, 1996, Philadelphia, PA: Lippincott. Copyright 1996 by Cecilia Doak. Adapted with permission.

of how they will be used and by whom, research to shape the programs and materials to the particular worker population, and evaluation of the materials during and after development. Publication of such evaluations and creation of accessible repositories of materials grounded in research will assist OSH practitioners in providing the best possible training for workers.

REFERENCES

Arcury, T. A., Estrada, J. M., & Quandt, S. A. (2010). Overcoming language and literacy barriers in safety and health training of agricultural workers. *Journal of Agromedicine, 15*, 236–248. http://dx.doi.org/10.1080/1059924X.2010.486958

Arcury, T. A., Lu, C., Chen, H., & Quandt, S. A. (2013). Pesticides present in migrant farmworker housing in North Carolina. *American Journal of Industrial Medicine, 57*, 312–322. http://dx.doi.org/10.1002/ajim.22232

Arcury, T. A., Marín, A., Snively, B. M., Hernández-Pelletier, M., & Quandt, S. A. (2009). Reducing farmworker residential pesticide exposure: Evaluation of a lay health advisor intervention. *Health Promotion Practice, 10*, 447–455. http://dx.doi.org/10.1177/1524839907301409

Argeseanu Cunningham, S., Ruben, J. D., & Venkat Narayan, K. M. (2008). Health of foreign-born people in the United States: A review. *Health & Place, 14*, 623–635. http://dx.doi.org/10.1016/j.healthplace.2007.12.002

Baer, R. D., & Penzell, D. (1993). Research report: Susto and pesticide poisoning among Florida farmworkers. *Culture, Medicine and Psychiatry, 17,* 321–327. http://dx.doi.org/10.1007/BF01380007

Bischoff, W. E., Reid, T., Russell, G. B., & Peters, T. R. (2011). Transocular entry of seasonal influenza-attenuated virus aerosols and the efficacy of n95 respirators, surgical masks, and eye protection in humans. *The Journal of Infectious Diseases, 204,* 193–199. http://dx.doi.org/10.1093/infdis/jir238

Bureau of Labor Statistics. (2011). *National census of fatal occupational injuries in 2010* [News release]. Retrieved from http://www.bls.gov/news.release/archives/cfoi_08252011.pdf

Bureau of Labor Statistics. (2012). *Foreign-born workers: Labor force characteristics—2011* [News release]. Retrieved from http://www.bls.gov/news.release/pdf/forbrn.pdf

Centers for Disease Control and Prevention. (2008). Work-related injury deaths among hispanics—United States, 1992–2006. *Morbidity and Mortality Weekly Report, 57,* 597–600.

Collins, J. (2004). Education techniques for lifelong learners: Principles of adult learning. *Radiographics, 24,* 1483–1489. http://dx.doi.org/10.1148/rg.245045020

Connell, J. (1993). *Kitanai, kitsui and kiken: The rise of labour migration to Japan* (Economic and Regional Restructuring Research Unit Working Papers, Issue 13). Sydney, Australia: University of Sydney.

Doak, C. C., Doak, L. G., & Root, J. H. (1996). *Teaching patients with low literacy skills* (2nd ed.). Philadelphia, PA: Lippincott.

Early, J., Davis, S. W., Quandt, S. A., Rao, P., Snively, B. M., & Arcury, T. A. (2006). Housing characteristics of farmworker families in North Carolina. *Journal of Immigrant and Minority Health, 8,* 173–184. http://dx.doi.org/10.1007/s10903-006-8525-1

European Agency for Safety and Health at Work. (2007). *Literature study on migrant workers.* Retrieved from http://osha.europa.eu/en/publications/literature_reviews/migrant_workers/view

Farquhar, S. A., Goff, N. M., Shadbeh, N., Samples, J., Ventura, S., Sanchez, V., . . . Davis, S. (2009). Occupational health and safety status of indigenous and Latino farmworkers in Oregon. *Journal of Agriculture Safety and Health, 15,* 89–102.

Flynn, M. A., Eggerth, D. E., & Jacobson, C. J., Jr. (2015). Undocumented status as a social determinant of occupational safety and health: The workers' perspective. *American Journal of Industrial Medicine, 58,* 1127–1137. http://dx.doi.org/10.1002/ajim.22531

Forst, L., Lacey, S., Chen, H. Y., Jimenez, R., Bauer, S., Skinner, S., . . . Conroy, L. (2004). Effectiveness of community health workers for promoting use of safety eyewear by Latino farm workers. *American Journal of Industrial Medicine, 46,* 607–613. http://dx.doi.org/10.1002/ajim.20103

Gentry, A. L., Grzywacz, J. G., Quandt, S. A., Davis, S. W., & Arcury, T. A. (2007). Housing quality among North Carolina farmworker families. *Journal of Agricultural Safety and Health, 13,* 323–337. http://dx.doi.org/10.13031/2013.23355

Glanz, K., Rimer, B. K., & Viswanath, K. (Eds.). (2008). *Health behavior and health education: Theory, research, and practice* (5th ed.). San Francisco, CA: Jossey-Bass.

Green, L. W., & Kreuter, M. W. (2005). *Health promotion planning: An educational and environmental approach* (4th ed.). New York, NY: McGraw-Hill.

Grzywacz, J. G., Arcury, T. A., Marín, A., Carrillo, L., Coates, M. L., & Quandt, S. A. (2009). Using lay health promoters in occupational health: Outcome evaluation in a sample of Latino poultry-processing workers. *New Solutions, 19,* 449–466. http://dx.doi.org/10.2190/NS.19.4.e

Hunt, L. M., Ojanguren, R. T., Schwartz, N., & Laperin, D. (1999). Applying pesticides without using protective equipment in southern Mexico. In R. A. Hahn & K. W. Harris (Eds.), *Anthropology in public health* (pp. 235–254). New York, NY: Oxford University Press.

International Labour Office. (2004). *Towards a fair deal for migrant workers in the global economy* (Report VI). Geneva, Switzerland: Author. Retrieved from http://www.ilo.org/public/english/standards/relm/ilc/ilc92/pdf/rep-vi.pdf

Knowles, M. (1973). *The adult learner: A neglected species.* Houston, TX: Gulf.

Knowles, M. S. (1980). *The modern practice of adult education.* New York, NY: The Adult Education Company.

Lane, C. M., Jr., Arcury, T. A., Quandt, S. A., & Marín, A. (2003a). *Como controlar plagas* [Spanish language cartoon video]. Winston-Salem, NC: Department of Family and Community Medicine, Wake Forest University School of Medicine.

Lane, C. M., Jr., Arcury, T. A., Quandt, S. A., & Marín, A. (2003b). *Dígale adios a las plagas* [Spanish language comic book]. Winston-Salem, NC: Department of Family and Community Medicine, Wake Forest University School of Medicine.

Loh, K., & Richardson, S. (2004). Foreign-born workers: Trends in fatal occupational injuries, 1996–2001. *Monthly Labor Review, 127,* 42–53.

Luque, J. S., Monaghan, P., Contreras, R. B., August, E., Baldwin, J. A., Bryant, C. A., & McDermott, R. J. (2007). Implementation evaluation of a culturally competent eye injury prevention program for citrus workers in a Florida migrant community. *Progress in Community Health Partnerships: Research, Education, and Action, 1,* 359–369. http://dx.doi.org/10.1353/cpr.2007.0040

Marín, A., Carrillo, L., Arcury, T. A., Grzywacz, J. G., Coates, M. L., & Quandt, S. A. (2009). Ethnographic evaluation of a lay health promoter program to reduce occupational injuries among Latino poultry processing workers. *Public Health Reports, 124*(Suppl. 1), 36–43.

Menéndez, C. K. C., & Havea, S. A. (2011). Temporal patterns in work-related fatalities among foreign-born workers in the US, 1992–2007. *Journal of Immigrant and Minority Health, 13,* 954–962. http://dx.doi.org/10.1007/s10903-010-9379-8

Migrant Health Promotion. (2009). *Camp health aide program manual.* Saline, MI: Migrant Health Promotion.

Quandt, S. A., Arcury, T. A., Austin, C. K., & Cabrera, L. F. (2001). Preventing occupational exposure to pesticides: Using participatory research with Latino farmworkers to develop an intervention. *Journal of Immigrant Health, 3,* 85–96. http://dx.doi.org/10.1023/A:1009513916713

Quandt, S. A., Arcury, T. A., Austin, C. K., & Saavedra, R. M. (1998). Farmworker and farmer perceptions of farmworker agricultural chemical exposure in North Carolina. *Human Organization, 57,* 359–368. http://dx.doi.org/10.17730/humo.57.3.n26161776pgg7371

Quandt, S. A., Arcury, T. A., Rao, P., Snively, B. M., Camann, D. E., Doran, A. M., . . . Jackson, D. S. (2004). Agricultural and residential pesticides in wipe samples from farmworker family residences in North Carolina and Virginia. *Environmental Health Perspectives, 112,* 382–387. http://dx.doi.org/10.1289/ehp.6554

Quandt, S. A., Arcury-Quandt, A. E., Lawlor, E. J., Carrillo, L., Marín, A. J., Grzywacz, J. G., & Arcury, T. A. (2013). 3-D jobs and health disparities: The health implications of Latino chicken catchers' working conditions. *American Journal of Industrial Medicine, 56,* 206–215. http://dx.doi.org/10.1002/ajim.22072

Quandt, S. A., Austin, C. K., Arcury, T. A., Summers, M., & Saavedra, R. (1999). Agricultural chemical training materials for farmworkers: Review and annotated bibliography. *Journal of Agromedicine, 6,* 3–24. http://dx.doi.org/10.1300/J096v06n01_02

Quandt, S. A., Grzywacz, J. G., Talton, J. W., Trejo, G., Tapia, J., D'Agostino, R. B., Jr., . . . Arcury, T. A. (2013). Evaluating the effectiveness of a lay health promoter-led, community-based participatory pesticide safety intervention with farmworker families. *Health Promotion Practice, 14,* 425–432. http://dx.doi.org/10.1177/1524839912459652

Richardson, S. (2005). Fatal work injuries among foreign-born Hispanic workers. *Monthly Labor Review, 128,* 63–67.

Robinson, E., Nguyen, H. T., Isom, S., Quandt, S. A., Grzywacz, J. G., Chen, H., & Arcury, T. A. (2011). Wages, wage violations, and pesticide safety experienced by migrant farmworkers in North Carolina. *New Solutions, 21,* 251–268. http://dx.doi.org/10.2190/NS.21.2.h

Robson, L. S., Stephenson, C. M., Schulte, P. A., Amick, B. C., III, Irvin, E. L., Eggerth, D. E., . . . Grubb, P. L. (2012). A systematic review of the effectiveness of occupational health and safety training. *Scandinavian Journal of Work, Environment & Health, 38,* 193–208. http://dx.doi.org/10.5271/sjweh.3259

Rubel, A. J., & Hass, M. R. (1996). Ethnomedicine. In C. F. Sargent & T. M. Johnson (Eds.), *Anthropology: Contemporary theory and method* (pp. 113–130). Medical Westport, CT: Praeger.

Salminen, S. (2011). Are immigrants at increased risk of occupational injury? A literature review. *The Ergonomics Open Journal, 4,* 125–130. http://dx.doi.org/10.2174/1875934301104010125

Singer, A. (2012). *Immigrant workers in the U.S. labor force*. Retrieved from http://www.brookings.edu/research/papers/2012/03/15-immigrant-workers-singer#2

Weller, S. C. (1983). New data on intracultural variability: The hot-cold concept of medicine and illness. *Human Organization, 42*, 249–257. http://dx.doi.org/10.17730/humo.42.3.v485x5npq050g748

Weller, S. C., Baer, R. D., Garcia de Alba Garcia, J., & Salcedo Rocha, A. L. (2008). Susto and nervios: Expressions for stress and depression. *Culture, Medicine and Psychiatry, 32*, 406–420. http://dx.doi.org/10.1007/s11013-008-9101-7

Worksafe. (2012). *Dying at work in California: The hidden stories behind the numbers.* Retrieved from http://www.worksafe.org/Dying_at_Work_in_California_2012.pdf

8

THE WORK, FAMILY, AND HEALTH NETWORK ORGANIZATIONAL INTERVENTION: CORE ELEMENTS AND CUSTOMIZATION FOR DIVERSE OCCUPATIONAL HEALTH CONTEXTS

ELLEN ERNST KOSSEK, BRAD WIPFLI, REBECCA THOMPSON,
KRISTA BROCKWOOD, AND MEMBERS OF THE WORK,
FAMILY, AND HEALTH NETWORK WRITING TEAM

Interest is growing in the occupational health field regarding workplace interventions targeting the work–family nexus and addressing the growing diversity in occupational health contexts. *Work–family conflict*, which refers to incompatible expectations between work and family role demands, is a growing occupational and public health concern that impacts employees, employers, and families (King et al., 2012). Growing numbers of employees of all cultural backgrounds, ages, and marital and family status are reporting rising levels of work, family, and other nonwork conflicts, and stress in

We would like to thank these other members of this paper's Work, Family, and Health Network Writing Team who contributed significantly to this chapter in some way. They are: Phyllis Moen, Leslie Hammer, Erin Kelly, Kent Anger, Ryan Olson, Cassandra Okechukwu, Lisa Burke, and Georgia Karuntzos. This research was conducted as part of the Work, Family, and Health WFHN, which is funded by a cooperative agreement through the National Institutes of Health and the Centers for Disease Control and Prevention: The Eunice Kennedy Shriver National Institute of Child Health and Human Development (Grant Nos. U01HD051217, U01HD051218, U01HD051256, U01HD051276), National Institute on Aging (Grant No. U01AG027669), Office of Behavioral and Social Sciences Research, and National

http://dx.doi.org/10.1037/0000021-009

industrialized (Bureau of Labor Statistics, 2011) and developing (Baral & Bhargava, 2011) countries. Despite a burgeoning literature, work–family research has had limited impact on occupational health and organizational change practice (Kossek, Baltes, & Matthews, 2011).

The goals of this chapter are to provide a literature review integrating work–family and occupational health perspectives and to discuss the content, design, and customization of the Work, Family, and Health Network (WFHN) intervention. The WFHN intervention was created for one of the largest work–family randomized field control studies in U.S. history. Up until the WFHN study, there had not been a large-scale, rigorous, randomized work–family and health intervention study targeting how work organization can foster work–family conflict in occupational settings in the United States. By *work organization*, we refer to "the way work processes are structured and managed, such as job design, scheduling, management, organizational characteristics, and policies and procedures" (DeJoy, Wilson, Vandenberg, McGrath-Higgins, & Griffin-Blake, 2010, p. 139). We define *work–family interventions* as comprehensive organizational interventions designed to foster a healthy psychosocial work environment by preventing stressors in the organization of work that can lead to work–family conflict (Kossek, Hammer, Kelly, & Moen, 2014).

The WFHN intervention represents a rare and innovative effort to proactively change organizational structure and culture to reduce (and ideally prevent) work–family conflict and improve employee and family health. From the perspective of integrating occupational health, diversity, and organizational change, we focus on the development of interventions that target change in the work environment to influence work–family and personal life conflicts as pathways to employee health and performance. We use the term *work–family* broadly to include work and nonwork roles (caregiving, exercise, personal time) for all employees, even those without families, as many researchers have suggested (Casper, Weltman, & Kwesiga, 2007). After a literature review on work–family interventions and occupational health, we describe the intervention and the training content developed to implement the intervention

Institute for Occupational Safety and Health (Grant No. U01OH008788). The contents of this publication are solely the responsibility of the authors and do not necessarily represent the official views of these institutes and offices. Special acknowledgement goes to Extramural Staff Science Collaborator, Rosalind Berkowitz King, PhD (NICHD) and Lynne Casper, PhD (now of the University of Southern California) for design of the original Workplace, Family, Health and Well-Being WFHN Initiative. Dr. W. Kent Anger of Oregon Health & Science University (OHSU) and NwETA developed the cTRAIN system, which was adapted for one intervention component used in this study. There could be financial benefit for Dr. Anger and for OHSU if this study and others like it produce useful results. The nature of this financial interest and the design of the study have been reviewed by the OHSU Research Integrity Office to ensure the results of this research are not affected by the financial interest (for more information, contact 503-494-7887).

(see Table 8.1). We provide examples from field sites in two industries (information technology [IT] and health care) to show how the intervention was adapted across two diverse organizational contexts that have systemic variation in workforce stressors. A key point of this chapter is that the work context and the nature of the supervision may need to be adapted to support diversity in occupational health contexts. Most interventions target the individual, but here we discuss how to change the structure of the higher level work organization as a way to improve occupational health contexts for women and minorities.

LITERATURE REVIEW

In the literature review, we first briefly discuss links between work–family conflict and occupational health to provide context. We then discuss the need to customize interventions to address diversity in occupational health contexts.

Work–Family Interventions: Moving Toward Occupational Health Perspectives

The literature on creating healthy workplaces is largely in the areas of job stress and occupational health (Tetrick, Quick, & Gilmore, 2012) and generally does not directly address work–family conflict (Bambra, Egan, Thomas, Petticrew, & Whitehead, 2007). Work–family conflict, also known as work-to-family and family-to-work interference, remains one of the most studied concepts in the work–family field (Greenhaus & Allen, 2011) and has been consistently linked to adverse mental, behavioral, and physical health outcomes (Greenhaus & Allen, 2011; Hammer & Sauter, 2013; Hammer & Zimmerman, 2011). Further research has suggested that organizational interventions focusing on job stress and improving relationships between work, family, and other nonwork roles could be considerably improved (e.g., Kelly et al., 2008; LaMontagne, Keegel, Louie, Ostry, & Landsbergis, 2007; Parkes & Sparkes, 1998), and intervention research needs to be more deliberate to foster organizational and member learning in design and implementation (National Institute for Occupational Safety and Health [NIOSH], 2002).

Although not always evaluated as "interventions," reviews (Kossek, 2006; Kossek & Distelberg, 2009) have identified a three-legged stool of work–family initiatives. This includes (a) informal support for work and family roles arising from supervisors, coworkers, and the organization's work–family culture and norms (Allen, 2001; Kossek, Pichler, Bodner, & Hammer, 2011); (b) formal work–family support, such as the flexibility to allow for

TABLE 8.1

A Listing of STAR Intervention Components, Audience, and Timing for Organizations
in Information Technology and Health Care Industries

Step	Audience	Stage	Participatory session type	Manager training and employee outside activities	Length of time
			STAR in the IT Industry (Tomo)		
1	Managers	I. Preparing for change	Leadership education		2 hours
2a	Managers			Computer-based training	1 hour
2b	Managers			Supportive behavior tracking, 1st round	2 weeks
3	All employees	II. Setting change in motion	Kickoff		2 hours
4a	All employees		Sludge		2 hours
4b	All employees				2 weeks
5a	All employees		Culture clinic	Sludge poll	2 hours
5b	All employees				2 weeks
6a	Managers		Managers only	"Do something scary"	2 hours
6b	Managers			Supportive behavior tracking, 2nd round	2 weeks
7	All employees	III. Sustaining the change	Forum		1.5 hours
			TOTALS		
			Managers		12.5 hours
			Employees		7.5 hours

STAR in the long-term care industry (Leef)

	Phase	Participants	Activity	Duration
	I. Preparing for change			
1		Managers	STAR readiness	1 hour
2		Steering team	Steering team #1 overview	30 minutes
3		Managers	Management team induction/ sludge	2.5 hours
4a		All employees	Team induction/sludge	1.5 hours
4b		All employees		2 weeks
5a		Managers	Sludge tracking	1 hour
5b		Managers	Computer-based training	2 weeks
	II. Setting change in motion		Supportive behavior tracking, 1st round	
6		Steering team	Steering team #2 review	.5 hour
7		Managers	Manager Culture clinic	2.5 hours
8a		All employees	Culture clinic	1.5 hours
8b		All employees		2 weeks
9		Managers		2 weeks
	III. Sustaining the change		"Do something different"	
			Supportive behavior tracking, 2nd round	
10		All employees	Forum	1 hour
11		Steering team	STAR moving forward	1.5 hours
			TOTALS	
			Managers	9.5 hours
			Employees	4 hours
			Steering team (nonmanagers)	6.5 hours

Note. STAR = Start. Transform. Achieve. Result.

employee control of work time, load, or place (e.g., flextime, part-time work, teleworking; see Kossek & Michel, 2011, for a review) or access to care-giving resources (on-site and near-site child care, information and referral, financial subsidies; Butts, Casper, & Yang, 2013); and (c) links to formal HR job design, such as empowering employees to control job tasks and processes to ensure they do not negatively influence one's ability to meet nonwork demands (Perlow, 2012).

Relatively little research has integrated any of these components in interventions to prevent work–family conflicts emanating from the work organization. Yet Kossek, Lewis, and Hammer (2010) argued that for work–life initiatives to foster organizational change, they must not only enhance the availability of formal organizational policies and structures but also foster informal cultural support of positive work–family relationships for employees. Unfortunately, studies are unclear on what is meant by a work–family intervention, its theoretical underpinnings, and how to design and evaluate these interventions.

Work–Family Intervention Change Targets

There are three key elements to target to create an overall healthy workplace: the workplace itself, the individual, and the interface between the work and family roles (Quick, 1999). Although there is a growing research literature on the importance of improving employee perceptions of organizational support for work and family (Allen, 2001; Kossek, Pichler, et al., 2011), there has been a shortage of work–family interventions and almost no evaluation research studies using randomized controlled or rigorous quasi-experimental designs examining the roles of the key elements of occupational health interventions (Casper, Eby, Bordeaux, Lockwood, & Lambert, 2007; Kelly et al., 2008; Tompa, Dolinschi, de Oliveira, & Irvin, 2009; for an exception, see Hammer, Kossek, Anger, Bodner, & Zimmerman, 2011). Organizational work–family interventions to improve occupational health are key to creating a healthy workplace. Examples of targets for occupational health interventions would be to give employees greater control over work schedules (e.g., Kelly, Moen, & Tranby, 2011), to train managers and coworkers to provide employees with support for family and personal life (e.g., Hammer et al., 2011), and to redesign jobs and work processes so that employees can focus on results and tasks that are the most critical for performance.

Customizing Work–Family Interventions Across Diverse Occupational Health Contexts

Customization of the intervention design to address unique workforce demands is a key principle that has been used in the occupational health field but has been underused in the work–family field (Kossek et al., 2014). Specifically, interventions can be tailored to the organization to improve health and well-being outcomes of employees while meeting the needs of the employer. Intervention customization can take many forms, from modified content for various job types, to enhanced delivery techniques using new technology (e.g., web-based methods), to targeting problem areas that need additional attention or resources. For example, Ard and colleagues (Ard et al., 2010) examined a culturally enhanced behavioral weight loss intervention for an organization consisting predominantly of African American women, arguing that this group is disproportionately at risk for obesity. The authors contended that tailoring the dietary intervention program allowed for meaningful weight loss results, reducing disparities in obesity for a traditionally high-risk population (Ard et al., 2010).

Customization may be particularly salient for organizations with diverse employee populations across various job domains and requirements. For example, there has been a historical underrepresentation of workers of color in professional job domains, as well as an overrepresentation in blue-collar and service jobs (Bowman, 2005; Murray, 2003). Similarly, there is an overrepresentation of women in lower level clerical and service jobs, and more single-parent workers with children living in poverty are likely to be women (Kossek & Distelberg, 2009). Different job domains are typically susceptible to occupational health risks at disproportionate rates (Ard et al., 2010; Gany, Novo, Dobslaw, & Leng, 2014; Marín et al., 2009). As Presser (2003) explained, non-Hispanic African Americans (compared with Hispanics or Whites) are more likely to be employed in jobs with nonstandard work hours, lower levels of pay, and increased associated health risks. Individuals working in these jobs are likely to be at greater risk of exposure to work–family and work–life related health hazards than individuals in other jobs, which may be overrepresented in occupational health research.

Yet it is important to not oversimplify within-group demographics similarly. For example, workers of color or women in clerical jobs are not necessarily at higher risk for all negative occupational health and well-being outcomes (Murray, 2003; Shelton, Danes, & Eisenman, 2008). Health disparities are frequently discussed as issues of racial or ethnic inequalities. However, there is diversity across socioeconomic groups as well as in the morbidity and mortality rates for minority individuals (Stoddard et al., 2005). Jackson and Stewart (2003) explained that much of the occupational health research for Black individuals has focused on the severely disadvantaged; however, researchers should examine the risks associated with all socioeconomic levels (e.g., the middle class). Depending on the job and workplace culture and context, individuals from different racial/ethnic and gender groups experience differential exposure to workplace stressors (Bergman, Palmieri, Drasgow, & Ormerod, 2012).

Yet occupational health research has done little to identify the role that workplace interventions have on mitigating these negative outcomes for specific subgroups (Park et al., 2004). It is critical for research examining workplace interventions designed to improve employee health and well-being to consider both the individual and job domains when designing intervention content. This is particularly of concern for groups such as single parents (mostly female or ethnic minorities and immigrants) who may face added workplace stress because of racial and ethnic discrimination and/or language barriers (Deitch et al., 2003; Jamieson & O'Mara, 1991; Jones, 1993; Sparks, Faragher, & Cooper, 2001). Because women still handle more of the work–family caregiving demands than men in dual-career families and are less likely to have a stay-at-home caregiver, women in dual careers, or dual-earner families, may face more stressors on average than men in similar jobs (Kossek & Distelberg, 2009). Similarly, many individuals responsible for caregiving may have blue-collar or service industry jobs rather than professional jobs because of the career penalties or reduced opportunities often associated with caregiving demands (Wyatt-Nichol, 2009). As minority mothers are particularly likely to work while providing caregiving for young children, understanding how occupational interventions are designed to improve health and well-being for this specific cross-section is particularly appropriate (Odom, Vernon-Feagans, & Crouter, 2013). However, much of the research examining occupational health interventions target professional jobs that already offer a great deal of flexibility and may provide additional benefits such as child care (Kossek et al., 2014), as these are more most suitable for intervention design and implementation.

Most work–family interventions have not been customized on the basis of individual, demographic, or job-demand differences (Kossek et al., 2014). Many work–family interventions target whole job domains (e.g., professional jobs), rather than identifying multiple solutions to various types of jobs (e.g., blue collar, service), and rarely examine gender or racioethnic and family demography and systematic trends in the workforce and job populations. Because of the one-size-fits-all approach to many work–family interventions, this research has been criticized for the lack of consideration of individual and contextual concerns (Martins, Eddleston, & Veiga, 2002). Because of the complexity of problems facing diverse populations in organizations, researchers examining occupational health initiatives cite the need for training and interventions to combat the unique issues facing women, minorities, and culturally diverse populations within the workforce (Lillie-Blanton & Laveist, 1996; Murray, 2003; Sparks et al., 2001).

In a review of the effectiveness of training programs for the protection of workers, NIOSH identified demographic factors such as ethnicity as key moderators in the relationship between training and outcomes (Robson et al., 2010). Gender is also a critical moderator. The review authors noted that although it sometimes may not be politically and practically feasible to include these factors in an organizational study examining a training intervention's effectiveness, particularly if confidentiality and involvement by women and minorities may be negatively affected, for work–family interventions these factors may be increasingly important. Although some interventions have been designed to target specific groups (e.g., blue-collar female employees; Campbell et al., 2002), we could not identify any occupational health interventions addressing the work–family nexus that were specifically customized for unique minority, gender, and job groups while maintaining fidelity for all groups within an organization. Our main focus in this study was on diversity in job groups between the demands of being an IT worker (with more virtual work) and those of being a direct health care worker (with more patient face time). As we discuss next, these job groups had systematic differences in covariation with racioethnic, gender, and income groups.

THE WORK, FAMILY, & HEALTH NETWORK INTERVENTION

The Work, Family, & Health Network (WFHN)[1] is a national research collaboration of scholars with backgrounds in public health, epidemiology, family studies, organizational psychology, occupational health psychology, sociology, economics, and many other fields. The WFHN is made up of a team of scientists from seven institutions (Bray et al., 2013; King et al., 2012; Kossek et al., 2014).

To help advance future work–family and health intervention research and practice, the WFHN integrated the occupational health job stress intervention and work–family literatures to create and evaluate best practices, such as piloting intervention components, targeting multiple levels of change (e.g., supervision, structure of work), and identifying key ingredients in the organization of work that need to change to reduce work–family conflict (Kossek et al., 2014).

In the piloting phase, the WFHN developed and tested key components of the intervention via separate studies on different core elements of two interventions examined in two contexts: (a) training of supervisors to engage in family supportive behaviors for hourly workers in a grocery store setting (Hammer et al., 2011; Hammer, Kossek, Yragui, Bodner, & Hanson, 2009) and (b) participative cultural training of workers and managers to change norms to increase employee schedule control (Kelly & Moen, 2007; Kelly et al., 2011), thus moving toward a results orientation to eliminate low value work for office workers in a white-collar corporate headquarters. These interventions have

---

[1]A toolkit and more detailed information can be found at a public website: http://projects.iq.harvard.edu/wfhn/toolkits-achieve-workplace-change.

also been referred to as FSSB (Family Supportive Supervisor Behaviors) and ROWE (Results Only Work Environment), respectively.

The research teams, with the assistance of a consulting group, CultureRx, that originally developed ROWE at Best Buy, integrated the FSSB and ROWE elements into a single intervention, ensuring that essential elements were complemented by and supported each other. This new intervention was called STAR (Start. Transform. Achieve. Results).[2] Figure 8.1 shows the different time periods during which data were collected pre- and postdelivery of the STAR intervention to evaluate its effects in a group randomized control study. In the following section, we provide an overview of the STAR intervention and its customization.

Organizational Contexts

During Phase II, the WFHN chose to investigate this intervention in two different industries with highly contrasting occupational demands and work organization. One industry was an IT firm (called *Tomo*), and the other was a for-profit extended-care organization (called *Leef*).[3] Each industry had unique client and employee concerns and organizational demographics. Tomo had relatively higher professional status and more skilled, salaried employees with college and often advanced degrees. Leef had overall relatively lower status, with less-skilled employees paid by the hour. Organizational job groups and demographic population groups often covary in systematic ways that shape work–family and job demands, work schedules, and face-time demands, with implications for intervention design. The health care employees not only had lower socioeconomic income and education levels, but they also had to do the majority of their job tasks face-to-face in 24–7 continuous service industries. In contrast, employees at Tomo could often do at least part of their jobs virtually.

The racioethnic minorities systematically differed between Tomo and Leef in ways that often correlated with job groups. At Tomo, a majority of the racioethnic minorities (many highly educated, foreign born workers) tended to be in organizational job groups that were higher status, such as managers, directors, and team leaders, whereas the racioethnic minorities at Leef (also many foreign born workers, with a majority without advanced degrees or college) tended to be in lower status job groups, such as nursing assistants.

Another systematic difference in occupational context involves gender. The nursing home staff in the study was about 90% female, whereas the gender profile of the employees in the IT company was more balanced (close to 40% female workers), with a higher percentage of male managers.

---

[2]Persons interested in learning more about WFHN should go to http://projects.iq.harvard.edu/wfhn.
[3]Tomo and Leef are pseudonyms to protect confidentiality.

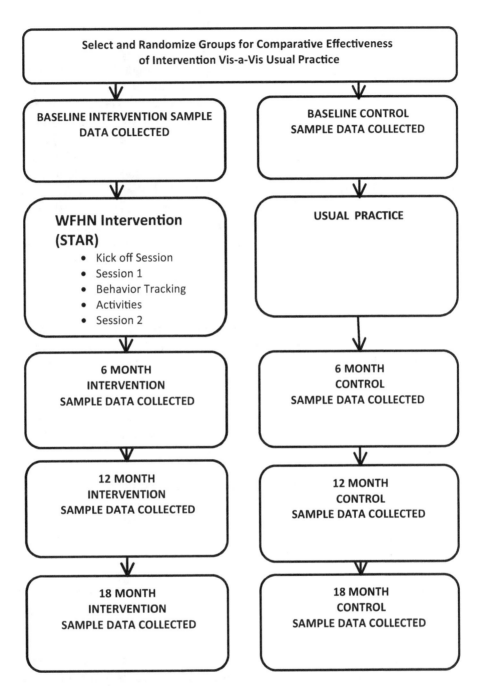

Figure 8.1. *Study design and example of timing for collection of evaluation data in a randomized control field design.* WFHN = Work, Family, & Health Network; STAR = Start. Transform. Achieve. Results. Adapted from "Changing Work and Work-Family Conflict: Evidence From the Work, Family, and Health Network," by E. L. Kelly, P. Moen, J. M. Oakes, W. Fan, C. Okechuckwu, K. D. Davis, . . . L. Casper, 2014, *American Sociological Review, 79*, p. 496. Copyright 2014 by Sage Publications. Adapted with permission.

Intervention Targets

The STAR intervention had three primary targets. The first target focus was on increasing support and understanding at the workplace for work–family issues from supervisors (FSSBs) and coworkers alike. FSSBs are supervisor actions that validate and facilitate employees' fulfillment of family roles. FSSBs comprise four dimensions or types of behaviors: (a) emotional support, (b) instrumental support, (c) role-modeling behaviors, and (d) creative work–family management or actions managers implement to facilitate employees' abilities to be successful in both their work and family roles (Hammer, Kossek, Bodner, & Crain, 2013; Hammer et al., 2009). Also included was training on performance support, such as ensuring employees clearly understand work objectives and had the resources to achieve these objectives. Although the main focus of social support training was supervisors, group activities were also conducted to promote coworker support for family and performance.

The second target focus was on organization-level change in employees' schedule control, whereby control over when, where, and how many hours employees worked systematically increased (Kelly & Moen, 2007). Schedule control is a job element that complements job control (Kossek, Lautsch, & Eaton, 2006), allowing an employee to control a key aspect of his or her work to accommodate both work and family roles. This facilitated change in the third target, job redesign that focused on results (e.g., patient outcomes or products), rather than on a time-focused orientation (e.g., hours worked), and reduced unproductive face time and low-value work.

Overall, unlike most work–family studies, which view work–family conflict as an individual employee problem targeting only workers in need, STAR focused on whole-systems change in the organization of work to reduce work–family conflict, targeting an entire worksite or work unit. Although the intervention had the same goals in both organizational sites, the process and content were adapted (customized) for each industry.

Occupational Job Context Customization for Core Change Targets

The research team developed consensus that the intervention design was to have the same principles across the two industries and work-unit contexts even as it needed to be adapted to local needs and customized to each industry. Given the diversity in work and family and occupational health contexts, a key challenge the research team faced was whether and how to customize the design of intervention components that had been developed in unique contexts. For example, how could an intervention focused on schedule control and implemented with white-collar corporate professionals (Moen, Lam, Ammons,

& Kelly, 2013) be adapted to hourly workers in a 24–7 patient-centered work system? Or how should intervention components developed largely in an hourly workforce setting (Hammer et al., 2011) be adapted to a professional IT context? What does schedule control look like for lower level, hourly workers with place-bound jobs (Haley-Lock, 2011), compared with IT workers who have high connectivity to work and family via cell phones and the Internet? The intervention in each industry followed similar goals (increase support, control, and job design for results orientation), yet was changed to modify content, timing, and sequencing to adapt common goals and processes to each. Next, we discuss the intervention and identify six areas that researchers and practitioners should attend to in customizing work–family interventions to address diversity in occupational health contexts. They are training content, delivery, cultural framing supplemental content, dosage/exposure time, workforce inclusion decisions, and managing workforce diversity.

INTERVENTION DESIGN: CORE CONTENT AND ADAPTATION

As Table 8.1 shows, the intervention that was rolled out in each industry included the common components of (a) participatory face-to-face sessions with staff and managers, (b) participatory face-to-face sessions for only managers and supervisors, (c) on-the-job activities for all employees to reinforce learning from sessions, and (d) manager-only computer-based training and behavioral self-monitoring. To maintain fidelity, the researchers and consultants worked together to prepare a facilitators' guide for participatory sessions using semistructured scripts as well as on the job application activities. These sessions encouraged supervisors and employees (either jointly or separately) to reflect on current practices and identify strategies to increase supervisor support and work-time control, leading to reduced work–family conflict while continuing to meet or exceed business goals. A supervisor computer-based training and a self-monitoring activity were implemented to teach ways of supporting work and family and to ensure transfer of family and performance support to on the job behaviors.

Formative Research Stage

To customize the intervention for each industry, we conducted focus groups and interviews in each industry with employees, supervisors, and other key personnel (i.e., scheduler in extended care) to determine the major issues likely to surface during the intervention and to be able to create relevant examples. We found that at Tomo, telecommuting was officially "not allowed" but some managers allowed certain employees to work from home, and this practice was very unevenly applied. It is interesting, though, that many workers were expected to take work calls at home and often very late at night because they were from workers in India and other countries in opposite time zones from the United States.

At Leef, we conducted our formative research in two very different care facilities, one urban and one rural. In both, we found that a major issue, not surprisingly, was scheduling and coverage for workers who called in sick. In the urban setting, the care staff was very culturally diverse and included many recent immigrants, whereas the staff in the rural center was almost exclusively White. This difference influenced scheduling in many ways, including when people most wanted to take time off (e.g., hunting season) and for how long. Those who were immigrants often wanted to be able to take all their time off at once because they frequently traveled long distances to visit family. This was counter to corporate policy and caused some friction for these employees. Also, the concept of "work and family" was often not something many immigrants had ever really thought about explicitly, and the links between work and how that could affect one's health were also often not familiar.

Intervention Design and Stages

The STAR intervention had a dual agenda (Bailyn, 2011) that focused on redesigned work to jointly reduce work–family conflict and enhance work performance. STAR was participatory in enactment, yet required top management support for the change. It was delivered during work time as part of normal business practice with the expectation that all employees and managers in the unit or site would be involved. Management support was also necessary for the randomized, experimental nature of the intervention delivery and the parallel (but separate) longitudinal study evaluating it (see also Kossek et al., 2014).

Because the work environments at Tomo and Best Buy, where ROWE was initially developed, were very similar (e.g., white collar, computer-based work), STAR needed only a small amount of customization relative to Leef. Next, we present the STAR process for Tomo, then how it was adapted for Leef, focusing especially on cultural and diversity issues.

Intervention Process Flow

As Table 8.1 shows, STAR is a change process involving participatory sessions, some with just managers and supervisors and others with everyone (i.e., employees and supervisors together). The first sessions orient the participants to the goals and the change process. At the beginning of the STAR rollout, supervisors and managers are exposed to the STAR philosophy and business case and are provided with an overview of the program, its key elements, and an open forum to ask questions, similar to methods described in Kelly et al. (2011).

The next set of sessions focuses on changing how people think about work hours and how work is done. This is accomplished partly by highlighting the negative toxic language in a workplace where qualitative judgments are made on how employees spend their work time, which consequently may divide employees or reinforce and maintain established views about work time rather than create new ones. After the completion of the session, workers are instructed to track the number of times they find themselves making a judgment about a coworker regarding when the person arrives or leaves.

At the next meeting, workers brainstormed possible changes at the workplace that would empower workers and facilitate a mind-set from being *time* oriented to being *results* oriented. For example, instead of thinking about performance as being measured by face time spent at work, workers were encouraged to rethink about performance in terms of completing tasks and accomplishing results. Employees and supervisors developed and implemented their own solutions, rather than having them dictated from consultants or top management. Although the focus was often on work scheduling, participants were also encouraged to think about improvement in work processes as well. To help assist with this new way of thinking, everyone was instructed to do an activity between sessions that they wouldn't normally do, such as working from home in the morning without asking permission for Tomo, or finding coverage for a few hours to attend a child's recital during normally scheduled work hours for Leef. Finally, after the completion of this activity, workers came back together to discuss what they tried, what worked, and what didn't, and to problem solve and come up with a plan for keeping the change momentum moving into the future, creating a real culture change within the organization.

Between training sessions, employees completed group-level behavioral self-monitoring activities to transfer training principles into workplace behavior change. The target behaviors for group-level self-monitoring were centered on reducing *sludge* (i.e., value judgments about coworker behaviors) and increasing *doing something different* (e.g., scheduling a personal errand during typical work hours). In both of these self-monitoring activities, group-level feedback was visible to all participating employees.

Additional Training for Supervisors

In addition to the participatory sessions, managers also had computer-based-training and behavioral self-monitoring or tracking, largely derived from FSSB (Hammer et al., 2011). It was designed to educate and motivate supervisors to increase their support for employees' family and personal lives and job performance, and to provide technology to support those changes. Hammer and colleagues (2011) found that employees with higher family-to-work conflict were most likely to benefit from having supervisors trained in FSSB. These employees had significantly more favorable job satisfaction, physical health reports, and lower turnover intentions. Supervisors first completed computer-based training and self-monitoring of supportive behaviors, followed by a second round of self-monitoring near the end of the intervention process, similar to Hammer et al. (2011). By tracking specific supportive behaviors, supervisors are more likely to transfer what they learned during the computer training into actual practice.

The training content gave examples of supervisor strategies for providing more support for employees' family and personal lives and to facilitate employees' control over work time. These included expressing appropriate and genuine interest in employees' lives outside of work, sharing accurate information on the company's work–life policies and benefits, modeling work–life balance in their own work patterns, establishing standard procedures for managing scheduling conflicts in a fair and transparent manner, posting schedules (Leef only) as far in advance as is feasible, and facilitating cross-training that allows for easier management of schedules. Examples of supervisor-support strategies for maximizing employees' work-time control while still meeting business goals were also provided. These included self-scheduling systems; establishing standard procedures for requesting schedule changes or trading shifts (Leef only); cross-training to increase backups within the work group; standard procedures for requesting an experienced floater/utility person (Leef only); designated "no-meeting hours" policies (Tomo only); and a shift to laptop computers, when feasible, to allow more work to be done remotely (Tomo only).

Immediately after the training, supervisors were asked to begin the first of two trials of behavior tracking using iPod devices. Each trial with the iPods lasted for 2 weeks and involved goal setting, daily self-monitoring of family- and performance-supportive behaviors, and individual and group feedback loops. The tracking process was informed by current best practices in self-monitoring methods (Korotitsch & Nelson-Gray, 1999; Olson & Winchester, 2008). Examples of the practices incorporated included goal setting, alarm cues for self-monitoring, high-frequency automated individual feedback, and normative group feedback provided at follow-up. All feedback loops highlighted gaps between actual supportive behaviors and personal goals. On the basis of the social-cognitive theory of self-regulation and behavioral motivational theory, feedback about "performance gaps" is expected to function as a motivational stimulus (or motivating operation) for supportive supervisory behaviors (Bandura, 1991; Laraway, Snycerski, Michael, & Poling, 2003).

Customization at Leef

Many of the adaptations made to STAR for Leef were done for practical reasons, as it was very difficult to take too many nurses and nurse assistants off the floor to attend sessions. For example, the essential content of two sessions was combined into one, ensuring the core elements were still present. Another critical customization for Leef involved creating steering teams that received training and were charged with communicating the information about STAR to employees in their units and championing the culture change. These teams were designed to have representation across all levels, including the facility director down to nurses' aides, and a racial and ethnic composition reflective of the facility as well.

There was also a follow-up session at the end for the steering team facilitated by the Leef Center administrator. The focus was on identifying challenges, discussing solutions, and developing and implementing an action plan to carry them forward. Table 8.2 shows specific examples of how training content from Tomo, the white-collar IT workforce, was customized at Leef, the nursing and nursing assistant workforce, in regards to the three main intervention change targets: (a) increasing social support for work, family, and performance; (b) increasing control over work and work time; and (c) improving the design of work conditions to become results oriented and reduce face time. As the table shows, these concepts can be carefully adapted to a nursing home setting that has 24–7 scheduling with many federal and state patient regulations (for a discussion of the scheduling and work–life challenges of the low-income workforce, see Kossek, Pisczcek, McAlpine, Hammer, & Burke, 2016).

ADAPTIVE CHANGE: OTHER ISSUES TO CONSIDER IN INTERVENTION CUSTOMIZATION TO INDUSTRY OCCUPATIONAL CONTEXTS

Besides customizing training content, the intervention was customized to each industry to address differences in expected supervisor behaviors and delivery methods. For example, at Tomo some employees teleworked off-site regularly, and most office jobs did not require 24–7 regulations for patient coverage. Consequently, training delivery at Tomo could be scheduled in a webinar and conference room. In contrast, at Leef, just getting workers off the floor to go to the training was a major challenge, as round-the-clock patient coverage had to be maintained so not everyone could be trained at the same time. Not all night-shift or weekend workers were included. Table 8.2 gives another example of how many core training concepts had to be adapted at Leef; for example, supervisor family support for time off had to involve consideration

TABLE 8.2

Examples of Customization at Leef

Key component of intervention	Need for customization	Resulting issue	Delivery adaptation
Increase social support for work–family interface and performance (supervisors and coworkers).	In the caregiving environment, with strict regulations on number of employees per resident, there is less schedule flexibility, as well as less control over work hours. Managers can be supportive of scheduling flexibility, but for one person to take time off, someone else has to provide coverage.	Importance of peer support, because of the nature of the work and necessity of shift swapping/other coverage strategies to achieve some scheduling flexibility. When an employee takes time off or calls out, someone else needs to cover that shift. Although a manager may be the one supporting the employee's scheduling needs, another person will be affected as well.	Inclusion of a "steering team" as an important part of the STAR rollout in the Leef workplace. This is a group of managers and peer leaders, who meet to understand STAR and the guidelines of the initiative, and are expected to "champion" the initiative. STAR in this environment was especially dependent on employee involvement and peer support.
Increase control over work and work time.	Providing care to residents by definition requires working on-site; coverage is necessary 24/7, and the number of each type of direct care staff is highly regulated by the state in which the facility is located.	The idea of changing where work is done is less relevant in this environment. As a result, how work is done is the focus of the change initiatives—work practices and also how employees interact with managers and with other employees.	More emphasis on process issues and working more productively and efficiently together, because working "off-site" is not relevant for most employees at Leef. STAR participants were enthusiastic about the idea of eradicating "sludge"—negative toxic language in the workplace. The reduction in sludge can lead to better teamwork and a more positive work environment.

Improve design of work conditions and support cultural processes to become results oriented and reduce low-value work and unnecessary face time.

Because of state regulations, there is less opportunity to eliminate redundant documentation and strict guidelines regarding the number of employees required to be working at any time.

Compared with a corporate work environment, many of the lower wage workers in Leef were less educated, some spoke English as their second language, and many were not as technologically savvy.

It was necessary to empower employees to work differently within a regulated structured environment. The STAR rollout included handouts with key ideas to reinforce learning. Also, the employee activities (Sludge Eradication and Do Something Different/Do Something Supportive) were done on posters with stamps rather than online through a website.

It was especially important to encourage employees to think creatively. Leef corporate required the inclusion of guidelines for employee ideas—all changes had to be "safe," "legal," and "cost neutral." These words were repeated in sessions and on handouts. This attempted to address concerns around employees leaving the facility short staffed.

When considering work inefficiencies, the lack of access to computers and less knowledge of technology by some employees needed to be factored in.

Note. STAR = Start. Transform. Achieve. Results.

of worker replacement coverage for workers with jobs involving direct patient care. The results-oriented work training materials developed at Tomo had to be adapted for Leef in supplemental materials to use language that took into account patient safety needs regarding care quality and to account for unique workforce diversity and literacy levels of workers, some of whom were recent immigrants from Caribbean and other countries.

Customizing Supervisor Behaviors in Computer-Based Training and Self-Monitoring

The supervisors component of the intervention was customized for Leef in two ways: (a) supportive supervisory behaviors unique to the Leef work environment were identified through formative research, focus groups, and interviews with supervisors and workers, and then incorporated into training and tracking; and (b) the beta version of the iPod application for tracking was tested with supervisors and modified for usability based on that feedback.

As an example of differential customization for the Leef and Tomo environments, consider the family supportive supervisory behavior construct of functional or instrumental support. For Leef, this category was renamed *daily problem solving*. Example behaviors (derived from formative research described previously) were different within the category as well; for Leef, an example was "Posting work schedules on time so employees can plan for family and personal commitments," whereas at Tomo, the example was "Telling employees about existing company resources or policies that support family or personal needs." Another example of a Leef-specific supportive behavior in the *creative management* category was "rewarding or praising employees who solve problems or cover work shifts/tasks when a coworker has an urgent/emergency family or personal issue," whereas the corresponding Tomo example was "encouraging employees to experiment with new ways of doing work that benefit their family or personal lives." The Leef versions of these supportive behavior examples were irrelevant at Tomo because work shifts were not part of the environment.

Customizing Employee Behavioral Self-Monitoring

Because employees at Tomo are frequently on computers, both group-level behavioral self-monitoring activities were conducted via a daily e-mail poll. For the activities (Sludge Eradication and Do Something Different), each of which was 2 weeks in duration, employees received a daily e-mail with a link to answer yes/no poll and qualitative questions. Group-level feedback was displayed immediately after employees submitted the survey. However, computer and e-mail access among employees was much less frequent in Leef. We customized the activities by printing large posters and posting them in employee break rooms. We attached rubber stamps to the posters and asked employees to stamp the poster whenever they completed one of the activities. This method still allowed group-level feedback in a way that fit how work was organized at Leef.

Delivery Challenges: Identifying Appropriate Work Unit and Scheduling

The organization of the collective for intervention delivery, defined as the *work unit*, were teams of employees at Tomo who reported to the same manager. At Leef, the work unit was the entire health care facility. The main training delivery issue at Tomo was adaptation to a virtual workplace and linking training to formal policies. Remote workers had teleconference access to participatory sessions. Web-based polls and forums were scheduled as repeating Outlook events to provide easy employee access to self-monitoring activities. Remote managers were given access to the computer-based training.

The biggest delivery issues at Leef were organizing and scheduling training delivery, given the time-sensitive nature of the health care work environment. It was challenging to set training schedules in advance, socialize workers to get off the floor for training, and ensure coverage of patients during training without increasing overtime work and pay. Group-based, work–family intervention training of this scale had never been tried in this context. To ensure that the intervention was widely delivered at Leef facilities, change advocates from all departments and all levels were identified and were responsible for bringing employees up to date if they missed sessions, and a steering team was implemented with members that included managers from different departments and frontline employees.

Although the steering team format helped with communication when sessions were cancelled for bad weather or if some workers were unable to attend face-to-face training sessions, it also reflected the somewhat less bottom-up organic nature of the intervention design that was necessary at Leef. Because long-term care facilities are often highly hierarchical in structure and top-down in decision making, the steering team was developed as a way to allow for representative participation in leadership roles for workers from lower level employee groups.

Supplemental Training Materials to Bolster Intervention in Context

In both industries, some employees were not able to attend the facilitated sessions because of absences or because they were not scheduled to work during the times that sessions were offered. This was particularly true of night-shift workers at Leef or those who worked a weekend or 3-day schedule that did not overlap with the training sessions. Handouts with key messages were shared by the steering team members at Leef and also left with the administrator for dissemination. This was also thought to be important for those workers, particularly for some of the immigrants who may have had difficulty understanding the oral presentations during sessions. The research team ensured that the language was easily understandably by nonnative English speakers (e.g., avoiding colloquialisms) and provided pictures of diverse peoples.

Dosage Challenges: Paid Time and Training Trade-Off and Inclusion Design Issues

A key issue in both industries was determining how to conduct delivery during paid work time, as the intervention training and activities took employees away from their work. At Leef, the paid-time customization involved agreement with management that the training would not lead to overtime, or if overtime did occur it would be allowed to support training participation. At Tomo, management came up with a special billable code that employees used to track training time. This adaptation resulted in slightly less time spent in formal intervention training at Leef than at Tomo. The research team did not want intervention training to increase work intensification by causing Leef employees to have less time available to complete the same amount of work.

Cultural Framing: Language, Symbols, Visioning

For all training components, in each industry, care was taken to include examples, language, and pictures appropriate for the work context. For example, although there was a high degree of overlap in target supportive behaviors across industries, customization required different target behavior examples in certain behavior categories. In the health care industry, an example of instrumental support was "posting work schedules on time so employees can plan for family and personal commitments." In the IT industry, where shift work and schedules are less relevant to workers, an example of instrumental support was "adjusting or facilitating work assignments to support employees' family or personal needs."

Similarly, language in the facilitated sessions was changed. For example, at Tomo, a visioning principle used in the orientation session was "Every day feels like Saturday." At Leef, because some hourly workers work on Saturday, the guidepost was changed to "Every day feels like my day off." Examples that were used at Tomo, such as taking several hours off to get a pedicure during the workday, were dropped at Leef because workers have less discretionary income and schedule flexibility. Examples of leaving for long periods during the workday were also less effective for workers who had long commutes or who were less able to extend or restructure their 8-hour shift.

In addition to the guidepost vision statement adjustment previously mentioned, other statements used at Tomo were eliminated at Leef because they did not fit with the hourly wage workforce. This change in vision was compensated by innovation in the change tenets of the intervention. For example, a Leef-only guidepost statement was created that employees were able to work in the way that was best for them as long as it was "safe, legal and cost neutral." These principles helped set worksite boundaries about how far culture change and work redesign could go. Overall, slightly more experimentation, trial and error, and customization were needed in the lower wage workers' context, an overbounded system (Alderfer, 2011) with many occupational health challenges (Murray, 2003).

Exploring Intervention Workforce Diversity Considerations

Our intervention provided opportunities to challenge some assumptions about work–life issues and increase sensitivity to the differing needs of various job groups. This customization resulted in a greater sensitivity and awareness of the nuances of work life specific not only to occupational contexts but also to the exploration of racioethnic minority concerns. For example, at some of the Leef facilities, direct care staff who had immigrated from other countries requested more days off when they took vacation for holidays with family in their native country. Yet Leef had strict rules and policies regarding the number of vacation days that could be taken at one time, so these individuals faced situations in which they had many hours of travel and expensive plane tickets, and they were asking to take more time off than was permitted. The STAR sessions encouraged employees to take more control over their work time. In this example, STAR may have encouraged an employee to find his or her own coverage for the extra days needed, whereas previously the employee might have believed quitting was the only way to take an extended period of time off. This shift in how one approaches a work–life conflict may seem relatively minor; however, it is a highly meaningful and symbolic change to employees who ordinarily may not feel much control over their schedule. We also conducted exploratory descriptive analyses to determine how future intervention effectiveness research might consider the distinctive racial and ethnic composition of the organizations studied.

Racioethnic Intervention Design Considerations at Tomo

There was good representation of employees of Asian and Asian American background in the IT industry, as nearly one fourth (23%) of the sample at Tomo were of Asian ethnicity. The disproportionate presence of

Asian employees and managers in this corporation conforms to the number of Asians in IT occupations. According to the Bureau of Labor Statistics (2013), Asians made up only 5% of all employed workers in the United States in 2011 but made up 27% of software developers. Employees with an Asian ethnicity at Tomo were distinctive from the 67% who were non-Hispanic White and the 11% who were Hispanics, Blacks, or "other," pointing to the difficulties of using conventional White/non-White dichotomies. For example, as Moen et al. (2013) found using a 5-point scale with 1 reflecting little or no levels and 5 reflecting high levels, Asian respondents reported considerably less burnout (racioethnic subgroup mean 3.78) than did White, non-Hispanic (racioethnic subgroup mean 4.48) or Black, Hispanic, or "other" ethnic groups (racioethnic subgroup mean 4.06). They also reported less job insecurity (2.13 on a 1–4 scale with 1 reflecting low levels of job insecurity and 4 reflecting high levels of job insecurity. In contrast, Black, Hispanic, and "other" races and ethnicities reported higher levels of insecurity (2.46 mean), and non-Hispanic White respondents had a group mean of 2.30 (Moen et al., 2013).

Moreover, at Tomo, 17% of employee respondents reported to an Asian manager. Multivariate analyses (see Lam et al., 2015) revealed that employees reporting to an Asian manager (as opposed to a White manager) were more likely to report lower job insecurity. This may reflect the relatively more powerful and secure positions of Asian managers in teams engaged in IT work. Related to this, Asian respondents were found to be likely clustered together in teams (Moen et al., 2013). The fact that Asian respondents were more apt to be in teams engaged in direct IT work versus other business support functions such as human resources or finance (60% were in teams doing direct IT work compared with only 31% of non-Hispanic Whites and 20% of Blacks, Hispanics, and those in the "other" category) might have affected their responsiveness to the intervention as well as how well their team adapted to the new ways of working and the supervisor support the intervention offered them (Moen et al., 2013).

Age and gender composition are other key markers of diversity that should be taken into consideration in the customization of interventions and the analysis of their effectiveness. For instance, at Tomo, the IT workforce was middle-aged with an average age of 46, and only 39% were women. Further, many of the Asian employees at Tomo had immigrated to the United States to work at the firm (or another technology company in the IT industry). Because of visa restrictions, some of their spouses are not able to work, which likely has a direct impact on work–family issues and conflicts compared with other Tomo employees who are nonimmigrants.

There are also possible effects of the intersections of these social locational markers related to age and family status. For example, in the Tomo sample, only 23% of the Asian respondents were women, compared with 40%

of the White non-Hispanic respondents and 66% of the Black, Hispanic, and "other" respondents. At Tomo, the Asian employees tended to be younger, and if they had families their children tended to be younger than those of the other employee racioethnic subgroups. For example, one fifth (20%) of the Asian respondents were under 40 with no children, and another two fifths (40%) had preschool children at home. This contrasts with White non-Hispanics and the Black, Hispanic, or "other" respondents, of whom less than 10% were under 40 with no children. Only 14% of the White non-Hispanic respondents and only 16% of the Black, Hispanic or "other" category were parents of a preschooler.

The cultural value of family may be different across racial and ethnic groups as well (Lam, Moen, Kelly, & Kojola, 2013). For example, in a different firm used in a pilot study, one 32-year-old married Asian engineer with a young child observed that he did not understand work–family conflict, as he always prioritized his family over his work, explaining the contrast he saw between family and work life in India compared with that in the United States:

> Family is very different in India than here. Family is always first and is the most important thing in your life. Extended family either lives with each other or very close and they all help the young couples raise kids.

Racioethnic Considerations in Computer-Based Supervisory Training and Behavior Tracking

There is a lack of research on whether different self-monitoring methods are more effective for increasing participation and behavior change among different ethnic and racial groups (Korotitsch & Nelson-Gray, 1999; Olson, Schmidt, Winkler, & Wipfli, 2011). Contrasting participation rates across trials revealed that nonminority supervisors were approximately 15% less likely to drop out during Trial 2. In another analysis of participation, we examined the number of times a supervisor opened the app and made a submission during each trial (in contrast to the behavior counts reported). Minority supervisors made 30.0 ($SD = 18.0$) submissions in Trial 1 and 26.2 ($SD = 25.8$) in Trial 2, compared with 31.1 ($SD = 19.2$) and 28.4 ($SD = 23.6$), respectively, for nonminority supervisors. A 2×2 repeated measures analysis of variance revealed no significant differences between groups in this measure of app usage. Overall, these participation rates show that minorities and nonminorities participated equally in behavior tracking, whereas minority supervisors had slightly higher retention rates in the second trial of the activity. This suggests that in our case the activity did not have an adverse impact on minority participation. To ensure this kind of outcome for other studies, researchers and practitioners should conduct formative and developmental activities with both minority and nonminority users and then monitor for any differences across groups. In addition, inspecting data on participation and dropout rates during implementation may identify opportunities to improve activities for maximum minority engagement. Overall, however, adopting a general focus on user-friendliness and tailoring activities to the unique culture of the occupational working population at hand may be more practical than making specific customizations based on race or ethnicity, unless language and translation issues are impeding training participation and involvement and data suggest that particular groups are not engaged or are dropping out at higher rates.

In terms of participant reactions to behavior tracking, there were somewhat more favorable reactions from White managers than non-White managers. Specifically, the non-White supervisors in Leef indicated that the behavior tracking designed to increase self-monitoring of targeted behaviors was less useful to them as supervisors than the White supervisors at Leef. Although these findings are exploratory, future research should gather qualitative information on the cross-cultural valence of individual goal setting and tracking across multicultural groups.

Future Research Directions

Organizational interventions need to be designed to address how the organization of work contributes to occupational health disparities and work–family conflict, which may differ across organizational contexts. As this chapter shows, change targets vary depending on work organization contexts that systematically differ across racioethnic, gender, and class groups. Although professional office employees at Tomo could be empowered to work nearly wherever and however they want, shift-working health care employees' at Leef were encouraged to give input to having greater control over work processes, such as how schedules are made, or having some say regarding how work is done. Thus, interventions can use similar design principles across two very different industries, yet must be customized in delivery and enactment to meet occupational and cultural needs.

More research is needed that investigates the role of primary prevention interventions in preventing outcomes associated with work–family conflict. We have noted that there is relatively little research that has examined how intervention efforts targeting change at multiple levels can improve health and work outcomes for employees. This chapter describes intervention content considerations in addressing these gaps in the design of the WFHN's randomized controlled field experiment to improve occupational health by reducing work–family conflict in the organization of work across diverse industries. Not only has there been a shortage of work–family intervention studies to improve occupational health across industries, but there have been virtually no evaluation studies using randomized controlled or rigorous quasi-experimental designs examining the roles of the key elements of these occupational health interventions. Future research should specifically consider whether multilevel workplace interventions, involving both leaders and employee work groups to improve the organization of work to reduce work–family conflict (i.e., increasing job control, redesigning work to reduce low value work, and increasing support for work and family roles), can improve employee and family health and organizational outcomes. More research is also needed to compare the effectiveness of these work–family intervention components to improve occupational health across industries.

Overall, this chapter identifies the necessity of considering the unique context in which the work–family intervention occurs as well as the individuals and groups receiving the interventions. Many job contexts, as well as demographic groups of employees within those job domains, are likely to face specific challenges that require tailored interventions to address the unique issues these individuals face. Yet the preponderance of work–family and heath interventions to date have not been customized on the basis of individual or demographic differences specific to the populations in which they are targeted.

Our research suggests that customization of work–family interventions is critical to improve occupational health. Yet most work–family interventions focus on one kind of employee population (e.g., those in professional jobs), rather than identifying multiple solutions to various types of jobs (e.g., blue collar, service). We need to move away from the one-size-fits-all approach to designing work–family interventions. Future studies need to seriously increase consideration of variations in demographic concerns and how these intersect with the job positions held across occupational contexts. Future research should identify how customization of intervention content, delivery, structure, and length may improve intervention success and address the workforce needs of women and minorities.

We have also suggested that rather than being evaluated as ad hoc policy, work–family initiatives should be evaluated rigorously as organizational change interventions. Such studies would link the design of work–family policies to changes in issues of control, support, and work redesign over time. Studies would need to include measures of both formal structural and policy change, such as the adoption of workplace flexibility policies and job redesign to allow for flexible scheduling, as well as informal change in organizational culture and norms to allow for greater worker perceptions of their level of job control and leader social support for family and job demands.

Implications for Practical Design

This study demonstrates that having diversity in occupational health contexts allowed the team to take a more holistic approach to promote understanding of the commonality and distinctiveness of principles and processes of work–family organizational change to improve occupational health. Kossek et al. (2014) identified the main principles and strategies that emerged in the development of robust work–family interventions.

All interventions should begin with identifying theoretically derived key intervention ingredients that target the reduction of occupational risk factors for work–family conflict. Intervention scholars and practitioners should also attend to a design approach that conscientiously seeks to prevent work–family conflict in the organization of work. This primary prevention approach is critical to the implementation of organizational change that averts work design issues related to work–family conflict, rather than reactively dealing with problems after they have been allowed to develop. Second, commitment from both top management and workers at all levels to support implementation of the work–family intervention is vital to intervention success. One reason work–family policies may have had limited impact on reducing stress is that they have been implemented largely without significant top management support, and they have not been implemented as joint employer–worker participation initiatives.

Third, ameliorating work and family conflict involves multiple streams of knowledge, and the integration of knowledge from multiple disciplines in the design and evaluation of interventions is also valuable. This could be done at different stages of the research if resources are limited. For example, colleagues from disciplines outside the core research team, such as health and family researchers, could be consulted on measures or intervention design features. Workplace change researchers could focus on intervention design and delivery. The WFHN intervention was developed on the basis of the understanding that the employees and the organizations would plan and designate resources (e.g., time outside of sessions) specifically to ensure transfer of training (e.g., new employee and supervisor norms and behaviors) to the work environment.

Fourth, given that much of the intervention research is conducted at the individual level of analysis, such as job stress training (LaMontagne et al., 2007), the integration of multiple levels of analysis, referred to as a high-systems approach (LaMontagne, Noblet, & Landsbergis, 2012), will yield the most effective intervention to reduce work–family conflict. Future researchers should take a primary prevention approach and consider ways of leveraging the organizational-level programs, such as work–life supports, policies, and benefits, in addition to individual-level targets for stress reduction, to ideally lead to the most effective organizational intervention. Work–family conflict occurs across multiple organizational levels from personal stress to job design to supervision.

CONCLUSIONS

Designing organizational interventions to prevent work–family conflict is increasingly necessary as government support for the work–family interface remains relatively low in the United States (Kelly, 2006; Kossek & Distelberg, 2009) and is uneven and faces reductions in many countries—even those with traditionally high levels (Varney, 2011). Consequently, it is increasingly important to shift the lens in work–family interventions to focus not only on individual strategies to reduce work–family conflict after it occurs, but also on the prevention approach to organizational change initiatives to reduce work–family conflict in diverse workplace and job contexts to proactively improve occupational health. This focus is critical because organizational groups and demographic (gender, racial, ethnic) identity groups often systematically overlap, which has implications for linkages between family and personal demography and occupational health.

REFERENCES

Alderfer, C. (2011). *The practice of organizational diagnosis: Theory and methods.* New York, NY: Oxford University Press.

Allen, T. D. (2001). Family-supportive work environments: The role of organizational perceptions. *Journal of Vocational Behavior, 58,* 414–435. http://dx.doi.org/10.1006/jvbe.2000.1774

Ard, J. D., Cox, T. L., Zunker, C., Wingo, B. C., Jefferson, W. K., & Brakhage, C. (2010). A study of a culturally enhanced EatRight dietary intervention in a predominately African American workplace. *Journal of Public Health Management and Practice, 16*(6), E1–E8. http://dx.doi.org/10.1097/PHH.0b013e3181ce5538

Bailyn, L. (2011). Redesigning work for gender equity and work–personal life integration. *Community, Work & Family, 14,* 97–112. http://dx.doi.org/10.1080/13668803.2010.532660

Bambra, C., Egan, M., Thomas, S., Petticrew, M., & Whitehead, M. (2007). The psychosocial and health effects of workplace reorganisation. 2. A systematic review of task restructuring interventions. *Journal of Epidemiology & Community Health, 61,* 1028–1037. http://dx.doi.org/10.1136/jech.2006.054999

Bandura, A. (1991). Social cognitive theory of self-regulation. *Organizational Behavior and Human Decision Processes, 50,* 248–287. http://dx.doi.org/10.1016/0749-5978(91)90022-L

Baral, R., & Bhargava, S. (2011). HR interventions for work-life balance: Evidences from organisations in India. *International Journal of Business, Management and Social Sciences, 2,* 33–42.

Bergman, M. E., Palmieri, P. A., Drasgow, F., & Ormerod, A. J. (2012). Racial/ethnic harassment and discrimination, its antecedents, and its effect on job-related outcomes. *Journal of Occupational Health Psychology, 17,* 65–78. http://dx.doi.org/10.1037/a0026430

Bowman, K. (2005). Racial and ethnic disparities in the workplace—effects on worker health and safety. *AAOHN Journal, 53,* 198–201.

Bray, J. W., Kelly, E., Hammer, L. B., Almeida, D. M., Dearing, J. W., King, R. B., & Buxton, O. M. (2013). *An integrative, multilevel, and transdisciplinary research approach to challenges of work, family, and health* (RTI Press Publication No. MR-0024-1302). Research Triangle Park, NC: RTI Press.

Bureau of Labor Statistics. (2011, March 28). Employment characteristics of families, 2010. *The Economics Daily.* Retrieved from http://www.bls.gov/opub/ted/2011/ted_20110328.htm

Bureau of Labor Statistics. (2013, October). *Labor force characteristics by race and ethnicity, 2012* (BLS Report No. 1044). Retrieved from http://www.bls.gov/opub/reports/race-and-ethnicity/archive/race_ethnicity_2012.pdf

Butts, M., Casper, W., & Yang, T. (2013). How important are work-family support policies: A meta-analytic investigation of their effects on employee outcomes. *Journal of Applied Psychology, 98,* 1–25.

Campbell, M. K., Tessaro, I., DeVellis, B., Benedict, S., Kelsey, K., Belton, L., & Sanhueza, A. (2002). Effects of a tailored health promotion program for female blue-collar workers: Health works for women. *Preventive Medicine, 34,* 313–323. http://dx.doi.org/10.1006/pmed.2001.0988

Casper, W. J., Eby, L. T., Bordeaux, C., Lockwood, A., & Lambert, D. (2007). A review of research methods in IO/OB work-family research. *Journal of Applied Psychology, 92,* 28–43. http://dx.doi.org/10.1037/0021-9010.92.1.28

Casper, W. J., Weltman, D., & Kwesiga, E. (2007). Beyond family-friendly: The construct and measurement of singles-friendly work culture. *Journal of Vocational Behavior, 70,* 478–501. http://dx.doi.org/10.1016/j.jvb.2007.01.001

Deitch, E. A., Barsky, A., Butz, R. M., Chan, S., Brief, A. P., & Bradley, J. C. (2003). Subtle yet significant: The existence and impact of everyday racial discrimination in the workplace. *Human Relations, 56,* 1299–1324.

DeJoy, D. M., Wilson, M. G., Vandenberg, R. J., McGrath-Higgins, A. L., & Griffin-Blake, C. S. (2010). Assessing the impact of healthy work organization intervention. *Journal of Occupational and Organizational Psychology, 83,* 139–165. http://dx.doi.org/10.1348/096317908X398773

Gany, F., Novo, P., Dobslaw, R., & Leng, J. (2014). Urban occupational health in the Mexican and Latino/Latina immigrant population: A literature review. *Journal of Immigrant and Minority Health, 16,* 846–855.

Greenhaus, J., & Allen, T. (2011). Work–family balance: A review and extension of the literature. In J. C. Quick & L. E. Tetrick (Eds.), *Handbook of occupational psychology* (pp. 165–183). Washington, DC: American Psychological Association.

Haley-Lock, A. (2011). Place-bound jobs at the intersection of policy and management: Comparing employer practices in U.S. and Canadian chain restaurants. *American Behavioral Scientist, 55,* 823–842. http://dx.doi.org/10.1177/0002764211407831

Hammer, L. B., Kossek, E. E., Anger, W. K., Bodner, T., & Zimmerman, K. L. (2011). Clarifying work-family intervention processes: The roles of work-family conflict and family-supportive supervisor behaviors. *Journal of Applied Psychology, 96,* 134–150. http://dx.doi.org/10.1037/a0020927

Hammer, L. B., Kossek, E. E., Bodner, T., & Crain, T. (2013). Measurement development and validation of the Family Supportive Supervisor Behavior Short-Form (FSSB-SF). *Journal of Occupational Health Psychology, 18,* 285–296. http://dx.doi.org/10.1037/a0032612

Hammer, L. B., Kossek, E. E., Yragui, N. L., Bodner, T. E., & Hanson, G. C. (2009). Development and validation of a multidimensional measure of family supportive supervisor behaviors (FSSB). *Journal of Management, 35,* 837–856. http://dx.doi.org/10.1177/0149206308328510

Hammer, L. B., & Sauter, S. L. (2013). Total worker health and work-life stress. *Journal of Occupational and Environmental Medicine, 55*(Suppl. 12), S25–S29.

Hammer, L. B., & Zimmerman, K. L. (2011). Quality of work life. In S. Zedeck (Ed.), *APA handbook of industrial and organizational psychology* (Vol. 3, pp. 399–431). Washington, DC: American Psychological Association. http://dx.doi.org/10.1037/12171-011

Jackson, P. B., & Stewart, Q. T. (2003). A research agenda for the black middle class: Work stress, survival strategies, and mental health. *Journal of Health and Social Behavior, 44,* 442–455. http://dx.doi.org/10.2307/1519789

Jamieson, D., & O'Mara, J. (1991). *Managing workforce 2000.* San Francisco, CA: Jossey-Bass.

Jones, T. (1993). *Britain's ethnic minorities.* London, England: Policy Studies Institute.

Kelly, E. L. (2006). Work-family policies: The United States in international perspective. In M. Pitt-Catsouphes, E. Kossek, & S. Sweet (Eds.), *Work-family handbook: Multi-disciplinary perspectives and approaches* (pp. 99–123). Mahwah, NJ: Erlbaum.

Kelly, E. L., Kossek, E. E., Hammer, L. B., Durham, M., Bray, J., Chermack, K., . . . Kaskubar, D. (2008). Getting there from here: Research on the effects of work-family initiatives on work-family conflict and business outcomes. *The Academy of Management Annals, 2,* 305–349. http://dx.doi.org/10.1080/19416520802211610

Kelly, E. L., & Moen, P. (2007). Rethinking the clockwork of work: Why schedule control may pay off at work and at home. *Advances in Developing Human Resources, 9,* 487–506. http://dx.doi.org/10.1177/1523422307305489

Kelly, E. L., Moen, P., Oakes, J. M., Fan, W., Okechuckwu, C., Davis, K. D., . . . Casper, L. (2014). Changing work and work-family conflict: Evidence from the Work, Family, and Health Network. *American Sociological Review, 79,* 485–516.

Kelly, E. L., Moen, P., & Tranby, E. (2011). Changing workplaces to reduce work-family conflict: Schedule control in a white-collar organization. *American Sociological Review, 76,* 265–290. http://dx.doi.org/10.1177/0003122411400056

King, R. B., Karuntzos, G., Casper, L. M., Moen, P., Davis, K. D., Berkman, L., . . . Kossek, E. E. (2012). Work–family balance issues and work–leave policies. In R. J. Gatchel & I. Z. Schultz (Eds.), *Handbook of occupational health and wellness* (pp. 323–339). New York, NY: Springer.

Korotitsch, W. J., & Nelson-Gray, R. O. (1999). An overview of self-monitoring research in assessment and treatment. *Psychological Assessment, 11,* 415–425. http://dx.doi.org/10.1037/1040-3590.11.4.415

Kossek, E. E. (2006). Work and family in America: Growing tensions between employment policy and a changing workforce. In E. Lawler & J. O'Toole (Eds.), In *America at work: Choices and challenges* (pp. 53–71). New York, NY: Palgrave Macmillan. http://dx.doi.org/10.1057/9781403983596_4

Kossek, E. E., Baltes, B. B., & Matthews, R. A. (2011). How work–family research can finally have an impact in the workplace. *Industrial and Organizational Psychology: Perspectives on Science and Practice, 4,* 352–369. http://dx.doi.org/10.1111/j.1754-9434.2011.01353.x

Kossek, E. E., & Distelberg, B. (2009). Work and family employment policy for a transformed work force: Trends and themes. In N. Crouter & A. Booth (Eds.), *Work-life policies* (pp. 3–51). Washington, DC: Urban Institute Press.

Kossek, E. E., Hammer, L. B., Kelly, E. L., & Moen, P. (2014). Designing work, family, & health organizational change initiatives. *Organizational Dynamics, 43,* 53–63. http://dx.doi.org/10.1016/j.orgdyn.2013.10.007

Kossek, E. E., Lautsch, B., & Eaton, S. (2006). Telecommuting, control, and boundary management: Correlates of policy use and practice, job control, and work-family effectiveness. *Journal of Vocational Behavior, 68,* 347–367.

Kossek, E. E., Lewis, S., & Hammer, L. B. (2010). Work-life initiatives and organizational change: Overcoming mixed messages to move from the margin to the mainstream. *Human Relations, 63,* 3–19. http://dx.doi.org/10.1177/0018726709352385

Kossek, E. E., & Michel, J. S. (2011). Flexible work schedules. In S. Zedeck (Ed.), *APA handbook of industrial and organizational psychology: Vol. 1. Building and developing the organization* (pp. 535–572). Washington, DC: American Psychological Association.

Kossek, E. E., Pichler, S., Bodner, T., & Hammer, L. B. (2011). Workplace social support and work-family conflict: A meta-analysis clarifying the influence of general and work-family-specific supervisor and organizational support. *Personnel Psychology, 64,* 289–313. http://dx.doi.org/10.1111/j.1744-6570.2011.01211.x

Kossek, E. E., Pisczcek, M., McAlpine, K., Hammer, L., & Burke, L. (2016). Filling the holes: Work schedulers as job crafters of employment practice in long-term health care. *Industrial and Labor Relations Review, 69,* 961–960. http://dx.doi.org/10.1177/0019793916642761

Lam, J., Fox, K., Fan, W., Moen, P., Kelly, E. L., Hammer, L., & Kossek, E. (2015). Manager characteristics and employee job insecurity around a merger announcement: The role of status and crossover. *The Sociological Quarterly, 56,* 558–580.

Lam, J., Moen, P., Kelly, E. L., & Kojola, E. (2013). *Managing change: Managers' practices in the face of an organizational merger.* Unpublished manuscript.

LaMontagne, A. D., Keegel, T., Louie, A. M., Ostry, A., & Landsbergis, P. A. (2007). A systematic review of the job-stress intervention evaluation literature, 1990–2005. *International Journal of Occupational and Environmental Health, 13,* 268–280. http://dx.doi.org/10.1179/oeh.2007.13.3.268

LaMontagne, A., Noblet, A., & Landsbergis, P. (2012). Intervention development and implementation: Understanding and addressing barriers to organizational level interventions. In C. Biron, M. Karanika-Murray, & C. L. Cooper (Eds.), *Improving organizational interventions for stress and well-being: Addressing process and context* (pp. 21–38). New York, NY: Routledge.

Laraway, S., Snycerski, S., Michael, J., & Poling, A. (2003). Motivating operations and terms to describe them: Some further refinements. *Journal of Applied Behavior Analysis, 36,* 407–414. http://dx.doi.org/10.1901/jaba.2003.36-407

Lillie-Blanton, M., & Laveist, T. (1996). Race/ethnicity, the social environment, and health. *Social Science & Medicine, 43,* 83–91. http://dx.doi.org/10.1016/0277-9536(95)00337-1

Marín, A., Carrillo, L., Arcury, T. A., Grzywacz, J. G., Coates, M. L., & Quandt, S. A. (2009). Ethnographic evaluation of a lay health promoter program to reduce occupational injuries among Latino poultry processing workers. *Public Health Reports, 124*(Suppl. 1), 36–43.

Martins, L. L., Eddleston, K. A., & Veiga, J. F. (2002). Moderators of the relationship between work-family conflict and career satisfaction. *Academy of Management Journal, 45,* 399–409. http://dx.doi.org/10.2307/3069354

Moen, P., Lam, J., Ammons, S., & Kelly, E. (2013). Time work by overworked professionals: Strategies in response to the stress of higher status work and occupations. *Work and Occupations, 40*(2), 79–114.

Murray, L. R. (2003). Sick and tired of being sick and tired: Scientific evidence, methods, and research implications for racial and ethnic disparities in occupational health. *American Journal of Public Health, 93,* 221–226. http://dx.doi.org/10.2105/AJPH.93.2.221

National Institute for Occupational Safety and Health. (2002, April). *The changing organization of work and the safety and health of working people* (DHHS [NIOSH] Publication No. 2002-116). Available at https://www.cdc.gov/niosh/docs/2002-116/

Odom, E. C., Vernon-Feagans, L., & Crouter, A. C. (2013). Nonstandard maternal work schedules: Implications for African American children's early language

outcomes. *Early Childhood Research Quarterly, 28,* 379–387. http://dx.doi.org/
10.1016/j.ecresq.2012.10.001

Olson, R., Schmidt, S., Winkler, C., & Wipfli, B. (2011). The effects of target behavior choice and self-management skills training on compliance with behavioral self-monitoring. *American Journal of Health Promotion, 25,* 319–324. http://dx.doi.org/10.4278/ajhp.090421-QUAN-143

Olson, R., & Winchester, J. (2008). Behavioral self-monitoring of safety and productivity in the workplace: A methodological primer and quantitative literature review. *Journal of Organizational Behavior Management, 28,* 9–75. http://dx.doi.org/10.1080/01608060802006823

Park, K.-O., Schaffer, B. S., Griffin-Blake, C. S., Dejoy, D. M., Wilson, M. G., & Vandenberg, R. J. (2004). Effectiveness of a healthy work organization intervention: Ethnic group differences. *Journal of Occupational and Environmental Medicine, 46,* 623–634. http://dx.doi.org/10.1097/01.jom.0000131793.44014.91

Parkes, K. R., & Sparkes, T. J. (1998). *Organizational interventions to reduce work stress: Are they effective? A review of the literature.* Sudbury, England: Health and Safety Executive Books.

Perlow, L. (2012). *Sleeping with your smartphone: How to break the 24-7 habit and change the way you work.* Boston, MA: Harvard Business School Press.

Presser, H. B. (2003). *Working in a 24/7 economy: Challenges for American families.* New York, NY: Russell Sage Foundation.

Quick, J. C. (1999). Occupational health psychology: The convergence of health and clinical psychology with public health and preventive medicine in an organizational context. *Professional Psychology: Research and Practice, 30,* 123–128. http://dx.doi.org/10.1037/0735-7028.30.2.123

Robson, L., Stephenson, C., Shulte, P., Amick, B., Chan, S., Bielecky, A., . . . Grubb, P. (2010). *A systematic review of the effectiveness of training & education for the protection of workers.* Toronto, Ontario, Canada: Institute for Work & Health and Cincinnati, OH: National Institute for Occupational Safety and Health. (DHHS [NIOSH] Publication No. 2010-12). Retrieved from http://www.cdc.gov/niosh/docs/2010-127/pdfs/2010-127.pdf

Shelton, L. M., Danes, S. M., & Eisenman, M. (2008). Role demands, difficulty in managing work-family conflict, and minority entrepreneurs. *Journal of Developmental Entrepreneurship, 13,* 315–342. http://dx.doi.org/10.1142/S1084946708000983

Sparks, K., Faragher, B., & Cooper, C. L. (2001). Well-being and occupational health in the 21st century workplace. *Journal of Occupational and Organizational Psychology, 74,* 489–509. http://dx.doi.org/10.1348/096317901167497

Stoddard, A. M., Krieger, N., Barbeau, E. M., Bennett, G. G., Fay, M. E., Sorensen, G., & Emmons, K. (2005). Methods and baseline characteristics of two group-randomized trials with multiracial and multiethnic working-class samples. *Preventing Chronic Disease, 2*(4), A10.

Tetrick, L. E., Quick, J. C., & Gilmore, P. L. (2012). *Research in organizational interventions to improve well-being: Perspectives on organizational change and development* (pp. 59–76). New York, NY: Routledge/Taylor & Francis.

Tompa, E., Dolinschi, R., de Oliveira, C., & Irvin, E. (2009). A systematic review of occupational health and safety interventions with economic analyses. *Journal of Occupational and Environmental Medicine, 51*, 1004–1023. http://dx.doi.org/10.1097/JOM.0b013e3181b34f60

Varney, S. (2011, July 27). *Egalite for bebe? France's free child clinics at risk* [Radio broadcast]. Retrieved from National Public Radio website, http://www.npr.org/2011/07/27/138748747/egalite-for-bebe-frances-free-child-clinics-at-risk

Wyatt-Nichol, H. (2009). Blue-collar mother/White-collar daughter: A perspective on U.S. policies toward working mothers. *Journal of the Association for Research on Mothering, 11*(2), 111–121.

AFTERWORD: RESEARCH AND POLICY IMPLICATIONS FOR ADDRESSING HEALTH DISPARITIES

CHU-HSIANG (DAISY) CHANG, J. KEVIN FORD,
AND RUBÉN O. MARTINEZ

Occupational health disparities reflect the stratification features of U.S. society. These disparities are evident in the differences across racial and ethnic groups in occupational illness and injury incidents, and in morbidity and mortality rates resulting from work exposures (National Institute for Occupational Safety and Health [NIOSH], 2012). Occupational health disparities are often associated with the overrepresentation of racial and ethnic minority workers in the more hazardous industries, such as agriculture and construction. For example, in 2012, the fatal injury rate for farming, fishing, and forestry workers was 24.8 per 100,000 full-time equivalent workers and 12.9 per 100,000 full-time equivalent workers for construction workers (Bureau of Labor Statistics, 2014). In the United States, more than 80% of hired farm workers are Hispanic, and a majority of them are foreign born (NIOSH, 2012). These workers are exposed, more than workers in other occupations, to physical, chemical, and biological hazards that may directly cause occupational illnesses and injuries.

http://dx.doi.org/10.1037/0000021-010
Occupational Health Disparities: Improving the Well-Being of Ethnic and Racial Minority Workers, F. T. L. Leong, D. E. Eggerth, C.-H. Chang, M. A. Flynn, J. K. Ford, and R. O. Martinez (Editors)

In addition to exposure to occupational hazards, social, cultural, and political factors also contribute to occupational health disparities. Minority workers tend to face discriminatory employment practices or hostility from supervisors or coworkers, which may cause stress and exacerbate the negative health effects associated with exposure to workplace hazards. Racial and ethnic minorities also face additional cultural and language barriers that render the existing occupational health and safety programs aimed at protecting workers less effective because of communication difficulties and cultural insensitivities (NIOSH, 2012). Finally, occupational health disparities tend to reflect the general health disparities associated with individuals' socioeconomic status and access to health care.

The authors in this volume have approached occupational health disparities from different perspectives, including identifying disparities associated with particular racial and ethnic groups and the risk factors leading to occupational health disparities, as well as considering the implications these differences have for occupational illness and injury rates. In this concluding chapter we summarize these implications and how they may inform future research, practice and interventions, and policy decisions.

A NUMBER OF RESEARCH DIRECTIONS

The chapters herein have provided various strategies or avenues for understanding and addressing health disparities. For example, in Chapter 3, Tetrick pointed to several ways in which organizations may intervene to help reduce the disparities. First, Tetrick proposed that better social integration between dominant and minority group members and stronger structural support may help reduce health disparities. In this case, organizations can contribute to better diversity integration by adopting policies and practices, such as demonstrating respect and value for diversity and promoting sensitivity toward diverse group members, that foster high-quality relationships among organizational members of diverse backgrounds. Second, Tetrick pointed out that organizational interventions that are designed to promote health-related behaviors (e.g., smoking cessation programs, lunchtime walking groups) may offer another venue to reduce health disparities. Finally, as stress is an important factor in explaining relationships between occupational status and health disparities, Tetrick suggested that organizational programs that help employees better manage and cope with stress may be helpful in reducing occupational health disparities.

In Chapter 4, Arcury and Quandt described a participatory action approach to the study of health disparities that brings researchers and community members together in the coproduction of knowledge. This research approach led to a successful intervention to reduce exposure of Latino immigrant agricultural workers and their families to insecticides. The research efforts show what can be accomplished when there is a true research partnership between researcher and community. This effort challenges researchers to let go of their status as "experts" and embrace activities valued by their community partners. The chapter also illustrated how researchers can conceptualize their efforts within the context of social, political, and economic factors.

Roberts, in Chapter 5, highlighted the enormous potential benefits of taking steps to reduce stress as one strategy for reducing health disparities. Stress management programs (SMPs) are one such type of intervention. SMPs have three core components: (a) psychoeducation, (b) skill-building in stress arousal reduction, and (c) social support and active problem solving. Program customization is needed to accommodate variations in program and policy utilization. Culturally appropriate occupational stress management and prevention programs that are designed for and clearly accessible to African Americans are also needed. But researchers and practitioners should first develop a full understanding of the African American community's strengths, one of which is the Black church, the most important social institution in that community. Collaborating with the church to design community-based occupational stress interventions ensures that messages are communicated in a culturally appropriate manner. Future studies should take a fuller approach to understanding how the workplace psychosocial environment influences the health and safety status of African American workers. Occupational safety and health (OSH) professionals appear to have rarely worked with or collaborated with this population to design, deliver, and evaluate community-based occupational stress interventions.

Leong, Chang, and Mak (Chapter 6) called for more research on the linkages among risk exposure and health outcomes, with an emphasis on mediating variables. Further, given the relative lack of accurate data on the scope and nature of the problem, they called for improved surveillance of occupational health and safety issues relative to Asian Americans. They also recommended disentangling race and ethnicity with regard to occupational health disparities by going beyond using them as demographic variables to deep-level research that examines the psychological processes and mechanisms that may moderate or mediate the relationship between race–ethnicity and occupational health.

A VARIETY OF BEST PRACTICE INTERVENTIONS

Several of the chapters presented information and data on a variety of interventions that can be applied to address health disparities. For example, Quandt and Arcury (Chapter 7) provided a compelling argument for the greater use of research-based OSH training programs as one way of addressing occupational health disparities for the immigrant worker population. They reminded readers that the development of all OSH materials needs to begin with the reality of the lives of workers that will use them. They demonstrated how research can be used to ensure materials are appropriate for low-literacy audiences while still treating the workers as adults. Using the PRECEDE-PROCEED method, they invited readers to see the development of educational materials as part of an overall program and showed through concrete examples how this can be accomplished. In short, Quandt and Acrcury provided a comprehensive guide on how to create OSH training programs to address occupational health disparities, as well as a strong theoretical justification on why this approach to developing training programs is needed. The extensive treatment of the topic serves as a valuable resource for researchers and practitioners new to this work, as well as for those who have been doing it for a while.

Kossek and her colleagues in Chapter 8 clearly articulated the need for interventions focused on reducing work–family conflict to affect employee and family health. The unique, large-scale, randomized, field-controlled work–family and health study described in their chapter provides a wealth of information to inform research, practice, and policy regarding health and workforce diversity considerations. In particular, based on the results of the study, they highlighted the need to customize work–family interventions to develop approaches likely to resonate with the population in question and therefore improve occupational health. Kossek et al. identified six areas that researchers and practitioners should attend to in customizing work–family interventions to address diversity in occupational health contexts. These six areas include training content, training delivery, cultural framing, dosage/exposure time, inclusion decisions, and managing workforce diversity. They noted how most work–family interventions focus on one kind of employee group rather than on identifying multiple solutions for various types of jobs, and they highlighted the need to move away from the one-size-fits-all approach often taken by organizations. From a policy perspective, the researchers noted a need to move beyond individual strategies to reduce work–family conflict and to direct more attention to prevention-focused organizational change initiatives to reduce work–family conflict in diverse workplace contexts.

A MULTITUDE OF IMPLICATIONS FOR POLICY

The chapters also provided best practices that have direct policy implications. For example, OSH, as do all other areas of public health, values prevention over remediation of harm. However, most of these efforts have focused on engineering controls to reduce risk and/or the development of processes that reduce, if not eliminate, exposure to toxins—be they chemical or psychological. In Chapter 1, Martinez offered an entirely new direction for primary prevention of OSH failures—considering the possible adverse consequences that economic policies can have on worker health as part of the policymaking process. For those policies that are already in effect and that are causing problems, Martinez pointed us toward the need to disseminate research findings beyond the academy (and its usual publishing outlets) and to bring this important information to the attention of those making economic policy at the highest levels.

Leong, Chang, and Mak in Chapter 6 offered several policy recommendations for addressing the occupational health disparities experienced by Asian Americans. With regard to policy, they recommended going beyond the politics of numbers to ensure that occupational disparities among all groups are addressed irrespective of the size of a particular group. They suggested educating policymakers about the complex backgrounds of Asian Americans as a step toward overcoming the negative effects of the model minority stereotype. Finally, they recommended greater cooperation and coordination among the different professional groups and associations promoting Asian American health and greater community engagement in addressing occupational health disparities.

Moure-Eraso and Brunette in Chapter 2 emphasized the importance of targeting structural and community determinants of Latino occupational health for addressing workplace exposures, lack of access to occupational health care, insufficient income, and vulnerable population status. Interventions include strengthening regulations and improving education and health access at the structural level. They also recommended interventions at the policy and workplace levels to decrease differential workplace exposures. Interventions, however, will require political actions that promote collective organization among workers, regulatory controls on job outsourcing, antidiscrimination of immigrants, and incentives and sanctions relative to regulation compliance and violation. Ultimately, they argued, the state must promote more just social policies that regulate labor markets, and Latino organizations must assume the political will to promote a just society and join other organizations to do so.

Together, these studies and essays highlight the many research, intervention, and policy issues associated with the occupational health of racial and ethnic minorities in this country. Several of the authors pointed to the structural dimensions of occupational health disparities, and there is little question that the key leverage points for addressing the problem are to be found at the structural level. Still, research is needed to inform intervention and policy developments that will improve the conditions of employment and reduce the prevalence of occupational hazards.

REFERENCES

Bureau of Labor Statistics. (2014). *Fatal occupational injuries, total hours worked, and rates of fatal occupational injuries by selected worker characteristics, occupations, and industries, civilian workers, 2012.* Retrieved from http://www.bls.gov/iif/oshcfoi1.htm

National Institute for Occupational Safety and Health. (2012). *Occupational health disparities.* Retrieved from http://www.cdc.gov/niosh/programs/ohd/default.html

INDEX

Blacks. *See* African Americans; Non-Hispanic Blacks
BLS (Bureau of Labor Statistics), 76–78, 204
Braveman, P., 15
Brunner, E., 78–79, 83
Bureau of Labor Statistics (BLS), 76–78, 204
Burgel, B. J., 141, 144
Business ownership, among Asian Americans, 135

Cambodian Americans
    chemical risk factors for, 142
    ergonomic risk factors for, 141
Canada, racial inequities in health in, 81, 82
Caregivers, 188
Carson, S., 124
CBPR. *See* Community-based participatory research
Centers for Disease Control and Prevention (CDC), 124
Chang, C.-H., 14–15, 138–139
Chavez, G., 15
Chemical risks, 141–142
    for Asian Americans, 141–142
    in PACE project, 168–170
Chinese Americans, 134, 135
    chemical risk factors for, 142
    ergonomic risk factors for, 141
    nonreporting of concerns by, 145
    poverty among, 144
Chinese Exclusion Act of 1882, 134, 150
Chinese immigrants, 134
Churches
    African American, 122–124
    partnerships with, 113–114, 124
Citizenship, 29–30, 134
Civil rights movement, 134
Collective interventions, 60–62
Columbus County Community Health Center, 96
Commission on Social Determinants of Health, 51, 62
Community
    defined, 90, 91
    engagement of, 152–153
Community-based interventions, for occupational stress, 122–124

Community-based participatory research (CBPR), 89–107
    defined, 90–91
    elements of, 91
    operational model of, 93–94
    partners available for, 102–103
    on pesticide exposure among Latino farmworkers, 95–101
    power in, 104–105
    structure of partnerships in, 103–104
    topics and populations appropriate for, 101–102
    as translational science, 92–94
    translation of results of, 106
    with vulnerable populations, 94–95
Community Participatory Approach to Measuring Farmworker Pesticide Exposures (PACE3) project, 95–101
Community social determinants of health, 60–61, 66–68
Computer-based supervisory training, 205–206
Confirmatory factor analysis, 14–15
Confounding variables, 15
Côté, S., 81
Cubbin, C., 15
Cultural appropriateness, of training materials, 164
Cultural framing, 202–203
CultureRx, 190

Deaths. *See* Fatal work injuries
Demakakos, P., 79
Deregulation, 25, 27, 28, 30
Derose, K. P., 124
Differential item functioning analysis, 14
Discrimination
    against Asian Americans, 134, 145
    based on stereotypes, 149–151
    against Blacks vs. Whites, 119–120
    defined, 119
    against single parents, 188
Disease. *See* Illness and disease
Disentangling approach to research, 146–149
Displaced workers, 28, 29
Division of labor, racial, 29, 41
Doak, C. C., 174

Doak, L. G., 174
Duan, N., 124
Dunkel Schetter, C., 84
Dyrenforth, S., 83

Earnings. *See* Income
Eatough, E. M., 138–139
Economic restructuring, 9–10, 27
Economy
    recent changes in, 27–30
    underground, 143
Education. *See also* Training programs
    adult education principles, 165
    of Asian Americans, 135
    and emphatic accuracy, 81
    and health, 82–83
    immigrant workers' levels of, 174, 176
    of policymakers, 152
    social status associated with, 78
    and subjective social status, 79
Educationally appropriate safety
    training, 164–165
Egerter, S., 15
Eggerth, D. E., 30
Eliminating Health and Safety
    Disparities at Work conference
    (NIOSH), 9
Emphatic accuracy, 81
Employers' organizations, interventions
    by, 61
Employer-sponsored interventions, for
    occupational stress, 120–122
Employment. *See also* Unemployment
    among Asian Americans, 135
    by occupational categories, 31–34, 78
Employment conditions, 51–69
    and demographics of Latino OHDs,
        52–57
    domains of, 52
    and interventions to improve
        workers' health, 62–69
    as source of access to health services,
        61
    structural, community, and individual
        factors in, 57–62
Employment Standards Administration,
    U.S. Department of Labor, 8
Engelhardt, H., 82–83
Environmental health, 8

Environmental risk factors, 187
    behavioral responses to, 138, 147
    biophysiological, 136, 138, 147
    chemical, 141–142, 172–174.
          See also Occupational stress
    ergonomic, 138, 141, 145
    feedback loop from health effects
        to, 139
    in hazardous industries, 217
    psychological processes affecting
        impact of, 138, 147
    psychosocial, 138, 144–145
    research on, 146–147
    safety hazards, 142–144
Ergonomic risks, 141, 145
Ethic minorities. *See* Racial and ethnic
    minority groups
Ethnic composition of occupations,
    76–77
Ethnic discrimination, 119–120
Ethnicity
    as demographic variable, 149
    and training outcomes, 188–189
    and variation in stress, 84
Evidence-based OSH training, 166–170

Fahs, M., 118
Fairness, as mechanism underlying
    disparities, 79–80
Family, cultural value of, 205
Family-operated businesses, 5
Family Supportive Supervisor Behaviors
    (FSSB), 190, 195, 196
Family-to-work interference, 183.
        See also Work–family conflict
Farmworker Advocacy Network, 96
Farmworkers
    PACE3 project, 95–101
    PACE project, 168–170
    pesticide intervention materials for,
        172–174
    training programs/materials for, 163
Fatal work injuries
    among Asian Americans, 36, 140,
        143–144
    among Blacks, 36–39
    among immigrant workers, 162
    among Latino workers, 25, 35–41,
        45–47

Fatal work injuries, *continued*
    among Whites, 37, 38
    disparities in, 35–42
    in hazardous industries, 217
Feedback
    from health effects to environmental
        risk factors, 139
    on training materials, 174
Filipino Americans, 134
    job-related stress for, 144
    poverty among, 136
Flexible labor, 27
Flynn, M. A., 30
Fox, S. A., 124
FSSB. *See* Family Supportive Supervisor
    Behaviors

Galván, Leonardo, 100
GAO (U.S. Government Accountability
    Office), 30
Gee, G. C., 117
Gender differences. *See also* Men; Women
    in occupations, 77
    in stressors, 84, 188
    in training outcomes, 188–189
Global environment, conceptualizing
    social determinants of health
    in, 6
Globalization, 9–10
Government agencies, interventions
    by, 61
Grand, J., 150
Green, L. W., 166–168
Greene County Health Care, Inc., 96

Hammer, L. B., 186, 196
Harassment, 120
Harrison, R., 141
Hawes-Dawson, J., 124
Hawthorne effect, 7
Health and safety standards, pursuit of
    "economic freedom" and, 30.
    See also Occupational safety
    and health
Health care
    access to, 61, 218
    disparities in quality of, 151
    expenditures due to occupational
        stress, 115

Health disparities, 6, 187
    associated with socioeconomic
        status and access to health
        care, 218
    defined, 4
    and politics of numbers, 151–152
    research progress with regard to,
        12–13
    and social status, 75. *See also* Social
        determinants of health
    in the workplace. *See* Occupational
        health disparities (OHDs)
Health equity, structural and intermediate
    social determinants of, 62–65
Health inequity, 6, 66
Healthy People 2000, 10–11
Healthy People 2020, 4
Hidgson, M. J., 83
Hispanics. *See also* Latinas; Latinos
    employment by occupational
        categories, 78
    and gender composition
        of occupations, 77
    in racial/ethnic composition
        of occupations, 76–77
    as U.S. hired farm workers, 217
    in U.S. workforce, 161
    violent acts and assaults on,
        143–144
    in WFHN intervention, 204, 205
Hudson, K., 29–30
Human relations dimensions
    of productivity, 7

Illness and disease
    among Asian Americans, 140–144
    gender disparities in, 35
    lay-defined, 164
    racial/ethnic disparities in, 34–37,
        58, 140
    and work stress, 114–118
Immigrant effect, 40
Immigrants, 161–176. *See also individual
    groups, e.g.:* Asian Americans
    characteristics shaping training needs
        of, 165–166
    marginalization of, 69
    occupational health disparities for,
        34–35

Meyer, J. D., 82
Michigan State University (MSU)
    Symposium on Multicultural
    Psychology, 16
Migrant farmworkers, 172–174
Minority groups. *See* Racial and ethnic
    minority groups
Model minority stereotype, 150–151
Moen, P., 204
Money, as social determinant of health, 6.
    See also Income; Poverty; Wealth
Motivation, 7
MSU (Michigan State University)
    Symposium on Multicultural
    Psychology, 16
Murray, L. R., 76
Mutambudzi, M., 82
Myers, H. F., 12–13

National Center on Minority Health
    and Health Disparities, 12, 13,
    16
National Institute for Occupational
    Safety and Health (NIOSH), 3
    Eliminating Health and Safety
        Disparities at Work
        conference, 9
    implementation of, 8
    national strategy for work-related
        psychological disorders, 9
    Occupational Health Equity
        program, 4, 16, 147, 153
    OHP-promotion initiatives of, 9
    Total Worker Health initiative, 6
National Institute on Minority Health
    and Health Disparities, 12
National Occupational Research
    Agenda (NORA), 3, 13
Native Hawaiian and Other Pacific
    Islanders. *See also* Pacific Islanders
    in labor force, 31
    unemployment among, 135
    work injuries among, 140
Navarro, Vicente, xiii–xiv
Nazroo, J. Y., 76, 82
Nemoto, T., 143
Neoliberalism, 10, 26, 43
    defined, 26
    and deregulation, 25, 28, 30–31
    economic effect of, 27–30

and efforts for safety and health
    support, 42
impact on Latino workers, 26
issues emphasized in, 27
and workplace safety, 30–31
Nguyen, Q. C., 81–82
NIOSH. *See* National Institute for
    Occupational Safety and Health
Nonemployed, prime-age men as, 28
Nonfatal injuries
    among Asian Americans, 140–144
    among Blacks, 35–36, 58
    among Latinas, 35–36
    among Latinos, 56–57
    among Whites, 35–36, 58
    gender disparities in, 35
Non-Hispanic Blacks. *See also* African
    Americans
    coronary heart disease among, 116
    fatal workplace injuries among, 37–38
    hypertension among, 115–116
    nonfatal injury and illness rates
        among, 35, 58
Non-Hispanic Whites. *See also* Whites
    (White Americans)
    coronary heart disease among, 116
    fatal workplace injuries among, 37,
        38
    hypertension among, 115–116
    in labor force, 31
    nonfatal injury and illness rates
        among, 35–36, 58
    in WFHN intervention, 204, 205
NORA (National Occupational
    Research Agenda), 3, 13
North Carolina Farmworker Health
    Alliance, 95
North Carolina Farmworkers Project,
    95, 96
Numbers, politics of, 151–152

Occupational health
    customizing work–family
        interventions for, 186–189.
        See also Work, Family, &
        Health Network (WFHN)
        intervention
    jobs targeted in existing research
        on, 188
    key elements to target for, 186

Occupational health disparities
(OHDs), 217–218. *See also
specific groups, e.g.:* Latinos
best practice interventions for,
219–220
factors contributing to, 218
general health disparities reflected
in, 218
identifying mechanisms underlying,
15–16
multidimensional nature of, 139
NIOSH OHE program goal for, 4
NIOSH on, 13
policy recommendations for
addressing, 220–222
recent developments affecting, 10–13
in risk exposure, 217
social determinants of, 75–85
and stress, 116–117
Occupational health disparities (OHD)
research. *See also specific types of
research, e.g.:* Community-based
participatory research (CBPR)
assessment of factors explaining
disparity in, 15–16
developing training programs from,
166–170
disentangling approach to, 146–149
future directions for, 218–219
measurement equivalence in, 13–15
sample equivalence in, 15
Occupational Health Equity (OHE)
program, 4, 16, 147, 153
Occupational health psychology
(OHP), 4
goal of interventions in, 5
history of, 6–10
overview of, 4–6
Occupational safety and health (OSH)
approaches for addressing, 162
developing training programs for.
See Training programs
illness. *See* Illness and disease
injuries. *See* Fatal work injuries;
Nonfatal injuries
for migrant farmworkers, 172–174
practices for, 26
in public health field, 8
safety climate, 9

safety culture models, 5
safety hazards, 142–144
Occupational Safety and Health Act of
1970 (OSH Act), 8, 28, 30–31
Occupational Safety and Health
Administration (OSHA), 8, 30
Occupational Safety and Health Review
Commission, 8
Occupational segregation, 29, 41
Occupational stress, 9, 113–125
African American exposure to,
118–120
among Asian Americans, 144
community-based interventions for,
122–124
consequences of, 115
costs of, 115
differential exposure to, 187
employer-sponsored interventions
for, 120–122
and health disparities, 116–117
organizational interventions for, 183
prevalence of, 114
psychological and biophysiological
reactions to, 138–139
stress processes, 84
work–family conflict, 181–182
Occupations
of Asian Americans, 31–33, 78, 135
of Blacks, 31–34, 78
gender differences in, 77
health disparities related to, 140–141
of immigrant workers, 161–162
income variability among, 80
of Latinos/Hispanics, 31–34, 78
racial and ethnic composition of,
76–77
risk factors for hazards, 77
social status associated with, 75, 78, 82
and subjective social status, 79
of Whites, 31–33, 78
OHD research. *See* Occupational health
disparities research
OHDs. *See* Occupational health
disparities
OHE program. *See* Occupational Health
Equity program
OHP. *See* Occupational health
psychology

Quality of health care, disparities in, 151

Race
    as demographic variable, 149
    and variation in stress, 84
Racial and ethnic minority groups.
        See also individual groups
    employment by occupational
            categories, 31–34
    in hazardous industries, 217
    of less skilled, nonunionized
            workers, 5
    methodological approaches for
            research with, 3–4
    quality of health care for, 151
    recent developments affecting OHDs
            among, 10–13
    in supervisory training, 205–206
    workplace barriers for, 218
Racial composition of occupations, 76–77
Racial differences in health, 81–82
Racial discrimination, 119–120
Racial harassment, 120
Raymond, J. S., 9
Regulatory context of work, 26–31,
        41–43
Reigadas, E., 124
Research. *See* Occupational health
        disparities (OHD) research
Resources
    sharing, 94
    as social determinant of health, 6
Results Only Work Environment
        (ROWE), 190, 194
Retention, 5
Root, J. H., 174
ROWE (Results Only Work
        Environment), 190, 194

Safety. *See also* Occupational safety and
        health
    and deregulation, 27, 30–31
    issues of "lifestyle" vs., 6
    occupational safety practices, 26
    safety hazards, 142–144
Safety climate, 9
Safety culture models, 5
Safety hazards, 142–144
Safety performance, 9

Safety training, 145
Salazar, M. K., 144
Sample equivalence, 15
Sauter, S. L., 138
Scales, adaptation of, 14
Scenario of use (training), 171–172
Schult, T. M., 83
Scientific management, 6
Secondary labor markets, 28
Segregation, occupational, 29, 41
Self-employment, among Asian
        Americans, 135
Service sector, 27
SES. *See* Socioeconomic status
Sexual harassment, 120
Shin, C., 118
Siddiqi, A., 81–82
Siegrist, J., 84
Skill sets
    help in building, 121
    misalignment between jobs and, 29
Small businesses, 5
Smedley, B. D., 12–13
SMPs (stress management programs),
        120–122
Social class, as mechanism underlying
        disparities, 80–81. *See also*
        Socioeconomic status (SES)
Social class signals, 80–81
Social determinants of health, 5–6,
        75–85. *See also individual
        determinants, e.g.*: Occupational
        stress
    community factors, 60–61
    defined, 6, 51n1, 59
    employment conditions for Latino
            workers, 51–69
    gender differences in occupations, 77
    individual factors, 61–62
    mechanisms underlying disparities,
            78–85
    occupational hazards, 77
    racial and ethnic composition of
            occupations, 76–77
    structural factors, 58–60
    in WHO framework, 62–65
Social integration and support, as
        mechanism underlying
        disparities, 83

ABOUT THE EDITORS

Frederick T. L. Leong, PhD, is a professor of psychology and psychiatry at Michigan State University, and director of the Consortium for Multicultural Psychology Research. He has authored or coauthored over 290 journal articles and book chapters and either edited or coedited 20 books. He is editor-in-chief of the *Encyclopedia of Counseling* and the *APA Handbook of Multicultural Psychology*. He is the founding editor of the *Asian American Journal of Psychology* and the associate editor of the *Archives of Scientific Psychology*. Dr. Leong served as associate editor of the *American Psychologist*, and the lead editor of the *Handbook of Asian American Psychology, Second Edition*. His major research interests center on culture and mental health, cross-cultural psycho-therapy (especially with Asians and Asian Americans), cultural and personality factors related to career choice, adaptability, and work stress. He is the recipient of the American Psychological Association (APA) Award for Distinguished Contributions to the International Advancement of Psychology, Stanley Sue Award for Distinguished Contributions to Diversity in Clinical Psychology from APA's Division 12, APA Division 45 Distinguished Contributions to Research Award, APA Minority Fellowship Program's Dalmas Taylor Distinguished Contributions Award, Lifetime Achievement Award from the Asian American Psychological

Association, and the APA Award for Distinguished Service to Psychological Science.

Donald E. Eggerth, PhD, is a senior researcher with the National Institute for Occupational Safety and Health. He received his degree in psychology from the University of Minnesota. Dr. Eggerth is a Fellow of the American Psychological Association (Divisions 17 and 45) and a recipient of the Dorothy Booz Black Award for outstanding achievement in health psychology. He currently manages a portfolio of projects concerning Latino immigrant worker safety and health.

Chu-Hsiang (Daisy) Chang, PhD, is an associate professor in the department of psychology at Michigan State University. She received her PhD in industrial and organizational psychology from the University of Akron. Her research interests focus on occupational health and safety, leadership, and motivation. Specifically, she studies issues related to occupational stress, workplace violence, and how employee motivation and organizational leadership intersect with issues concerning employee health and wellbeing. Her work has been published in *Academy of Management Review, Academy of Management Journal, Journal of Applied Psychology, Journal of Organizational Behavior, Organizational Behavior and Human Decision Processes, Psychological Bulletin,* and *Work & Stress.* She has served as an associate editor at *Applied Psychology: An International Review* and *Journal of Organizational Behavior,* and is currently serving as an associate editor with the *Journal of Applied Psychology.*

Michael A. Flynn, MA, is a social scientist with the National Institute for Occupational Safety and Health (NIOSH), where he serves as the project officer for a program of research to better understand and improve the occupational health of immigrant workers. He also serves NIOSH as the coordinator for the Occupational Health Equity Program. He is an applied anthropologist whose research interests include social determinates of health, organizational culture, and intervention effectiveness as they relate to occupational health. Mr. Flynn has a master's degree in anthropology from the University of Cincinnati, and is a research fellow of the Consortium for Multicultural Psychology Research at Michigan State University.

J. Kevin Ford, PhD, is a professor and associate chair of psychology at Michigan State University. His major research interests involve improving learning and retention in the workplace through training and other learning activities. Dr. Ford also concentrates on organizational change and how to build continuous learning and improvement orientations within organizations. He is a Fellow of the American Psychological Association and the

Society of Industrial and Organizational Psychology. He received his BS in psychology from the University of Maryland and both his MA and PhD in psychology from The Ohio State University.

Rubén O. Martinez, PhD, is a professor of sociology and director of the Julian Samora Research Institute at Michigan State University. He is the editor of the *Latinos in the United States* book series with the Michigan State University Press. He has coauthored several books, including *Chicanos in Higher Education* (1993), *Diversity Leadership in Higher Education* (2007), and *A Brief History of Cristo Rey Church in Lansing, MI* (2012); edited volumes include *Latinos in the Midwest* (2011) and he coedited a volume titled *Latino College Presidents: In Their Own Words* (2013). Dr. Martinez's research interests include neoliberalism and Latinos, diversity leadership in higher education, education and ethnic minorities, Latino labor and entrepreneurship, and environmental justice issues.